Your Best Health by Friday

How to Overcome Anxiety, Depression, Stress, Trauma, PTSD, and Chronic Illness

SECOND EDITION

By
Elizabeth Gould Morse
M.S.

Printed in the United States of America.

First Printing: October, 2017
Rincon Star Press

Disclaimer

This book is not intended to be a substitute for the medical advice of a licensed physician. This book is meant for informational purposes only and the reader should consult with their doctor in any matters related to his/her health and/or diet. The content is the sole expression and opinion of its author unless otherwise noted. No warrantees or guarantees are expressed or implied. Neither the publisher nor the individual author shall be liable for any physical, psychological, emotional, financial, or commercial damages, including, but not limited to, special, incidental, consequential, or other damages.

ISBN 978-0-9969722-5-3

9 780996 972253

2

Praise for Your Best Health by Friday

RECOMMENDED by the US Review
The US Review of Books
reviewed by Megan Bain

"If you are anxious, depressed or chronically ill, please don't be discouraged about where you are."

This practical guide contains research on reducing chronic illness. These recommendations are to aid readers' medical plans. This simple plan is divided into five days of learning. Monday describes ways to reduce stress. Tuesday outlines understanding pain. Wednesday teaches how to stop reliving negative emotions that cloud your mind. Thursday stresses ways to develop breathing practices to control emotions, exercise, and how to use vision and thoughts to heal. Finally, Friday discusses how the digestive system and diet work together to aid your body in retaining nutrients needed for overall health.

Morse has lived with chronic illness her whole life due to a multitude of unfortunate circumstances. These illnesses had her on multiple medications, but the side effects were just as bad as the illness itself. Morse chose to start researching alternatives to modern medicine to heal her body, instead of just masking the troubles with medication. She shares her experiences in the hope of helping others in her situation. While Morse addresses the main issues of most individuals living with a chronic illness, she takes what doctors describe and breaks it down in ways the readers can understand.

At the end of each day's lesson, she even demonstrates ways the reader can start using this information by organizing ideas into easy, moderate, and harder steps so no reader is overwhelmed when starting this regimen. She emphasizes that no one should start all the steps at once but take a few actions toward a healthier way to heal one's body and when comfortable, add more. Morse has designed a simple, researched way to help readers heal and experience a better life.

Through her research, Morse has designed a simple way to help her readers heal and experience a better life. By sharing her personal experiences from childhood to adulthood, Morse builds a rapport with her readers, developing a trust in her knowledge of the subject. Throughout the book, she references other authors' works which she uses as a guide to her own course of action, lending sincerity to her study and ideas. Within each lesson, she directs her readers to other sites, books, and studies in order for the reader to learn more about the techniques and practices that most interest them and will fit best within their lifestyle, never promoting that her way is the best or only way. This shows the reader genuineness from Morse, proving she is truly sharing her experiences simply to help her readers gain a healthier, less painful, and more fulfilling lifestyle.

RECOMMENDED by the US Review

The following is an email the author received from the reviewer, which is included in this book with the reviewer's permission:

Subject: Your Best Health by Friday
Date: December 20, 2017 at 10:45:34 AM
To: <elizabeth@rightbrainuniversity.com>
From: Megan Bain

I am not sure if this email will find Elizabeth Morse, *Your Best Health by Friday* author, but I hope it does. This is the reviewer from US Book Review. I have never felt the need to contact an author before, but I must tell you this book spoke directly to me. I had been a teacher since 1999. Last December, I had to quit and was put on disability due to my fibromyalgia. I am 40, feel sad all the time due to my illness, and miss a lot of my children's events due to illness. I cannot wait to try the steps in your book. I feel like that review was sent to me by a higher power. I was meant to read your inspiring words. Thank you for letting me review your book. Not only did I get to review it, but I also get to grow from it which is something that has never happened before in my reviews. Thank you for sharing your personal experiences and research so those of us with this condition can relieve some pain, stress, and depression. I will be using all your suggestions and just want to thank you for sharing this with the world, so we can use your years of research and start healing now.

Thanks,
Megan

4

Dedication:

to Michael, for believing
to Alex & Dylan, for being

Table of Contents

Introduction: p 9
Chapter 1: How Chronic Stress Kills.... p 19
Chapter 2: How the Brain Works...... p 23
Chapter 3: Communicating with Your Body.... p 39

Monday: Reduce Stress, Increase Flow

Chapter 4: Finding Flow....   p 47
Chapter 5: Meditation 101...   p 55
Chapter 6: Try Yoga and Dance...p 61
Chapter 7: Resistance Stretching... p 69

Tuesday: Understand Pain

Chapter 8: Pain and Its Message.....p 75
Chapter 9: Musculo-skeletal Repair... p 85
Chapter 10: Muscle-Based Therapies Relief....p 93
Chapter 11: More Myofascial Help....p 101

Wednesday: Stop Reliving Emotions

Chapter 12: Emotions Made Easy....p 111
Chapter 13: Beyond Processing Emotions....p 121
Chapter 14: Acupuncture....p 127
Chapter 15: Specialized Kinesiology p131

Thursday: Develop Parasympathetic Breathing, Exercise, Vision, and Thoughts

Chapter 16: Breath Is More Than Just Taking in Air...p 189
Chapter 17: Improving How You Exercise....p 197

Chapter 18: Vision Therapy...p 203
Chapter 19: Rhythm and Timing Therapies...p 213
Chapter 20: Left-Brain Healing Therapies that Work...p 221

Friday: Improve Digestion and Nutrient Absorption

Chapter 21: Improving Digestion...p 231
Chapter 22: Nutrition You Can Live With...p 245
Chapter 23: Internal Repair...p 257
Chapter 24: Cognitive Hypnotherapy and HeartSpeak...p 273
Chapter 25: The Power of Intention...p 277

Bibliography... p 285
Acknowledgements...p 291
Index... p 293

Introduction

The Difficulty with Our Culture

Jill woke up one day three months ago and immediately had a panic attack. While a year ago she'd been enjoying her job as a regional manager for a large women's clothing manufacturer, COVID-19 had her locked down at home with her family. This was a particularly brutal day to have a panic attack because she had to attend a socially-distanced funeral later that morning. One of her teenage son's best friends had died by suicide the week before—in fact, he was the fourth teenager at the high school to do so that year.

Later, she had a phone call scheduled with her daughter Jenna, who was trying to get into medical school but had test anxiety and kept bombing the MCATs. Jenna was utterly depressed, had lost her self-confidence, and was talking about moving home.

Jill ran a shaky hand through her hair. She rolled over and reached out for her husband, but he wasn't there. She remembered with a start that he had his annual physical that morning and prayed that the doctor would find an easy fix for his racing heart episode last week. Heart disease ran on her husband's side of the family, and even though she'd been nagging him to quit again, he'd restarted his smoking habit to try to deal with the anxiety that lockdown had caused since closing his restaurant. He was in constant pain, increasingly stiff and tight, with his back often going out on him. Jill shook her head. She opened the Amazon app on her phone to check the status of a package that was supposed to arrive that day. And that's when she saw an ad for *Your Best Health by Friday 2nd Edition: How to Overcome Anxiety, Depression, Stress, Trauma, PTSD, and Chronic Illness.*

It was understandable that Jill felt so stressed. Months of unrelenting pressure and living life within the same four walls was getting to everyone around the globe, leading to an epidemic in increased anxiety, depression, stress, and suicide rates.

Not only that, but our culture focuses on the conscious and tends to ignore the unconscious. The rise of smart phones and video games has only made it easier to avoid processing the subconscious root of our negative feelings. Further, the unconscious is resistant to change and that can prevent the conscious mind from ever addressing underlying issues.

Research has shown that somewhere between 50% to 90% of all behavior is driven by the unconscious. While you think the conscious self that you know is the driving force behind your life, much of your life experience is being hidden from you. You don't even know what you don't know. Your unconscious hides things to protect you, and it is pulling many of the strings.

How You Can Have a Better Life, Too, Like Elizabeth

The year was 2010. I lay in my bed in agony, every nerve ending in my body feeling like it was exploding. I was exhausted. This kept happening to me, I didn't know why, and neither my doctor nor the doctors at the local emergency room had a clue what to do to help me. I was only forty-six, but I felt like ninety-six. My joints and muscles ached. The night before I'd sent up a prayer: "Please God, just take me. I'm done. I can't take it anymore," but I'd woken up the next morning the same as usual. I felt guilty that I'd asked God to be taken. My two young sons needed me. I had to be stronger. That night I sent up a different prayer. "Please God, if I can't leave, then let me find the answers to what's wrong with me. It would make everything I've gone through worth it if I can just help others avoid all this pain."

I'd chosen a husband who recreated the pathology of my childhood. I'd grown up with an active-duty combat vet for a dad, who vented his PTSD-level rage on me, my mom, and my younger sister. I could never please my dad, and I could never please my husband. Stress kept mounting because I was a perfectionistic people-pleaser. My husband kept threatening to end the marriage. Eventually my stress caught up with me. I had fibromyalgia, chronic fatigue, irritable bowel syndrome (IBS), and if I didn't figure out how to heal, I was at greater risk of lymphoma and other scary diseases. I felt like I was dying; I couldn't see how I was going to be around long enough to see my boys grow up.

In that moment, however, I realized something incredibly important, and within a couple of years, I had ended that marriage, was dating an incredible man, was going to hot yoga three times a week (and could outlast most of the twenty and thirty year-olds there), had a turnaround on pain and stress, arthritis symptoms, spinal stenosis, brain fog, and big improvements in focus, concentration, energy, and joy, joy, joy. The one realization that caused such a transformation for me has led to equally amazing outcomes for the clients I help, improving health, focus, concentration, test results, direction, happiness, peace, and joy, and is the basis of the book you hold in your hands today.

I spent most of my childhood with my stomach tied up in one knot after the other. But things changed for me when I made that discovery in my forties. Suddenly I had a growing toolkit, and I started to use it regularly. My health got better and better. Eventually, I knew it was time to share what I'd learned with the world. I realized I needed to get training in what had helped me most, so I could demonstrate it to audiences. It turned out that I was good at it and enjoyed helping others. Since those days, I've helped hundreds of people get the lives they wanted:

- Clients with anxiety and depression who notice big improvements in their quality of life.
- Clients with chronic illnesses who are able to lower their stress levels and support rebuilding their health.
- Clients who had failed their first attempts at the bar exam who are now practicing lawyers.
- An 800 on the SAT Math Subject Test and an early decision offer to the school of his dreams for the student who was stuck

in such bad test anxiety that he couldn't finish more than two-thirds of the practice test (and what he completed was only 50% right.)

- The LSAT test-taker who started off in the 65th percentile on practice tests but earned a score in the 99% percentile on the actual LSAT
- Hundreds of others whose lives were changed for the better, released from past traumas, able to make a fresh start.

As I mentioned earlier, I've completely transformed my life in the years since first making these discoveries, going from being so ill with autoimmune illness that I felt like I was dying to the vibrantly healthy woman I am today.

And Jill? She wanted more help, so she reached out to me, began educating her unconscious, and reduced her stress and anxiety. It helped turn around her life and that of her family as well. She sent her son to a psychologist and to me too, to help him cope with the body aspect of trauma from losing his friend. She sent her daughter to me for help with test-taking and she just found out that Jenna did well enough on the MCAT to get into medical school. She sent her husband to me for help with stress reduction and he's successfully quit smoking again. His stiffness has stopped, and his back stays comfortable between chiropractic visits.

This book is going to explain to you in a simple way why it is that your life is not going optimally, and it will help you transform your future. It contains insights into how to reduce stress and improve your health and has a link to further free content within to help you lower your stress levels within the first few minutes of use.

What Most People Have Overlooked
There are many people like Jill who are perfectionists, people-pleasers, or type A overachievers. They often struggle with anxiety and panic attacks. And what many people with these issues often do to overcome them is try harder and attempt to control more. In a

sense, this becomes a cascading failure, for this approach just doesn't work. You can't control life, no matter how much you try to pretend you can. Furthermore, the unconscious is always waiting to step in and mess up any attempts you make to change.

But what can you do instead? If becoming more controlling is flawed because it eventually burns through the adrenals, destroys digestion, and leaves you a sitting duck for whatever your genetic weak links are, then you can begin to be calmer and start leading happier lives if you instead educate your unconscious.

In our culture, we act as if the conscious mind is the only mind to educate, yet the education of the unconscious mind is what will determine our illness or wellness, our academic ability, our ultimate success or failure in business, and the quality of the relationships we attract into our life. To achieve good health, academic and business success, and attract great relationships you must educate your unconscious mind. And in *Your Best Health by Friday*, you will learn how to educate your unconscious in a way that will create buy-in, so that change will become easier and easier.

You likely remember how Jill went from suffering panic attacks to educating her unconscious. What was it that Jill did? She worked with me to overcome her unconscious fear of change and get her unconscious on board with her life goals.

Now people don't show up at conferences where I'm speaking, read my book, or visit my website because they care about abstract knowledge. They do so because they care about the possibility of change. And it was the possibility that Jill was being prevented from changing by her own unconscious that sparked her to pick up the phone and give me a call for help. I helped Jill by looking for where I could see she favored one side of the body or the other, knowing that is linked to trauma. I asked Jill for internal feedback on how it felt in her body when she walked, bent down, stood on her toes, swayed forward and back and side to side while she thought about her goal. Through self-observation, acupressure, and other techniques, these areas correct themselves. And by explaining the goal in a different

13

way from the conscious mind's perspective, we educate the unconscious and help to overcome its fear of change. Once the unconscious understands a goal fully and integrates it, then we will have its cooperation.

The simple truth is you will achieve good health, academic and business success, and attract great relationships when you educate your unconscious mind.

Educating the Unconscious

But who ever heard of educating the unconscious?! And what does that involve?

I had a client who was a talented upper-level manager at an international corporation. We'll call him Joe. He had to have been putting in a hundred hours a week at his job. And over the years, he kept seeing the same number over and over in different contexts, 10:54 or 1054. He said it always preceded something horrible happening to him, like a car accident. Lately, he had begun to see that number every day—on the clock, on the computer, on paperwork. It kept him up at night, worrying about what might happen to him. He wanted to know what it meant and if there was anything he could do about it.

I did some research before his appointment and found out 10-54 is police code for possible dead body. A tall, slim man with cropped blond hair, Joe looked both exhausted and like he hadn't been eating or exercising enough. I told him of the meaning I'd discovered and asked if that made sense to him. He slumped in the chair, shocked at the echo of his innermost thoughts: he was so overworked and overwhelmed that he could barely feel his body anymore. I helped him come up with a goal that he liked, "I effortlessly create work/life balance," and asked him to walk and notice sensations within his body. We cleared away resistance to the goal—those unconscious beliefs that kept him working harder than he needed to because he felt unworthy of success—and he left a different man: energized, vital, and hopeful.

Now most people would probably prefer to just dip a little deeper into the wine vat rather than explore the Pandora's box of the unconscious. Instead, they'd double down on trying to control themselves and their behavior more, or that of their spouse or children. But that's what you've always tried, and it doesn't work. It just adds another layer of stress. You overcome your greatest struggles not by imposing protocols on yourself but by asking the body what it needs to heal.

When my clients embraced the concept that they could partner with their unconscious to produce change, everything clicked, and they saw a night and day difference in how much better they felt, how productive they were, and how much less stress they felt.

Over the next twenty-five chapters, I will show you what you must do in order to begin educating your unconscious and get the most out of the rest of your life. You'll find that increased health, happiness, and productivity are some of the benefits. Others are increased joy, self-esteem, wisdom, impulse control, and reduced suicidal ideation.

1. First, I'm going to simply explain some things so that you may understand what gets us into this mess. Second, I'll divide the information into five lessons, which I've listed under the five days of the week, and tools to learn them. Once you understand the lessons, you can check in anytime you want to make sure you've incorporated them into your daily life, and if you haven't, reset your intentions. All of these aspects contribute to the calming of the body and mind, so that we can spend more time in our higher-level thinking.

The daily focus:

Monday	Reduce Stress, Increase Flow
Tuesday	Understand Pain
Wednesday	Stop Reliving Emotions
Thursday	Develop Parasympathetic Breathing,

Exercise, Vision, and Thoughts
Improve Digestion and Nutrient
Absorption

2. Each chapter will include information and stories, along with easy, moderate or harder action steps you can choose from to better your life. If you are pressed for time, I suggest that you just read the action steps and see what resonates with you to start incorporating small changes into your daily life.

3. There are many people struggling with unhappiness, anxiety, depression, stress, chronic illness, pain, trauma, and PTSD. Most of them are going to try to use willpower yet again to turn things around. But you know that willpower, which is run by the conscious mind, is no match for the automatic programming of the unconscious mind.

4. How do you take on the task of creating change when the part of you which fears change is always on guard to prevent it? You can do it through the steps outlined in this book along with free tools on my YouTube channel and by visiting my website, www.rightbrainuniversity.com. As challenging as this work may be, my experience, as well as those of my clients, demonstrates that it is not only possible, but the rewards are enormous.

Join the movement to gain more out of your life. Start reading *Your Best Health by Friday* today.

Your Free Gift

Included in this book purchase is a resource guide with a free Adverse Childhood Experiences (ACE) test to help you determine your and your children's risk for autoimmune illness, stroke, heart disease, obesity, suicide, drug and alcohol abuse, and more at www.rightbrainuniversity.com/guide.

The links provided in the book will be kept updated online on my website's resource guide page. Be sure to sign up and take the ACE test!

Chapter 1
How Chronic Stress Kills

Outer Chronic Stress

We likely think of stress as being a bad thing and that chronic stress is even worse. Stress is any situation that motivates us to act or change, and as such, it can be neutral, good or bad. Hunger is an example of a stress and feeding ourselves the right amount of healthy food is a good outcome.

Outer chronic stress is when we have the motivation to act or change our environment but for some reason, we feel unable to do so; whether it is because of external conditions in our lives, like being repressed in some way during our childhood years, being stuck in a toxic relationship, or needing to keep our job in order to pay our mortgage.

Inner Chronic Stress

We put a lot of pressure on ourselves with negative self-talk and how we think about ourselves. This is inner chronic stress.

Inner chronic stress can be the most insidious because we often believe that without constantly pushing ourselves, we will be lazy or useless and amount to nothing. So many of us have a streak of perfectionism that constantly beats up our inner child, our unconscious self.

We harangue and berate ourselves at times to win the love and approval of our parents, teachers and friends, and it can become a habit because it seems to have worked in the past. Because it is self-generated, it is easily turned around, however we must learn to listen to how we speak to ourselves:

"I'm such an idiot!"

"Dad was right; I'm a failure"

"I'll never lose this weight!"

Children Want to Please

I believe that we need to understand that most children are born eager to please. If children are given love and positive encouragement along with tools to help with self-discovery and personal growth, they will develop a balance between being true to themselves and their calling, as well as finding joy in making others happy.

Children are often taught more by the unconscious teachings of the adults in their lives through nonverbal communications rather than by the verbal. It's said that most of communication happens nonverbally. As parents, we are often unaware of what we "say" nonverbally. The emotional stress that we feel when our children are up all night with a fever, and then bounce back, while we suffer from lack of sleep, can result in overreaction to our children's behavior.

Even if we do not overreact visibly, the stress we feel is in our brain state. This helps explain why our kids often start to act out when we are having a bad day. In addition to biochemical cues, I believe they are reacting to the painful feelings from their mirror neurons caused by our own emotional state, and they do not know what to do about it.

Similarly, I think we react to our children's distress, anger and fear because it is generated unconsciously within our mirror neurons when we see it in them. How nice it would be to have the skills to reset our emotional state, so we do not have to keep reacting to each other in a negative way when we are having a bad day.

Our Unconscious Mind Runs the Show Under our Noses

Our unconscious beliefs are not easy to access, but they drive most of our behavior. Most of those patterns and beliefs were formed before we were seven years old, according to molecular biologists such as Dr. Bruce Lipton of Stanford. I don't know about you, but I am uncomfortable at the thought that most of my behavior is being run by that childhood self of mine. It doesn't have to be that way; the work I do can help you grow past that. More information on what I do is in chapter 15.

Adverse Childhood Experience (ACE) Test

I first heard about the ACE test in 2015 from an NPR piece. For those who haven't heard of it, doctors have realized that traumatic events from our childhood increase risk factors for poor health in later life. The likelihood of our having problems with issues as diverse as smoking, drug and alcohol use disorders, missing work, obesity, diabetes, heart disease, cancer, depression, suicide attempts, and COPD (chronic obstructive pulmonary disorder) increases based on how traumatic our childhoods were. Things like abuse, neglect and household dysfunction impact us long after our childhoods are over.

As Donna Jackson Nakazawa reports in *Childhood Disrupted*, "chronic stress leads to dysregulation of our stress hormones, which leads to unregulated inflammation. And inflammation translates into symptoms and disease." Many other factors go into whether we will get sick, but the right hemisphere of the brain doesn't have a sense of time. Until the emotions from these traumatic events are processed and released, they are stored in our body and we will continue to suffer. Remember, if you'd like to take the ACE Test to find out your score, you can get your free bonus at www.rightbrainuniversity.com/guide. In addition to answering these questions for yourself, I suggest you think about how your parents would answer these questions, as well as your grandparents. I believe it has a bearing that I'll go into later in the book. It's clear that what we don't face from our childhoods is contributing to us getting sick, which gave me a great deal of motivation to look back at those early years.

Why I Needed Healing

I was born into a military family during the Vietnam War, while my dad was on active duty in Vietnam. His combat stress translated into PTSD for me. It doesn't take much to put babies into a freeze state that is easily re-triggered. My unconscious patterns brought nothing but increasing amounts of fear, restriction, isolation, and ultimately pain from fibromyalgia.

Fibromyalgia feels like an overloaded circuit board that is about to ignite. To give an example, if my body were a house, it would have been a house with all the lights on, all the appliances running, everything churning, grinding and wearing out. I needed to find help. I had been frozen in a state of chronic stress for over 40 years and I was about to discover the consequences. I needed answers before it was too late.

Medication gave me too many side effects to deal with. I needed to find the root of my problems, so I could heal.

Chapter 2
How the Brain Works

My Friend Jessie's Story

I had a friend from hot yoga who was diagnosed with kidney cancer. Doctors assured her she had three years to live, yet she was dead within six months. Why? I think a big part of it was her self-talk. One day not long after the diagnosis, we talked in the yoga locker room. "Unless I get hit by a bus, I know this cancer is going to kill me," she said cheerfully.

"But what about positive thinking?" I asked, wondering how she could be so cheerful with such negative thinking. "You know how the unconscious gets its instructions from the thoughts we think."

She shook her head. "I need to face things straight up," she said. "No sugar-coating it."

And there was nothing more that I could say. Her mind was made up. The way I see it, the unconscious is made up of parts of us from the age of conception to the age of seven, so an average age of three-and-a-half years old. Would you tell a three-and-a-half-year-old that unless they got hit by a bus, their cancer was going to kill them? I sure hope not. In Jessie's case, I think the uncertainty of hope was more pain than she could bear. But we have to be brave for the sake of our unconscious. Without the possibility of hope, I believe her unconscious stress levels soared, leading to the suddenly rapid progress of her cancer.

Read on for more information on how to get the best you can out of your own brain.

The Three Layers of the Brain

The newest part of the human brain is the outermost layer and is called the cortex. The part behind our forehead is called the prefrontal cortex. The second oldest part generates our emotions and it is the middle layer; it is called the limbic system or the emotional brain.

The oldest part is at the base of the skull, closest to the top of the spine and continues into the spinal cord. It is called the brain stem and controls the autonomic nervous system (ANS).

Left/Right Handshake

There are two sides to the brain, called hemispheres. Their jobs are not so delineated as we've been told, but to simplify it, the left side is mostly in charge of the academic: things like speech, math, and symbolic language. The right side uses metaphoric language, oversees attention, processing of visual shapes, and processing unconscious data from both hemispheres, whether it is social, emotional, or sensory information.

Since most of our brain capacity is unconscious, the right side of the brain is important. The right brain handles our sensory processing: vision, smell, taste, touch, hearing, balance (this is called the vestibular system, which is based in the inner ear), as well as internal sensations such as the feedback from our body as it sits in a chair. These internal sensations of gravity are called the proprioceptive system. The proprioceptive system is responsible for taking the input from our senses and acting on them to keep us safe.

The right brain is also in charge of processing all nonverbal communication, which accounts for the majority of the communicating we do. This means it oversees our social success. For those who have high functioning autistic spectrum issues, key areas of the right brain are underdeveloped and can't process the social input fast enough, so the information is ignored. The right brain also processes information connected to heart rate, breathing, blood pressure, digestion, body temperature and metabolism. The left brain does a vitally important job: the logical thinking, verbal, analytical, math and writing skills that are all critical. It makes sure we eat and are productive so we as individuals survive. It has a voice—it is our conscious self, and it makes its needs known, often very insistently.

The right brain is always plugging along as the silent partner whose needs are ignored, or at best, the last ones met. Lots of us are Type-A workaholics who ignore impulses to play or are so busy being responsible adults that we shame ourselves into disconnecting from our creative passions.

It's probably simplest to think of the left-brain state as analytical and our right-brain state as emotional. Think of what we get rewarded for: our analytical abilities or our emotionality? See what I mean? We often get punished for our emotionality. If you have no emotionality, it's likely you've suppressed it enough that you can't connect with it consciously. That doesn't mean you don't have it. It means that your body builds up emotional neurochemicals and stores them in the body without your awareness. I've noticed in my practice and in my life that these types of people are often very stiff and inflexible, as if the muscles are in spasm, tight, or rigid. This is why I recommend therapy with someone who does Focusing or a Jungian analyst who uses dreams, active imagination, creative expression, and Sandplay therapy in the tradition of Carl Jung and Dora Kalff to honor the body's wisdom, along with the type of body connection work that I do. More information on that in Chapter 20.

Conscious vs Unconscious
A portion of the cortex of the left brain is considered the home of the conscious mind. (A small percentage of people are wired the opposite way.) The conscious mind is a small part of the left hemisphere. It's thought to consist of a portion in the part directly behind the left temple, a part deep in the center of the brain, and a tie-in to the brain stem. The rest of the brain is the unconscious. As I mentioned earlier, it is fully mature by the age of seven. Those first seven years, it accepts all information that it is given as fact.

In this book, I will refer to the conscious mind as the left-brain state and the unconscious mind as the right-brain state. I do this because the term unconscious can have a negative association and I'd like everyone to have a fresh look at the material I'm presenting.

The conscious mind is capable of so much: for example, our logical thinking, critical thinking, and short-term memory. Think of what humanity has created with that part of the brain. I'd like people to realize that the unconscious mind has layers to it too. It consists of the brain stem and emotional brain from both hemispheres, as well as the cortex and prefrontal cortex of the right hemisphere. The difference between the cortex and prefrontal cortex of the left and right hemispheres is that the conscious mind announces itself with speech, ideas and action, while many of us don't know how to connect to the higher functioning part of the unconscious mind. I think of it as the driver behind intuition, creativity, and the home to our connection to that which is greater than us, whatever you choose to call it.

In 1996, neuroscientist Dr. Jill Bolte Taylor had a severe hemorrhage in the left hemisphere of her brain. Her experience of the stroke and her road back to recovery was documented in her TED talk, *My Stroke of Insight* and book of the same name.

Her work provides a framework of understanding the way I was using neuroplasticity to help myself, the byproduct of which provided insights for me to heal from autoimmune illness.

While it's been shown in MRIs that we all use our hemispheres equally no matter our artistic or engineering temperaments, Dr. Taylor's work has opened our eyes to the concept of left- and right-hemisphere states of mind, which I simplified to call the left-brain state and right-brain state.

Taking that one step further, we can think of individuals as fitting in somewhere on a bell curve between that left-brain and right-brain state. Children who easily pay attention in class and comprehend lessons naturally fit into this societal orientation towards valuing the left-brain state. Children who primarily daydream and doodle have a right-brain state of mind. Our Western society greatly values that left-brain state because it's the productive one. We can think of world cultures as fitting somewhere on this bell curve, with the United States currently leading the way in left-brain state development by reducing the amount of time children spend in right-brain state activities such as play, art, and music, and instead packing their school days with left-brain state activities such as reading, writing, arithmetic, and homework—lots and lots of homework.

The downside of the left-brain state is that if someone is traumatized, the mind can orient towards fear-based judgment. With trauma, fear leads to vigilance. If life continues to be scary, the cycle leads to hypervigilance. The same cycle can happen with trauma-based anger, where the mind is oriented towards anger-based judgment, often with fear underlying the anger. If inciting events keep occurring, it can lead to ever-increasing vigilance and incite increasingly angry responses. These sorts of responses can then lead to overtaxing the adrenal system and impacting the digestive response.

The right-brain state takes in these same events and doesn't judge. Instead, it accepts. It's where we find peace no matter our current circumstances. We need the input of the left-brain state to keep us aware of our survival needs, but we also need the balancing effect of the right-brain state, so we can reset from the overdrive that can burn out our adrenal system and damage our health.

This book teaches the importance of flexibility of brain states for health and wellbeing, as well as providing action steps to teach how to become more flexible. I've found that learning how to change brain states fluidly has been the key to relieving stress, recovering from trauma, healing from chronic illness, enjoying better digestion, and saying goodbye to anxiety and depression.

A word about hemisphere use—I was diagnosed by a neurologist-chiropractor (look for diplomates of the American Chiropractic Neurology Board if you need one) as having a brain imbalance that probably played a large role in my autoimmune symptoms. At the time of my first visit to him, my right-hemisphere's brain stem had enough extra effort needed of it to keep up with the left that my blood pressure reading was ten points higher on the right than the left (blood pressure for each side of the body is handled by the same side brain stem.) He said it put me at an increased risk for stroke unless it was corrected.

Because of this, I've done exercises designed to equalize my right brain stem's capacity. I've also taken care to change how I use my computer, which had exacerbated the problem and caused headaches in the right-side brain stem from the increased blood pressure on that side. It's important that everyone take breaks every 20-30 minutes to shift visual focus in order to relieve overuse of eye muscles, but it's critical for people like me with a hemispheric imbalance. I doubt I'm alone in this issue; I would think it could be a combination of genetic predisposition as well as living under chronic stress and PTSD from early childhood throughout most of my adult life. If you're facing health issues that have autoimmune symptoms, asking your doctor to test blood pressure simultaneously on both sides could provide important information.

For Our Best Health, Both Mental and Physical
For perfect health, we need both sides of our brain to be fully developed because they need to work together. For example, many of the functions of the immune system and digestive system need to be cross-coordinated. The digestive tract is muscle-based and needs to be able to hand off from the muscles of the right half of the body to those on the left half of the body as food moves through the intestinal tract.

If we have one hemisphere that is underdeveloped, it is not possible to have an optimal digestive system. This is because the nutrients necessary for building and repairing our body are only provided by a healthy, fully developed left and right brain so that we have optimal digestion.

Every step of the process of food being absorbed, and of the body being able to repair the digestive tract requires a balanced brain.

It's also not possible to have an optimal immune system if one hemisphere is underdeveloped because both hemispheres control its proper functioning.

I think of the brain as being in a lifelong three-legged race. When I think back to childhood experiences of three-legged races, it wasn't the children paired with the adults (which is the equivalent of an underdeveloped hemisphere paired with a fully developed one) who won. The winners were always a pair of children with similar leg length (the equivalent of two equally developed hemispheres), which made it easier for them to operate with a paired stride.

When we are stressed, we use our dominant hemisphere, which is the most developed. This gives us the fastest reaction time possible to get away from a predator. In modern times, the stress might be taking a test or giving a presentation at work. For example, if our dominant hemisphere is the right brain (which does not house speech, symbolic language, or math), we can imagine just how much of a handicap that would be. People with a dominant right hemisphere often have a problem with text anxiety.

There are always connections to the opposite hemisphere, so it is not like we often go completely blank, but for some people it can get close.

The Power of Repetitive Movement

Learning begins with something called our primary, also known as primitive, reflexes. Primary reflexes are a way that babies automatically start learning about the world; these reflexes start in utero and build on each other. Each type of primary reflex is supposed to start at a specific age and last for a certain number of months. These time-tested patterns of movement allow synapses to make vital connections. They also allow development of the fatty sheath coating called myelin that gets laid down around a motor neuron every time it is used, which helps signal travel through it faster.

Signals can travel up to five times faster through myelinated neurons than unmyelinated ones. The faster the signals travel, the faster we can process information and our reactions. The more myelin coating, the stronger our grip will be.

IQ is a Measure, in Part, of Processing Speed

Since IQ is a measure of processing speed among other factors, the thicker (and therefore stronger) the myelin sheath, the better we can perform on IQ tests. Myelin destruction is common in many central nervous system disorders like Parkinson's disease and multiple sclerosis. Repetitive movement is the key to the development of healthy amounts of myelin. The brain is efficient at pruning unused connections. If we have not used a connection in seven years, it is removed. If we haven't frequently balanced with our eyes closed, ridden a bike or taken dance classes in a long enough time, we will notice a decline in our ability to balance. I believe the mental decline that some people experience as they age is largely because they move less, challenge their balance less and therefore the thinking process is happening on a slower circuit as there is less and less myelin coating.

Brain Growth Through Challenging Balance

Many of us think we maintain good balance by running but running presents a limited challenge to our brain. Running challenges our forward balance, but provides limited challenge to our balance going backward, up, down, or side to side. Different layers of our brain handle each of these types of movement. The more we repeat a movement, the more synaptic connections are made and the more dendrites (short branched extensions of nerve cells) are made. It's all brain growth, and that's a huge positive for us.

Myelin is added to a part of the neuron called the axon so that the whole system is in peak working order. If you have not been good about cross training in yoga or dance and you are in your thirties or older, hold onto a counter and close your eyes. Cautiously let go and see how good your balance is, then stand on your tiptoes and sink into a crouch and stand up. Chances are it is more of an effort than it used to be. Now try challenging yourself by asking a friend to spot you, so you do not fall. Can you close your eyes, bend over, and touch your toes? Can you close your eyes, stand on your tiptoes, and turn around with good balance or are you shaky?

Couch potatoes can see trouble with this at a much younger age. It's part of the slippery slope that leads so many people to using walkers or wheelchairs at far too young an age. Fear of losing their balance leads to people further restricting their activity which only accelerates the decline. Restricting activity means not producing as much myelin. This will make movement, balance, and thinking become ever more challenging.

It is never too late. My eighty-seven-year-old father took up yoga five years ago and he loves it. He has gone from being unable to get up on his own if he fell (he had double knee replacement surgery ten years ago and never regained full mobility afterwards), to now easily being able to get up. He's much more limber, active and happy.

Our Left-Brain Culture

It is my belief that as a society we overly value the left-brain state. Our education system targets the left brain. Any problems that we experience in learning are addressed by strengthening our left-brain abilities.

Our children are expected to sit at a desk and learn to read at younger and younger ages with each passing generation. They are often punished for not conforming by having their freedom to play taken away, by being held in at recess. There is also less and less time for free play allowed for children, both at home and at school. Children receive less self-directed playtime; learning has a schedule and young minds are constantly turned to academic goals. All of this promotes the development of the left-brain state.

Developing Children's Right Brain State

Scheduled play dates that often center around video games do not allow for developing the right-brain state. The brain stem cannot tell the difference between real and imagined images, so all the gaming produces adrenaline, the same feeling as if the player were firing a gun in real life.

One of the big prerequisites for developing the right-brain state is the willingness to let children get bored so they can go inward and discover what causes them to begin practicing creative play rather than just being consumers of entertainment. Our left-brain culture has made academic learning the top priority. School tests are designed to test the left brain's skillset, so it appears that accentuating left-brain learning produces more concrete academic success; however, the right brain skillset is invaluable for seeing the big picture and being able to focus attention, among other things. (While it has long been associated with creativity, and the left hemisphere with logic, the best examples of creativity and logic come from the whole brain functioning together.)

Bringing Back Music, Art, and Daily P.E.
In many schools, physical education is only two or three days a week for one semester of the year. Students often stand in lines, bored, as they wait for instruction on how to play a game, rather than staying active in a game and getting pulled out for instructional game training. One suggestion is to let children use a jump rope while they wait. In elementary school, punishment for the bad behavior of one child is often taking away recess time for an entire class; this kind of thing needs to stop.

There are fewer art and music teachers and often entire music programs have been eliminated. The right brain learns through movement, art, music, and creativity. It is how we find flow (the state in which we are fully immersed in a feeling of energized focus, full involvement, and enjoyment in an activity) and get back in balance when we suffer from too much thinking, which tires us out and floods us with stress hormones.

Small wonder we are stressed; small wonder high school and college students report a lack of joy in their lives. There is too little unstructured time no matter our children's ages. It seems logical to think this lack of joy and hope could cause a rise in suicide rates.

Surrendering Ego Can be Difficult in Our Search for Help

Because of school and societal emphasis, because we get in trouble for daydreaming and rewarded for paying attention, we likely have a more developed left-brain state than a right-brain state, and trouble switching between them. Another downside of our logical, rational left brain is that it is constantly judging. If we are always in that state, there is no peace. Our right brain specializes in non-judgmental processing. When we are in that state, we are peaceful. Our stress can reset to calm. Many of us reach the limits of how much our left-brain can help us at some point in our lives. We spiral into anxiety or depression and do not know how to reorder our thoughts so that we don't keep spiraling downward. Using the right-brain state to reset to calm is not something we're taught in school, and it's often not something we're taught at home either.

Too much thinking, in and of itself, can be a big part of the problem. Overthinking leads to over-feeling and vice versa, both of which often fly beneath our conscious radar. This causes a release of chemicals in our body. Neurons in our brain release neuropeptides to communicate with other neurons. When we are very upset, too much thinking can generate too many neuropeptides, giving us a kind of woozy emotional hangover that can feel like having too much to drink. We often get caught in a negative thought loop where a negative thought can scare our unconscious, which then causes fear and anxiety, which in turn scares us consciously until we have another negative thought. It's a downward spiral. Unless we acknowledge the thoughts and feelings, we remain caught in the loop and the neuropeptides persist in our body. The neuropeptides are created by our emotional (limbic) brain, and are meant to increase our chance of survival, so they never release until we process and learn from them. Unfortunately, when they're stored in quantity, they can cause inflammation in our body, which can lead to illness.

Beyond the Ego-Self

That dominant left brain keeps us locked into our ego, our lonely self, and prevents us from engaging the right-brain state, which processes all the nonverbal social cues. I think most of us are wired to be at peace when we are in community, despite whatever traumas might keep us from consciously feeling comfortable in community. When our right-brain state is more active, we can see the big picture and how wonderful it is to be alive, even in the worst of times.

Our left-brain state is for the survival of the self. Our right-brain state is for connection to others. How ironic that too much self-thinking can spiral into thoughts of ending the self because we cannot bear the pain of the self when the self feels alone and abandoned.

From Suicide Ideation to Peace of Mind

While I talk so openly about how I've healed and shared so much about my life story, I've hesitated to talk about the full depth of my anxiety and depression in years past and the full healing I've experienced. With suicide rates rising so much during the COVID-19 pandemic, I thought it important to discuss. A CDC survey from June 2020 states that one in four young adults has recently thought about killing themselves, and the increase in stress, isolation, mental health problems, and substance abuse as a method of coping with emotions are impacting all age levels. With this as a background, I share this part of my story with you in the hopes it can help you if you need it.

I first wished I was dead when I was ten; moving back to the States from Taiwan was an incredibly difficult transition for me. We lived in the finished basement of family friends for several months because our assigned base housing was still being built. Because my parents' friends lived in housing for upper-level Air Force officers, there were no playgrounds, no children around, no libraries nearby, no transportation to get anywhere—in short, a lot like this pandemic, and a situation potentially similar to what children may be experiencing whose parents aren't coping well. Finally moving into our own housing and meeting new friends fixed my depression then, but it was a harbinger of rocky mental health during hard times. If you are a parent of young children now, it might give you insight into your children's struggles.

My mother struggled with anxiety and depression her whole life and I inherited that tendency. She went through a rough patch when I was sixteen, and I was so concerned that she'd kill herself that I sometimes stayed home from school to keep an eye on her, including the day she got taken to the hospital by ambulance after having a nervous breakdown.

Going through that with her gave me the empathy I needed for what family and friends would go through if I ever killed myself and kept me from ever trying it, though it didn't stop me from thinking about it or wishing myself dead during rough patches in my life, like going through seven years of infertility, as well as the multiple skid marks along the bumpy road of my first marriage.

These action steps in this book are what I've used to build a life I'm so happy to live, that I find a joy to be a part of, and to find my calling—to help others with the tools I've found and used to rebuild my life. I needed to learn how to develop kinder self-talk, to increase my ability to switch between a left-brain state and a right-brain state, and to release decades of stuffed emotions. Keep reading to find more about the tools you need within these pages in order to build your best life yet.

For those of you who are anxious, depressed, or suicidal, I have found life to get better with every decade, even without these tools, so keep on trying to find your footing in this life. Every life is precious. If you are suicidal, please call and talk to someone at the National Suicide Prevention Lifeline at 800-273-8255, find a good therapist who will help you love yourself the way you deserve to be loved, and look at the action steps at the end of this chapter for free videos on my YouTube channel to help release emotions using acupressure.

Celebrate Every Step Towards Developing the Right-Brain State
Many of us have had some sense of having a gut feeling or intuition at

some point in our lives. This is a part of the right-brain state talking to us. The more we acknowledge and act on our gut feelings, the more that window opens to us.

We are Body/Mind—the Heart and the Gut Also Must be Heard
We have neurons in three areas of our body: the mind, gut and heart. All three need to be in harmony. I've learned the hard way that health flies out the door when they are not. That part of our brain that we know as ourselves is only a small fraction of our whole self; our ego self is not in charge.

Once Body and Mind are in Sync, Health Can be Rebuilt
I have been humbled enough by life's circumstances to realize that my conscious self is not in charge of my life. My unconscious is the bigger part and my ego self can only try to act as a guide to that unconscious. I realize it is a lifelong process to parent my unconscious self. I must think of my greater good, of the positive way of communicating to myself. It's been my habit of negative communication with my unconscious that brought problems and disease into my life.

　　I noticed that once I could catch myself at being negative about 50% of the time, I had a huge momentum shift in health and happiness.

Action steps to reduce anxiety and depression:
Easy:
Read *Spark: The Revolutionary New Science of Exercise and the Brain*, by John Ratey, MD. See your doctor to get approval to start half an hour of gentle aerobic and balancing exercises every day. Daily time spent walking has been shown to help anxiety and depression.

　　If you are suicidal, please contact the National Suicide Prevention Lifeline at 800-273-8255.

Anxiety and depression can also be caused by inflammation, nutritional deficiencies, and lack of beneficial bacteria in our gut. Talk to an integrative, naturopathic, or Ayurvedic doctor, or a nutritionist to get help.

Moderate:
With your doctor's okay, progress to high intensity aerobic exercise.

Read Donna Jackson Nakazawa's book *The Last Best Cure* for tips on walking meditation, among other things. Walking mindfully is incredibly calming, reducing both anxiety and depression.

Harder:
Read the book *Positive Psychology* by Martin Seligman. Take his online quiz at authentichappiness.org and see if you're as optimistic as you can be. If you catastrophize, try to stop the habit. You are keeping your unconscious paralyzed in fear. In the absence of confirmed knowledge, assume the best outcome—that's one way to start getting braver.

Develop your gratitude practice. More details in Chapter Four.

For multiple sclerosis and Parkinson's, consider Interactive Metronome, which has been shown to help lay down myelin in everyone, including people with these illnesses. I offer help for people with multiple sclerosis and Parkinson's through Rhythm and Reflex®, my Interactive Metronome private practice. More at www.rhythmandreflex.com.

Look for my free acupressure tools and yoga postures on my YouTube channel to help reduce the anxiety, depression, and stress that can lead to suicidal thoughts. You can find the link at the bottom of my homepage at www.rightbrainuniversity.com; just look for the YouTube symbol. I also offer private and group sessions as well as classes.

Take art classes, writing classes (be sure to journal, too), or music lessons to help activate the right brain. Use your nondominant hand as much as possible to help develop your brain's less-used hemisphere. My lifelong anxiety began to turn around with daily journal writing and weekly meditation.

Chapter 3
Communicating with your Body

Spinning, Spinning, Spinning

I worked in a local school district a few years back as a substitute teacher to see how our community's kindergarteners were doing. Across the board, these children were struggling with physicality in ways I doubt happened a generation ago. I would go in and play some games with them such as having them stand up, lift a knee, and touch it with the opposite hand and repeat that from one side to the other. It's called the cross crawl.

Most often, it was little boys who could not do it, instead touching the same side knee, almost unaware of the opposite side of their body. They were always the ones the teachers had listed as problem children to be on the watch for. One little boy I'll call Jeff stood out. He was known for behavior that sounded like early Oppositional Defiant Disorder. When I asked the class to draw, Jeff refused. I began helping the other children, keeping an eye on Jeff, who seemed to want to get a rise out of me. I simply said, "okay," and walked away. He sat down in the teacher's chair and started spinning. The other children reported this, outraged. I said, "We're trying an experiment. Today it's not against the rules." After a few minutes of minutes of spinning, Jeff came up to me as I helped another child. "I want to color," he said. "Okay," I said. I went and got him the printout and handed it to him. He sat down and began to fill it in. His color choices and ability to stay within the line were way above his peers' abilities, and he stuck with it until the assignment was complete. For the rest of the day, he behaved well and stayed on task. Never mind that his teacher listed him as the primary behavior problem in the classroom, he was an angel for me. You'll see why a little spinning was important for him later in this chapter.

How the Brain Develops and How It Stays Healthy

We are born thinking with our entire brain. The way our brain interacts with the world is via the body moving and exploring. Babies react to stimuli with automatic patterns of behavior known as primary reflexes necessary to help them survive, such as sucking, swallowing, and hiccupping. Once each primary reflex is mastered it gets handed off to the more primitive regions of the brain so that the cortex is free for higher thinking. Most primary reflexes should not be present beyond a year or so of age but can be reactivated or never properly inhibited when the baby experiences trauma or chronic stress. These reflexes can be reactivated in anyone by trauma at any age.

We want to have the most efficient use of each region of our brain. We do not want any part to be overused. The brain is harmed by having the more primitive areas over-activated by constant angry or fearful thoughts. Overuse of the sympathetic nervous system (also called the SNS, our fight-or-flight system) creates an inflammatory body and brain state. The brain can also be harmed by not being fed correctly. Eating too much sugar or refined carbohydrates at one time can deprive the brain of fuel, triggering insulin production, which in turn causes cells to pull excess glucose out of the bloodstream and into fat storage.

Brain neurons are unable to store glucose, so they rely on a steady source from our bloodstream. Hours after a coffee break or chocolatey afternoon snack, once the caffeine and sugar high wear off, insulin has caused blood sugar levels to crash. Most people will notice that they are feeling spacey, weak, confused, or nervous. It is a signal that our brain has been harmed and that we have made poor nutritional choices.

The Vagus Nerve

The vagus nerve is the tenth cranial nerve. It supplies the parasympathetic motor connection for all the organs from the neck to the colon, except for the adrenal glands. The automatic processes of our bodies like heartbeat, breathing, blood pressure and body temperature are handled by our autonomic nervous system (ANS), which consists of the parasympathetic nervous system (PNS), the sympathetic nervous system (SNS), and our enteric nervous system (ENS). We need our PNS to be as strong as our SNS so that we can reset to calm after stress. The stronger our PNS is, the faster we return to calm after a stressful event. For those of us who have chronic stress, it usually means that the tone of our SNS is too high and our PNS is too low tone. I go into more details about developing the PNS in later chapters, but I also want to mention the PNS as being a central component to our social connection. Having low tone or having the myelinated part of the vagus nerve not sufficiently myelinated (as well as having other cranial nerves insufficiently myelinated) can reduce our ability to interact with others as well as decode nonverbal communication.

The information we receive from mirror neurons and non-verbal communication is processed by the right brain, which is another reason to make sure the right brain is fully developed.

In a study published by Psychological Science, the researchers, led by Barbara Frederickson and Bethany Kok, found that people who experience warmer, more upbeat emotions may have better physical health because they make more social connections. The study also found that it is possible for a person to generate positive emotions for themselves using loving kindness meditation to make themselves physically healthier. Our vagus nerve also plays a role in satiation after eating. For these reasons, we want strong vagal tone.

The Importance of the Right Brain

The right brain oversees all unconscious processes, such as digestion, our immune system, and much more. The more primitive areas of the brain are supposed to process vision if our primary reflexes have been properly mastered. When primary reflexes or gross motor skills (the ability to control the large muscles of the body for walking, running, sitting, and crawling) are not properly developed or integrated, the cortex gets involved. Using the cortex this way diverts it from academic or creative thought. Instead, it is used to keep us physically safe by constantly checking our position as we interact with our environment.

The prefrontal cortex on the right side of the brain oversees the rhythm and timing in the body—things like our circadian rhythms, for example, as well as attention, and impulse control. Rhythm and timing are critical skills.

A lot of children, particularly boys, suffer from impulse control problems, but the more active they are in rhythmic play like hopscotch, jump rope, swimming, basketball, and soccer, the more this region of the brain gets developed and myelinated.

Spinning and swinging is an essential motor skill and sensory input that allows the mind and emotions to settle, allowing focus.

Being able to automatically process the information that a healthy vagus nerve provides is part of what keeps us from being on the autistic spectrum. Every autistic brain is different in what areas are underdeveloped and overdeveloped, but in general, information that can't be processed quickly enough is ignored, and not processing social information is a hallmark of autism. I think this is partly why so many children on the autistic spectrum benefit from a diet that eliminates gluten and dairy—if they're underdeveloped in processing speed, it's more likely their two hemispheres can't team properly to digest more difficult foods. A healthy vagus nerve keeps our digestion and immune system optimal too, as well as keeping us socially engaged and connected.

The parasympathetic nervous system is also involved in warming us up after a sudden exposure to cold. It's very popular in Finland and Russia to use a sauna to heat up, then go jump in the snow to cool off and start the cycle again. I believe they are giving their PNS a good workout. I would never recommend someone to try this who has an autoimmune disease. Start slow. People with poor vagal tone (which means low activity of the vagus nerve) have a great deal of difficulty warming up, particularly in wintertime. I found it easier to start this process in the summer. I started with ice water splashed on my face (the vagus nerve runs through the face.) After I got used to that, I started working on increasing my tolerance for a shower with a cold-water blast. First, I take a warm shower, then I do a minute of cold water near the end. I particularly like this after a hot yoga session. I don't do it if I'm sick. People who are frustrated with having weak voices could likely use increased vagal tone, since it powers the larynx, pharynx, and lungs. They could try adding in a bit of cold-water exposure. I have more suggestions in the action steps at the end of this chapter.

The Steps Needed to Rebuild Health
If we find our health slipping, it is important to recognize the possible road to repair. What I have laid out are the most important things I've found to heal myself: flow, nutrition, internal repair, meditation, vision therapy, rhythm and timing therapies, left-brain healing therapies that have a right-brain connection, right-brain healing therapies, muscular/skeletal repair, and muscle-based therapy relief.

I have examined what worked for me and what didn't. However, just because a therapy did not work well for me doesn't mean it won't work for you. I'll provide you with the information about what I have tried; you can choose what sounds best for you. We all have different comfort levels with left-brain and right-brain healing methods, so honor your needs and pick what your intuition tells you to try first.

If life takes an unexpected turn and your coping mechanisms aren't effective, I hope this book will be a resource for new ideas to regain your emotional, mental, spiritual, or physical balance.

Action steps:
Easy:
Pay attention to your inner talk. When you feel anxious or depressed, look for the connection to the inner talk that caused it. Learning to notice these connections is a skill; it's the basis of starting the process of living your best life. Old thinking patterns slip in so quickly; they're automatic because they're what we've developed over the course of our life. Even one less negative thought about ourselves each day is a win.

Moderate:
Anxiety can be caused by histamine release. If you have lots of chronic stress, you may have leaky gut, and the histamine in your food could be causing anxiety and poor sleep. You might want to modify your diet. I go into more details in the Friday section of this book.

In addition to adding a minute of cold water at the end of a shower, or splashing the face in ice water, it's possible to increase vagal tone by doing the gentle breath-holding found in the meditation practice from Ligmincha that I teach. You can find out more about Ligmincha's inner and outer salung practice on my website, www.rightbrainuniversity.com, or take classes from them at www.ligmincha.org.

The vagus nerve can also be helped by things like humming and slow rhythmic breathing. As mentioned earlier, practicing loving-kindness meditation also increases tone. Remember, high vagal tone means your body can relax faster after being stressed. Low vagal tone means your body is likely stuck in chronic stress and unable to reset. I also found it helpful to gently add more social activity to help with vagal tone. It only works if you can find some type of social activity you don't mind, like volunteering for something that you enjoy, or if you're an introvert, going to the occasional party and helping the hosts if you feel more comfortable that way. Be sure to honor when your body wants to leave.

To help children like Jeff, bring Brain Gym® instruction to your school district. Ask for teachers to get trained in Brain Gym®. Contact Brain Gym® headquarters at info@breakthroughsinternational.org to discuss or find your local instructor through their website, www.breakthroughsinternational.org/programs/the-brain-gym-program. As a Brain Gym® instructor, I'm always available as well. Take a class yourself. It will change your life.

Read more about the vagus nerve and how to help it in *The Self Hacked Secrets*, by Joseph Cohen.

Read Barbara Frederickson's book *Love 2.0.*

Harder:

Try Interactive Metronome (IM), which grows synaptic connections in the brain. Ask your IM trainer to focus on developing whichever hemisphere is weaker. In our culture, it's typically the right brain. Once that's done, have them integrate the left and right hemispheres. I'm an Interactive Metronome provider. You can find out more about Interactive Metronome and my work at Rhythm and Reflex® in Chapter 19. You can find an IM trainer near you at www.interactivemetronome.com.

Monday:

Reduce Stress, Increase Flow

Chapter 4
Finding Flow

Being in Flow

I was thirteen when I took Home Economics, and I loved every moment of class. I still remember the first skirt pattern I cut out. I laid out the fabric and pinned the tissue paper pattern on it. I cut around all the paper and stacked up the resulting pieces. It wasn't until the last piece was cut that I realized I had been running my tongue over my upper lip for the entire ninety-minute class. I'd been so immersed in flow that I was unaware I had rubbed my upper lip raw.

What is Flow?

Flow is any activity in which we become fully immersed in the experience, where we feel energized focus and enjoyment. You may know it as being 'in the zone.' Flow is a term coined by the positive psychology movement. What researchers found is that if we don't allow ourselves to experience flow, we suffer a deterioration of our mental health. In one study where participants were asked to stop immediately during the day each time they felt a sense of flow, the study had to be stopped after two days because of the participants' emotional state.

Many of us who were raised by workaholics or authoritarians have a sense that if we are not producing something useful, it has no worth and therefore it isn't allowable. People like us feel guilty doing anything approaching play. It's taken a lot of doing the wrong thing (driving myself to get my novel completed is a good example) for me to learn that I have no choice about play. I need it and I am more productive if I get it. I'm also a lot happier and so is my family.

Any Activity Will Do
Being in a state of flow doesn't require we go out and buy art supplies. Each person is unique in what will create flow for them, and it can vary even within the same person from day to day. I get lost in flow when I am creating sculptures, writing, or walking on the beach. Some people find shopping at the supermarket to be incredibly stressful. I used to, but since completing vision therapy and Interactive Metronome treatment for ADHD (I'll go into detail in chapters 18 and 19), it's one of the highlights of my day if I am not overbooked. I've known people who find flow when they do the dishes, although I do not share this trait. I know others who find flow while driving a car. For years, driving required so much of my attention that it was anxiety-producing and exhausting. Vision therapy helped me so much that now I can find flow while driving too.

Even if we don't consider ourselves to be creative, it is essential that everyone have an outlet for flow. If we have no hobbies, no way to relax other than watching TV and the like, it's something we need to actively develop. Brené Brown, author of multiple books including *The Power of Vulnerability,* saw the handwriting on the wall and started cultivating creativity after a lifetime of putting down artsy things like scrapbooking. It's now a favorite hobby of hers. Many of us were shamed as children by our teachers for our attempts to be creative in art, dance, and writing. Once that happens, it becomes unsafe to be creative. We need to speak kindly to ourselves about our attempts at creativity.

Develop a Gratitude Practice
The positive psychology movement has given us tools to develop positivity and resilience. It's never too late—these skills can and should be learned by everyone. Positivity reduces our inner critic's activity and leads to resilience. I've found Martin Seligman's books

Authentic Happiness and *Learned Optimism* as well as Mihaly Csikszentmihalyi's book *Flow: The Psychology of Optimal Experience* to be essential reading.

As I suggested before, you can take a free strengths survey at www.authentichappiness.org to help identify which skills to lean on and which skills need growing. I'd always considered myself an optimistic person, but the strengths survey helped me realize I had areas I could improve in. Doing so made me happier.

Above all, take the time to focus on things you are grateful for every day. I've read some suggestions to list three different things a day that you're grateful for and others that say to list five things a day. Start with three and work your way up if five seems unmanageable. Tuning your mind towards gratitude grows your time spent in calm and tells your unconscious that you value calm and joy. Stewing in how unhappy you are increases the stress in your life and will only add to your tendency to dwell on the negative. These are habits of thought. Do you want to develop a healthy habit or continue an unhealthy habit? You have the choice to change.

Start Journaling

Journaling is promoted to lower anxiety, stress and improve sleep. It's said to be a way to heal emotionally, physically, and mentally, although I was skeptical of it. In case you are too, maybe you'll give it a try again after hearing how it's helped me. I have tried journaling multiple times, beginning in my childhood. I'd end up re-reading what I'd written a month or two later, judge it and rip it out. Whenever I find an old journal, the only thing left in it is a forlorn page or two.

I learned what journaling can do for a person after I turned forty. Journaling regularly is an opportunity to become your own best friend, to be able to figure out how you feel about something, and to experience saying anything and being loved no matter what. Once I finally understood this lesson, it helped me begin to thrive. Often, we don't know how we feel until we talk about what's happening in our lives. It's getting rarer that we have enough people in our lives who can bear hearing everything that we need to express. We move a lot, which can disrupt friendships. It's said that our electronic devices are making us less connected too. It's good practice to connect with one's gut and learn how to be positive and encouraging to oneself. There are a lot of daily complaints and stressors that come up in journaling, but once we release that, there's a lot of time spent noticing the intricacy and beauty of life. I find that gets overlooked if I'm not journaling and practicing gratitude.

Writing to Heal
Writing to heal is also valuable and helps the left and right brain to understand and assimilate traumatic events in our lives. If you took the ACE test that I mentioned earlier (available by signup at www.rightbrainuniversity.com/guide), you'll have a sense if you need writing to heal. I encourage everyone to try it. Life is hard for all of us; even the luckiest of us were helpless children at some point. Understanding how to reframe scary events so that we can see how we learned important lessons from them is something that leads us to personal growth and healing. It allows the right and left hemispheres of the brain to begin operating on the same frequency.

When we block the memory consciously in the left brain, the right brain is still reliving it under the radar. This way both hemispheres can go forward together. If you are interested in writing a book, both journaling and writing to heal provide a wealth of emotional material for developing one. It's important to let what you've written settle for some number of months to lose its emotional charge before using it for fiction work. I let mine sit for five months minimum.

Behavioral Epigenetics
Behavioral epigenetics is a study of cellular traits that change because of external or environmental factors. These factors can change not just within ourselves but can be passed along through multiple generations

without changing the DNA. A study with mice at Emory University showed that fear of the smell of cherry blossoms (which was paired with a shock to the foot) is inheritable through two generations. It's very likely that humans are impacted by this, but we've got a heck of a lot more brain than mice do, so it could impact many more generations. If so, that makes it even more important to learn to process trauma so that future generations won't be affected.

One of the biggest environmental factors we can change is how we think about ourselves, how patient we are with ourselves, and whether we shame ourselves for making mistakes. Negative thoughts create toxic changes in our bodies at a cellular level and yet we do it anyway. We wrongly assume being supportive of ourselves will cause an inflated ego. I am not suggesting that we do this in a narcissistic way, but rather like a loving parent or coach would. When we allow constant negativity towards ourselves, essentially, we are providing our own shock to the foot. Please understand I'm not talking about a free-for-all/anything-goes type of scenario. There's a middle ground. For too long, I was strongly in the toxic shame camp without understanding what I was doing to myself. It's taken me a long time to learn how to live in balance.

The Power of Nitric Oxide
In her book *Goddesses Never Age,* Christianne Northrup speaks of the power of nitric oxide, which is released in peak experience such as pleasure, creativity or orgasm. We want to make sure we have a peak experience of some kind every day. This is the flow that positive psychologists are talking about. To produce nitric oxide, we must have enough vitamin D. We also must allow ourselves the time to be unproductive, to get away from what "must" be done and have some play time, no matter what our to-do lists say. I speak as a recovering perfectionist and a recovering workaholic. It's still a challenge despite all I've learned to make sure I take an entire day off once a week. It's a challenge to build in flow/peak experiences every day. I'm also much lower in vitamin D than I should be, as are most Americans.

Rebuilding that level has been a top priority of mine. I want to support my body's ability to produce nitric oxide. I make sure to take vitamin D with vitamin K to avoid tissue calcification, as my integrative medicine doctor has advised.

Action steps:
Easy:
Take the time to identify what puts you into a flow state and think about how to add it to your life regularly.

Pick up a fresh piece of paper and a crayon every day and scribble something on it. Pay attention to how you feel as you do it, and also how you feel as you pat yourself the back for what you did. If you're uncomfortable doing childish things like patting yourself on the back, try to grow your tolerance for it.

If you love art, do a little every day.

Start journaling.

Start a gratitude practice.

Try writing to heal. Dr. James Pennebaker's book *Writing to Heal* is a great place to start learning how.

Moderate:
Take a class in something creative that you always wanted to do some day—-and make it a weekly priority to practice it.

Reading uplifting books or watching shows can put us in a flow state. I enjoy watching Oprah's *Super Soul Sunday* interviews on www.Oprah.com.

I also like Jack Canfield's *Chicken Soup for the Soul* series, along with Marci Shimoff's book *Happy for No Reason*. Think about what lifts you up and do more of that.

Meditation can put you into a flow state. Try Oprah and Deepak Chopra's free 21 Day meditation programs, which are wonderful.

Monitor self-talk in a loving way.

Harder:

Ask your doctor if you should get your vitamin D levels checked and prescribed a supplement if you're low. Ask if you should be given D with K to prevent calcification.

Chapter 5
Meditation 101

From Meditation Avoider to Teacher

When I first started taking yoga classes, I loved them...until it got to the last few minutes of class. That's when the teachers would lead us through meditation. Again and again, I'd try to meditate, only to start getting agitated. It completely ruined class for me. Everyone else seemed content, so it made me feel like there was something wrong with me.

Fortunately, in 2006 I found a form of Tibetan Bön/Buddhist Tsa-Lung meditation that worked for me, which I now teach. Bön combines meditation with movement and breaths that allow the body to calm down enough so that the mind can finally get quiet.

Why We Should Meditate

Meditation helps increase our ability to concentrate because it gives us practice in concentrating. It does not matter whether you succeed in having fewer thoughts or no thoughts. It is the repeated attempts to observe our thoughts that helps develop the ability to be mindful.

Meditation helps protect against aging as it builds additional grey matter in our brain, so our brain stays younger longer. It improves our ability not to be swept along by our emotions because we learn to observe ourselves and our thoughts. It also helps us to remain in our highest level of thinking, executive thought, rather than triggered into reacting with our emotional brain or brain stem.

The Benefits of Observing Ourselves

With practice, we will be able to observe ourselves, our thoughts and emotions and stay centered as higher levels of thinking stay active. Many of us pay attention to thoughts or feelings as being of primary importance in directing our lives. We think our thoughts and feelings are always right and should be acted upon. With regular practice, we can eventually realize that while it's important to honor and process our emotions, it is not good to act on them without rational reflection.

Meditation allows us to access our prefrontal cortex, so we can have that rational review. It allows us to be better at our jobs and in our relationships. Our thoughts and emotions are a constantly changing landscape. If we think of our right brain as a vast blue sky (since the non-judgment of the right brain is always peaceful and calm) and the left brain's anxiety and anger as storm clouds, we can see why it might be better to attempt to focus on the calming vastness of the clear blue sky than on the grey storm clouds of emotion and thought. The sky is always there, even if we can't see it. We can access it through meditation. The calm of the non-judgmental right brain is connected to our intention even when our left brain is ready to give up and act out. We can stay on a more even keel, a more level path, if we meditate.

Four Types of Meditation

Being able to remain calmer lowers stress and increases health by reducing use of the sympathetic nervous system's (SNS) inflammatory pathway. Once I mastered Tibetan Bön meditation, other types of meditation opened up for me. The five types of meditation that have been most helpful to me are:

1) Bön meditation, a type of Tibetan meditation, uses movement and breath-holding to calm the nervous system enough to allow stillness without panic, even for ADHD types like me. It changed my life. It's hard to explain, but easily followed. You can find YouTube links by searching for videos by Ligmincha, an institute

founded by my teacher's teacher Tenzin Wangyal Rinpoche. They have three main practices that I've enjoyed: the Outer Tsa-Lung, Inner Tsa-Lung and Secret Tsa-Lung. (Contact info for all five types is at the end of this chapter.)

2) Vipasana meditation at its simplest uses the basics of thinking, "Rising" on an *in* breath and thinking "Falling" on an *out* breath. It's normal to constantly be distracted and start thinking and feeling again. When we do, simply return to thinking, "Rising" on an *in* breath and "Falling" on an *out* breath. We can't get it wrong, it's all about eventually remembering to think "Rising" and "Falling." Some days my mind is so busy that I don't remember until a minute before the timer goes off at the end of the session—but there's no blame or shame because I've gotten my practice in by trying.

3) Open Focus meditation is proven to produce alpha waves (that's good) and reset the hypothalamic axis stress response (that's good too.) The shortest version of their meditation practice is only seven minutes long. I've found longer versions to be helpful in reducing pain as well as calming me. The idea is to focus on the space between things rather than focusing on objects.

4) Oprah and Deepak Chopra's meditation programs.

5) TAT meditation, created by John Douillard, gives multiple meditative tools using breathing. It's more to learn, but I've found it's always good in a crisis to have lots of tools to choose from.

Meditation and Impermanence of Emotions
Meditation is helpful for learning that feelings are impermanent. This was a revelation to me; I thought that bad feelings hung around, waiting to strike when least expected.

I learned this in 2006, when every Monday I attended a writing class at the Hudson Valley Writer's Center and every Tuesday I took a meditation class. My meditation teacher, Annegret Wolfe Rice, was trained at Ligmincha by Tenzin Wangyal Rinpoche. Annegret led us through meditation, readings, and recordings from his books *Tibetan Sound Healing,* as well as *Healing with Form, Energy and Light.*

Every week as I journaled and wrote, emotions came up that could have blocked me. But thanks to the meditation, I realized that I could feel utterly horrible at the start of a meditation practice and feel transformed and peaceful within a half an hour of practice. That changed my whole outlook on fear and anxiety. For my entire life, I had avoided doing anything that might scare me because I was so terrified of the feelings that would come up. But now I realized I didn't have to be limited in that way anymore.

I realized that my emotions weren't necessarily right. A lot of what I experienced as fear, anger or anxiety was because my brain stem was hijacking my mind and taking over my thinking process. That then generated a flood of potentially incorrect conclusions and emotions. I realized meditation was important to get to a state of calm and to not make decisions based on my brain stem and emotional brain's thinking.

Here's a weird thing that happened to me when I went to see Tenzin Wangyal Rinpoche in New York City. It was 2008 when he came to Tibet House to give a talk. My meditation teacher talked me into going with her to the city. The night before the event, I felt like I had come down with a mild cold. It was pre-Covid, so we went anyway and listened to the talk. Afterwards, my teacher asked me to come with her to get a blessing. I followed her lead as people knelt in front of Rinpoche and he laid hands on the crown of their head. Finally, it was my turn. He laid his hands on my head and I felt like my head suddenly developed a three-inch hole in the top of it. I thanked him and walked to rejoin my teacher, stunned to realize that my cold symptoms had completely gone away. The top of my head continued to feel like it had a hole in it for two days. On the third day, it felt normal, and my cold returned. True story.

Action steps:
Easy:
Try to focus on your breath every day when you wake up, go to sleep or get upset. This is a way to train yourself to stay in the moment. If you get upset, focus on breath rather than the volatility of your emotions. This can help calm you down. Over time, this creates a new habitual reaction.

Moderate:
Practice Bön, TAT or Open Focus by taking part in a once-a-week class. More on Bön at ligmincha.org, Oprah and Deepak Chopra's at www.chopra.com. TAT at www.lifespa.com, and Open Focus at www.openfocus.com. Check out my YouTube channel for meditation videos.

Harder:
Bring your practice into daily life. Go on a meditation retreat. Join me for one of mine. More info at www.rightbrainuniversity.com.

Chapter 6
Give Yoga, Dance or Drum Circles a Try

Yoga in the Seventies

My mom took up yoga when I was about thirteen. I was mortally embarrassed by anything that my parents did that seemed weird, like how my dad was always wearing a trench coat and aviator sunglasses, which was super normal when he worked at Langley Air Force Base in Virginia, also home to the CIA, and not so normal in a small beach town in Southern California. My friends kept asking if he was a spy. Anyway, Mom had a bad back from a fall when she was young and yoga helped her to increase range of movement and decrease pain, but it was humiliating because no one else's mom was doing pretzel moves. I somehow survived being thirteen, got over myself, and was doing yoga moves with my mom soon thereafter, something I wish I could thank my mom for today.

Yoga Today

Yoga still seems so foreign and strange to many people in America. Lots of people try it, but many don't stick with it because it's too different or appears to have too much of a learning curve. One way to get at the unprocessed emotions that are lodged in our bodies is through yoga, so it's worth the effort to develop a yoga practice.

Yoga has the potential to help or harm us. It can help us if we begin to connect to our bodies and start listening to what the body wants. Our body is our guide, so we must surrender our egos when we walk in the door. Yoga will grow our attention span for checking in with the body. If a pose feels hard to do, modify it. Keep checking in with the body. It will be hard to do at first. At some point, newcomers will notice that they've checked out. That's when they can bring their attention back to feeling into the body. There is no shame at checking out and going on autopilot. We just want to start shifting into being present as much as possible. The more we practice this, the better we get at it. This is one of the main benefits of yoga, this close connection to our body. Mostly we ignore the body until it hurts. We can take what we learn on the mat out into our daily lives and improve our ability to heal and be centered in the present moment.

If we don't work at increasing that connection, it's easy to overstretch. That's how yoga can harm us. Competing with other people to do or outdo what they're doing on their mat is the perfect way to get hurt.

Learning from our Emotions

Our bodies are constantly trying to get us to learn from our emotions. To understand this through a blend of chiropractic and Traditional Chinese Medicine, the idea is that neuropeptides for the same emotion are sent to the same regions of the body along the same meridian pathway.

Whenever something happens to us which is like something that happened to us before, the same muscles are activated as in the original incident, reactivating an old unprocessed emotion. The stretching in yoga allows for opportunity to process, learn, and release these emotions.

People who have negative associations to yoga might have sensed that uncomfortable emotions were coming up. Our brain stem fears emotions, so we may reject yoga in order to make our brain stem more comfortable.

It can take a lot of grit to start a yoga practice knowing that we might be emotionally uncomfortable, but the explanation of why it feels uncomfortable can encourage us all to stick it out. Over time, we'll release toxic, inflammatory neurochemicals, something we don't want in our bodies. Our health is too important.

Svaroopa Yoga

The easiest yoga I've ever tried is Svaroopa, a type of restorative yoga that is so comfortable and relaxing that I call it "Couch Potato Yoga." Instructors are trained to be aware of an individual's body alignment, so they can put us into the proper position to allow our bodies to relax.

In Svaroopa it is believed when the hips, shoulder blades and head are perfectly aligned and flat while laying on a comfortable blanket, the body can begin to release tension; it sure worked for me. I had a much higher level of muscle tension when I first started doing Svaroopa yoga and nothing came close to reducing muscle tension so directly, particularly in my head and shoulders. No other restorative yoga classes have ever done as much for me. While it's very easy, it's also profound in its ability to release. After the first class, it felt like I was coming down with the flu, only it consisted of aches of sadness and other emotions rather than the usual flu aches as these neurochemicals were released. I never experienced discomfort again after the first two classes, only deep comfort, and relaxation. I recommend drinking plenty of water to help process the neurochemicals that get released.

You can often get a lot from a yoga class at private studios in your hometown or at your local YMCA. Just keep trying out different styles of yoga until you find one that works for you, along with an encouraging teacher and friendly class vibe.

Russayog

One unique form of yoga is called Russayog, which has pop-up classes in Santa Barbara, as well as DVDs available online. It can provide as much or as little of a workout as you want. Their yoga practice combines yoga with ropes to help provide stability for people who are uncomfortable with their ability to balance. It also provides innovative movements which harness positivity in the body. The body responds to movement in a way that many of us don't understand--for example, holding our arms overhead in a v-shape generates a more positive mental state, while holding arms below the waist generates a more downcast state. This is something I learned from a Waldorf School's Eurythmy dance instructor, so I look for elements of that wherever I can find it. Russayog's warmup and cool-down hand and arm movements leave me uplifted.

Hot Yoga

I've gotten a lot of help from hot yoga. In 2011, while on a writers' retreat on Martha's Vineyard, I had an osteopathic physician-in-training, Andy Estrella, tell me my spine was near the point of no return from degeneration. He recommended Bikram Yoga to help me bring it back. At that point, 90 minutes of hot yoga sounded like a joke: I had chronic fatigue, fibromyalgia, and have always loathed being too hot. But I was desperate enough to try it because I'd had ongoing spinal stenosis symptoms for five months. After three months of Bikram in 2011, normal sensation returned. I've stuck with hot yoga ever since.

Most of the people I've met with fibromyalgia do not exercise. They feel like they can't; they are too tired. I totally understand that because I went through that, too. I found that my anxiety and ADHD symptoms worsened whenever I gave in to listening to how tired I felt. I hated feeling anxious more than I hated feeling tired, so I continued to try to exercise. It was very hard, but I always felt better for having done it. Even at times when I was at my worst levels of pain, anxiety, and depression, I would have these brief windows where I would feel normal from having gone to hot yoga, so I knew I was doing the right thing.

Putting up with Short-Term Humiliation for Long-Term Rewards

Because of the chronic fatigue, I've spent more time on my back in a hot yoga class than most people ever spend in a yoga studio in their entire lives. At first, I went once a week, and it took me about four hours to recover from class. But I felt normal for about half an hour later that first day, for the first time in eight years, so I was hooked. Once I could stay upright for an entire class, I then moved on to adding a second class per week. Once I could stay upright for both classes a week, I moved on to three classes a week. Three years ago, I switched to Core Power, a national hot yoga chain. I love it because classes are only an hour long and the teachers are kind and encouraging. I have more time for my day and find the class length to be perfect for energizing me.

I've also stuck with hot yoga because sweating is a good way to rid the body of toxins—autoimmune illness can cause the body to accumulate toxins—and I want to support their release.

The Benefits of Dance

Dance classes can also get our emotions moving and releasing. Unfortunately, many people are self-critical when it comes to their ability to dance, but if you can be a good coach to yourself, you can enjoy dance no matter your current skill level. If you consider yourself too uncoordinated, be sure to read about vision therapy in Chapter 18, since even people with perfect vision can need prism glasses to enable them to see 3-D.

Dance helps the brain to integrate itself. Moving forward, backward, up, down, jumping, and spinning around are all things that make the two hemispheres of the brain talk to each other and become better coordinated. Most towns offer lots of different types of dance to choose from, so try out whatever your town has available. Consider your local YMCA, recreation center and private studios, depending on your budget. In Santa Barbara, we are blessed to have an amazing Zumba teacher, Josette Tkacik, who has used Zumba as part of a program to heal herself from Advanced Rheumatoid Arthritis. Every day between 150-300 people attend her class, where she teaches about the importance of finding and following your passion, knowing you are here for a purpose, and living in non-judgment, all while delivering a terrific workout. People (yes, women and men) of all ages and abilities come together to share the joy of movement and community.

Bhangra Dance

If you're open to multi-cultural types of dance, the husband-wife team behind Russayog, Jasprit and Teresa Singh, who are always looking to help people develop a healthier mind-body lifestyle, have created Bhangra Dance, which is available online.

Drum Circles

Drum circles have been shown to have a great benefit to both mental and immune system health. In one study conducted in the UK on people who were using the mental health system but were not on medication, by the sixth week of drumming, participants experienced decreased depression and increased social resilience. At the ten-week mark, they saw further reduction in depression, as well as significant improvements in anxiety and mental health. They also saw a shift in their immune system from being pro-inflammatory to anti-inflammatory. Changes were maintained at the three-month follow-up. It's now known that many mental health conditions are connected to underlying inflammatory immune responses. It makes sense that people with conditions as varied as anxiety, depression, bipolar disorder, and more consider drum circles as a part of their toolkit for health when consulting their doctors and psychologists.

Watch Out for Histamine as You Increase Exercise

If you have unexplained weakness at times, going from feeling strong to feeling weak and exhausted, it's possible that the immune system is dealing with histamine sensitivity or mast cell activation. Exercise can activate histamine and mast cells. Be sure to pay close attention when reading the Friday section of this book. It turned out to be a huge help for me in my energy levels.

Action steps:

Easy:

If you're healthy, get your doctor's okay to try something simple like Svaroopa or another type of restorative yoga class.

Tune into how you're talking to yourself before a class, so that you are kind and encouraging. Be patient; reset your thinking in a positive, loving way before each class. I loved my Svaroopa teacher in NY, Sue Kessman-Krieger, who can be reached at suekk1@verizon.net.

You can learn about Russayog Yoga and Bhangra Dance through their YouTube Channel *Russayog Yoga*. DVDs are available at www.yogadancepower.com.

Find a dance DVD or YouTube video you like. One funny, upbeat YouTube video series is by The Fitness Marshall. He pairs hit songs with hip-hop moves and explains everything well. If you think you need to be thin to dance, think again, because one of his dancers is large-sized and inspirational in her fitness level and dance ability. Just get your doctor's okay before trying it.

Look for a drum circle near you. In Santa Barbara, try Sese Ntem's Ewe Drum Circle. The Ewe are a West African people. Ewe culture is about connection. Humans are a social species, and people with bigger social circles have been shown to be healthier. This means introverts are at a health disadvantage. An Ewe drum circle can help build back health. At the time of publication, Sese's drum circle is held Saturday mornings at 10 a.m. in Santa Barbara. You can reach Sese at sese.ntem@gmail.com.

Moderate:

Try a more active yoga class. Yoga styles vary from more constant movement to more static holds. Find something that feels comfortable for you with encouraging teachers. Avoid classes where teachers judge you or tell you to move in a way that feels unsafe. That's not real yoga.

Look for a Zumba class near you. If you're in Santa Barbara, you can find out more information about Josette, Santa Barbara's premier Zumba teacher, at www.josettetkacik.com.

Harder:
If you struggle with your health and have your doctor's blessing to try hot yoga, look for a studio near you. Heat can make us overstretch without realizing it, so monitor yourself and don't go too far your first few classes. Our bodies have developed fascia (discussed more in the next chapter) over the course of our lifetime to protect us, so tread cautiously. If you are not careful, you can go beyond what your body is ready for, which can either lead to injury or alarm in your body. Honor your body by being gentle with yourself. Go slow, drink plenty of water and lie down as often as needed.

Core Power Yoga has locations across the country. You can find them online at www.corepoweryoga.com. They offer unheated and moderately heated yoga classes too. If you're interested in Core Power Yoga, get your doctor's okay first. I'd suggest starting with their unheated classes and work your way into heated.

Chapter 7
Trying Resistance Stretching

What is Resistance Stretching?

When I lived in New York, a friend of mine's husband was a videographer. They had a special needs son and got very excited by a project that the husband was working on because it helped improve their son's flexibility. I tried it and got very excited too. Somehow, when we stretch a muscle while trying to prevent ourselves from stretching it, the muscle can lengthen. How people figured this out is only slightly less amazing to me than how the first person discovered how to make ice cream, and only slightly less important.

Most of us have not heard of resistance stretching before. There are different forms of it around the country. One type, called Resistance Flexibility Strength Training (RFST), was featured as Oprah's exercise of choice in the January 2016 issue of *O Magazine*. Resistance stretching is somewhat like yoga, only more profound in its ability to change us quickly, although it's important to be cautious in how fast we try to change. The trainers I've met make a point of trying to make it accessible to people who haven't exercised in years.

RFST has centers in Boston and Santa Barbara, as well as trainers in Los Angeles and New York. If you're not near these cities, you can benefit from buying Bob Cooley's book *Resistance Flexibility 1.0: Becoming Flexible in All Ways*, or by trying their online training videos at www.geniusofflexibility.com.

I would suggest looking at your local gym to see if some form of resistance stretching is offered; it doesn't need to be RFST to be beneficial; just make sure to feel into your body as you do it.

It's All About the Fascia

Bob Cooley began developing RFST in the 1970's after trying to recover from a devastating automobile accident. He had recovered from many of his physical injuries, but something was still very wrong. Only stretching with resistance made a difference to his health. In researching why, he learned about fascia, a network of tissue which attaches muscle to bone, skin to muscle, and surrounds our organs. Fascia is an instantaneous neural feedback network, but it can become dense and overgrown from physical injury as well as excess thinking or emotion. It's possible to break up the excess fascia and when you do, it feels wonderful, joyful, invigorating, and liberating. The best news is that there is no pain from breaking up dense fascia because it doesn't have nerve attachments to it.

Why We Have Dense Fascia

People with constant stress or who have had physical injuries from sports or auto accidents will have lots of dense fascia in their bodies. We accept these limitations because no one's taught us any differently. Bob's done enough research experimenting on himself to learn that dense fascia can impair the function of our internal and external immune systems. It can also impair our endocrine system and more, which can lead to pain and constriction, which can in turn impair our thought patterns and emotions.

Stretching under resistance contracts the muscle while the fascia resists, which helps reorient it and break it down. Breaking down dense fascia permanently changes it. We can re-grow it, but the practice of resistance stretching can help improve our thought patterns, which makes it less likely that we'd regrow the same amount of dense fascia. Other treatments such as chiropractic can give us immediate relief, but then our patterns of fascia generated from thoughts or emotional tension can shift our bones out of alignment again.

Our Dominant and Weakest Meridians

Bob also realized that our genetic profiles and our childhoods impact us as to which meridians are dominant and which are our weakest links. This helps to bring awareness to our way of interacting with the world. We all have patterns of interacting with the world: some of us do so in a thinking way, some of us in a feeling way, some of us in a spiritual way, some of us in a physical way. It can make it hard to understand other people when our experience of the world is so different. Doing resistance stretching allows us to integrate these different types of patterns into our minds and bodies so that we can be more whole and complete.

Attending trainings has helped me understand others' differences and appreciate them for what they've been through. I've heard many others in class say the same thing. They find it easier to be in the world. They notice how much happier, how much more physically comfortable, and how much more connected they are to their family and people in their community. I think it's especially good for thinking types as compared to some of the other techniques I have tried. Thinking types notice that they have less pain and more flexibility. As a result, they become more whole, rather than just being in their heads all the time.

Weekly Classes and Weekend Trainings

RFST centers offer weekly classes, as well as weekend trainings that I'd recommend. I've attended RFST's levels 1-3. At each level, I felt a sense of increasing freedom. Instead of being held prisoner in a straitjacket of fascia, I had more range of motion, a lighter body, and lighter, faster thoughts. Should this sound a bit too strenuous for your level of fitness, there's a gentle type of fascia stretching, and realignment called Advanced Release Therapy. It was developed by Lori Zeltwanger, who was a long time protogé of John Barnes, who developed what he calls John Barnes' Myofascial Release technique (MFR.) I'll go into this later in Chapter 11. I personally prefer Lori Zeltwanger's approach over MFR, and I also prefer ART over RFST, but everyone is different.

Just a word of caution with RFST: it's not uncommon for people to ask trainers to do too much too soon. For clients who come in from out of town, it's a way to save money and time on treatment. I've sometimes seen three, four, or more trainers work on one person and it's not always a positive experience for the client. Our fascia develops a certain way for a reason. I believe it is there to protect the neuropeptides formed from our emotional experiences until we can process and release them. We are emotional learners, and the body needs the information it contains and can feel stripped if it loses it too quickly. I haven't had a problem myself with two trainers working on me in a session, but I find that three or more is too much. For one thing, with that many people involved, it's hard to stay present with the body's sensations in order to absorb the neurochemical messages because so much effort is spent on physical effort. I know someone who developed a bursa from working with three trainers, and another person who felt he had emotional setbacks from too much being done too soon. There is a temptation to want to go quickly to lower the cost and time until feeling better, but I suggest going slowly and honoring the body, whomever you do the work with.

Action steps:
Easy:
If you're well, look into a local gym for a resistance stretching program. If there is none available, I'd recommend the book *Resistance Flexibility 1.0* to help you develop a regular stretching routine. Streaming videos are available online at www.geniusofflexibility.com if you need further guidance.

Moderate:
If your health could use improving, I'd recommend attending a weekly stretch class at your local gym or a weekend training program at one of the resistance stretch centers, whether it is RFST or another

highly regarded program.

Harder:
Begin working with a trainer. There's so much that resistance trainers can do to give you back the healthy body you were born with. I've done weekly sessions in Santa Barbara which have helped reset incorrect patterns of movement. I've also done a fibromyalgia-specific intensive. It quickly brought me to new levels of energy I haven't seen since before my auto accident. A friend of mine with ME/CFS, formerly known as chronic fatigue syndrome, has been getting a lot of help through RFST in Santa Barbara as well.

Tuesday:

Understand Pain

Chapter 8
Pain and Its Message

Listening to the Body

Our culture often trains us as children to ignore our own sense of what feels right for us to do and when to stop. It's something to become aware of, because ignoring this inner sense can lead to injuries that cause pain that we deal with for the rest of our lives. When I was seven, my mom signed me up for a judo class. The first day all the kids learned how to do a rolling fall to prevent injury when being thrown. I did a bunch of these rolls and the sensei complimented me. A few more times through, I got tired and sat down. The sensei told me to keep going. To please him, I ignored my body's request to recharge. The next time it was my turn, I fell and broke my collarbone. Think back to a time when you were told to ignore your own sense of safety as a child. You can rebuild your connection to that ability.

My Pain History

I had stomach pain growing up since I was eight. I thought it was normal. I slept poorly for most of my life and thought it was never going to change. My body, especially my neck, shoulder, and jaw, hurt more and more after I broke my collarbone since it led to increased facial tension. After a whiplash car accident when I was thirty-nine, my chronic shoulder and neck pain grew much worse and I started developing numbness, tingling and difficulty walking, as well as worsening bouts of stomach pain and IBS attacks.

Neurologists ruled out multiple sclerosis, but it took me years to finally get a diagnosis of fibromyalgia.

Fibromyalgia Pain
Research now suggests that the pain of fibromyalgia is due to extremely excessive amounts of a type of nerve fiber called arteriole-venule (AV) shunts. Doctors are talking about developing treatments based on this type of nerve fiber. I have a good friend with cerebral palsy, who says that by the age of forty, most CP patients also develop fibromyalgia. Since CP patients tend to suffer a great many falls over the course of their lives, it seems possible that an excess of AV shunts occur because of physical trauma as opposed to a purely genetic cause, particularly because many CP patients develop CP because of birth trauma rather than a genetic link.

This ties into the onset of many non-CP patients with fibromyalgia—onset happened after a whiplash car accident or multiple falls. I mention all of this because most people with fibromyalgia have been treated like our problems are imaginary, when really, medicine hadn't advanced enough to know what was wrong. Thank goodness for progress, though there is still much to learn. I think of fibromyalgia as a mind-body illness and am mostly healed without taking any medications thanks to the mind-body treatments I've talked about in this book.

Much of Our Pain is Hidden by Our Autonomic Nervous System
A lot of pain is hidden by the brain via endorphins, oxytocin, and dopamine; this means we frequently do not get a direct sense of cause and effect. We often don't become aware of pain until it reaches the point at which it can no longer be suppressed. Emotional pain becomes physical pain. Mental over-thinking can become physical pain. Our physical pain can become emotional and mental pain. It all runs on the same circuit board.

A healthy brain produces enough endorphins so that the connection between emotional, mental, and physical pain is hidden as we go about in our daily lives. This is a hidden form of fight-or-flight that we are living with. Years of holding onto emotions and thoughts build up until our bodies are toxic. Once we no longer have healthy levels of endorphins, the pain becomes constant. Physical pain can become emotional and mental pain as our physical state leads to depression or sadness or anger at our physical limitations or degeneration. We can get caught up in over-thinking as we try to figure a way out of the situation. As a result, another round of emotional and mental pain also gets stored in the body, adding to our pain and risk of disease as inflammatory neurochemicals continue to build up.

Picking up Other People's Emotional States
I've learned that my pain levels are activated if I'm around other people who are in a painful emotional state. Our mirror neurons can pick up other people's energy and hold it within us. That's a normal human reaction, but most people aren't aware of it because it's processed unconsciously. Our pain gets taken on by others in the same way—that's why it can sometimes feel so hard to be around people who are in emotional pain. Our healing lessens the load on others, as their mirror neurons pick up on our healed state and hold that healthy energy. We can then become a catalyst for change and healing in other people.

Understanding this is why I took on the task of fully healing. I want to live as healthily as I can for as long as I'm alive on this good earth, be an example for my children, as well as a catalyst for healing in others.

Sleep Quality is Essential
Sleep quality, soundness of sleep and the amount of Rapid Eye Movement (REM) cycle time is essential for keeping levels of pain at their lowest. REM cycle is the deep sleep we are in when we dream, typically 90-120 minutes per night. Chronic stress and nutritional deficiencies can impact our ability to sleep soundly which can then set

off an inflammatory cycle in our brain and body.

Pain is Stored in Muscle Memory

I believe that pain is stored in muscle memory as tension. You could say that the tension from injury or trauma causes pain, too. The emotion felt at the time of the injury also gets stored. Much of our physical pain is accumulated emotional pain. Much of our emotional pain is due to stewing over our thoughts. Since emotional pain gets stored in our bodies, our thoughts create physical pain too. The pain offers us the incentive to connect with the held pain and emotion in order to learn from it.

Judging thoughts about others and their actions create tension within us. And our judging thoughts about our own actions can lead to bad moods and a domino effect of further bad actions. It negatively impacts our own internal climate, family life and time with friends. I think we humans are basically judgment machines because judging is a basic survival mechanism. I've found that I feel better the less I judge others. It's a way of reducing my internal stress because our unconscious does not understand the difference between us and other. Our unconscious hides parts of ourselves from our conscious awareness to protect us.

When we were young children, anytime our parents or society rejected our behavior in a traumatic way, our unconscious hid that part away. When we judge another person, our unconscious knows that there is a part of us that is or was a little bit like that person. It causes stress for our unconscious and leads to dissociation, which is a lack of conscious connection to our thoughts or emotions. They get hidden from our conscious awareness by our unconscious in order to protect us. Debbie Ford's book, *The Dark Side of the Light Chasers,* has a more detailed explanation.

Becoming Aware of When We are Under Stress

It's important to become more aware of our stressed states, so that when we are causing our own stress, we can learn to let it go.

Have you ever lost or forgotten something that made you upset? Can you remember what you thought about yourself? Can you remember if you were kind?

Most of us have a usual pattern of getting down on ourselves for forgetting or losing something. We internally beat ourselves up for forgetting and berate ourselves to never forget again. Maybe there's a possibility of finding it, so we start stewing about the likelihood of it getting stolen before we can retrace our steps or contact someone to check if they'd found it.

Here's an example from my life. As you read it, think of how it might happen in yours:

One day in September a few years back, I ordered a latte and a bag of Pike's Place coffee beans at Starbucks, which I bought as a surprise for my second husband. I was in a huge rush. They took so long to make the latte and grind the beans that by the time the latte was ready, I was desperate to get out the door and had forgotten all about the ground coffee. I set off to my favorite massage place to get a gift certificate for my brother-in-law's birthday and give myself the gift of a half hour massage before heading back to the office.

Just as I was getting onto the massage table it flashed through my mind that I had forgotten the coffee. Immediately, every muscle in my body tensed up. There was no way that a massage could do me any good at that point. I could have done my usual pattern of getting down on myself for forgetting the coffee—internally beating myself up for forgetting and berating myself to never forget again, as well as stewing about the likelihood of it getting stolen before I could call and ask them to put it away for me, if it was even still there.

If I had started beating myself up internally, it would have made me feel bad about myself and that would have created internal tension which always (despite our best intentions) gets taken out on other people. Who am I around most? My husband and sons, all of whom would have suffered because of my loving my husband enough to want to surprise him with a gift of his favorite coffee. Since they would have suffered, so would I, because they would have reflected my stress back to me once I passed it along.

Instead of that usual pattern, I used it as an opportunity for personal growth. I turned it around and forgave myself for forgetting, patted myself on the head (figuratively while I was lying on the table; literally once I got back to my car) and said, "You did a good job Lizzie, for letting it go."

Because of that act of self-kindness, I was able to relax those muscles that had tightened up when I realized I left the coffee behind. Because of that forgiveness, I relaxed and got the benefits of massage that I desperately needed. I enjoyed the day, felt happy, and smiled way more than usual. I enjoyed the beauty of the people that I came across, all because of this loving act toward myself. I let go of whether the coffee would be there, and it was there when I went back for it.

I was so happy, all of me, my unconscious, and my conscious. I remembered to be grateful for ultimately remembering the coffee, to give thanks for what I have in my life and that I usually have a very good memory. By doing so I reduced my internal tension. Why would I live any other way than this? When you become aware of the options, it just doesn't make any sense, does it?

How Self-Judging Hurts our Loved Ones

To sum this up, when we started beating ourselves up internally, it makes us feel bad about ourselves and that creates internal tension which always gets taken out on other people. Who are we around most? Our family and friends. Who will be the bearer of our tension? Our family and friends. Because we've made them suffer, they will have higher stress levels, which rebounds back on us.

Next time you forget something, try using this exercise of self-love and compassion.

And yet so many people have the same pattern of beating the tar out of their inner selves in this way for making mistakes. The stats are that 3,999 people out of 4,000 want to please others; that is the ratio of normal people to sociopaths.

We are Parenting Ourselves Our Whole Life

Our unconscious wants to please us. We are the parent of our unconscious self for the rest of our life. Be a good one. Knowing that I am my own parent is a game changer for the quality of my life. I have found that making someone else "pay" for how they've treated me only generates long term harm for myself.

No matter how much someone else loves me, they are not going to be obsessing about how much harm or injustice they caused me. Either they feel bad and resolve to do better or they don't. Either way they end up moving on.

Meanwhile I have created a toxic environment in my body because of obsessing over the situation. Far better to process how I feel and either move on from the relationship or realize that someone else might have reacted differently to the same situation. Other people don't "make" me feel anything— my own unique history and neural pathways, plus the type of day I'm having all combine to generate my feelings. Same thing holds true for other human beings.

Interactions with Other People are a Mirror for Us to see Our Own "Stuff"

Seeing the same kind of emotions recur time after time in our life is a mirror for us to realize that we have anger (or whatever other emotion is coming up) that needs to be worked through. We might react in anger at all the many angry people we come across, not understanding that other people might react with compassion to the same situation. I believe that we all have default programming that we are put here to learn how to rise above when we are triggered.

Not being true to oneself puts one into pain, contraction, and inflammation. This is because of the increased brain stem and emotional brain activation. If, for example, someone stays in a relationship out of fear of the unknown, it means they are ignoring the emotional information from the unhappiness they feel that their needs aren't being met, rather than using their unhappiness as an opportunity to grow. Meanwhile, that unhappiness is causing pain, contraction and inflammation that can lead to disease. So is living with fear of the unknown rather than learning how to take steps to stop being frozen by fear in their lives.

Changing Our Response to Pain

I am all for working things out in relationships, but a clear-eyed view of a situation is also helpful. How can we become our best self in a way that might inspire others to be their best selves? How can we become our best self unless we learn to be kind to ourselves? I've realized that just because we have physical, mental, and emotional pain does not mean that we should allow ourselves to be immobilized by the pain or the fear of pain. When I was under emotional or mental tension, I needed to find a way to release the tension from my body. That tension was a wakeup call that something wasn't working in my life and needed to be addressed. Taking pain seriously as an indication of stress is an important part of the process.

Some people let go of outcomes and pray for help, which I believe really works. At a minimum, I suspect it activates something in the unconscious that takes pressure away from the ego self.

Action steps:
Easy:
Realize that thinking kind thoughts about yourself and redirecting negative or judging thoughts about others will help reduce contraction and pain in your body. Self-compassion was the biggest healer for me when I was depressed. Through self-compassion, I found the motivation and ability to act.

Try prayer. Even if you're an atheist or agnostic, try praying to the collective unconscious or to the unknown capacities of the human mind and heart. There is far more to our brains' abilities than science yet understands, and as I said before, I think it reduces pressure on our unconscious. For those who are not depressed, try the moderate or harder action steps below:

Moderate:
Try Open Focus meditation, developed by Les Fehmi, at www.openfocus.com. Open Focus meditation helps produce alpha waves in the brain and can reset the stress axis that keeps us in fight or flight mode. It helps us focus on the space between things, rather than on the objects we see around us. Taking in visual data and processing it into objects is a contractive process. This is because it can overuse our focal vision system, which activates our fight-or-flight sympathetic nervous system. Over time, constant contraction adds up to pain.

Harder:
Begin a resistance stretching program either locally or using RFST's book *Resistance Flexibility 1.0,* which helps release and realign the body where injury, thought and emotion have caused fascia growth and contraction. Some of RFST's online videos (available at www.thegeniusofflexibility.com) are specifically geared to stop neck or other specific pain.

Try learning Myofascial Release through one of Lori Zeltwanger's programs at www.advancedreleasetherapy.com. It helps reduce stress and connect you to your body. More information about her work in Chapter 11.

Try hot yoga or another form of yoga that you connect with. Most hot yoga studios offer cooler or unheated classes for beginners.

Try cognitive hypnotherapy to reduce conditioned responses to life's stresses.

Although it is geared towards training psychologists, I've found www.nicabm.com to have good programming and some free resources. Please note that these classes do not take the place of working with a professional.

Chapter 9
Musculo-skeletal Repair

Starting in Sleepy Hollow, New York

Sleepy Hollow was my home for fifteen years. It is a wonderful town filled with warm and welcoming people. Its annual Halloween festivities, held at historic Philipseburg Manor, draw thousands of visitors every year. I used to live a stone's throw from the spot mentioned in Washington Irving's *Legend of Sleepy Hollow*, where the Headless Horseman threw his jack-o'-lantern head after poor Ichabod Crane. My home was also a stone's throw to a lesser known but no less fabulous attraction of Sleepy Hollow: the office of Dr. Betty Gao, the physical therapist who started my body on the road to recovery. After decades of high tension, my body had started to break down. Here's what I've discovered that helped:

Physical Therapy

I learned the hard way to get multiple recommendations for a physical therapist. Even so, I've found a difference going to a physical therapist who has a PhD. As mentioned before, I broke my collarbone when I was seven and despite going to physical therapists off and on for help over the years, no one figured out that my arm was out of the socket because of that broken bone. It only took Dr. Gao two visits to realize that's why I had chronic shoulder and neck pain. There are plenty of wonderful physical therapists without a PhD; my current PT in California doesn't have one. Get your recommendations and if you don't feel better after treatment, move on to a new person. Try searching out someone with a PhD if you can't get relief.

Physical therapy helps to release muscle tension, increase strength, and educate clients about what is wrong with how we use our bodies. It works best when combined with a whole-body exercise like swimming, yoga or RFST, so that all the muscles get strengthened. Dr Gao gave me exercises that helped me unwind the high-tension wires that masqueraded as back muscles.

Chiropractic

From what I've read, medical researchers now think of meridians as nerve and fascia highways. Chiropractors think of meridian pathways as nerve pathways. I've gotten a lot of pain relief and increased mobility from going to a chiropractor. Their work corrects spinal alignment to allow for proper nerve flow. But why does the spine get out of alignment? Very likely because of dense fascia. Why does fascia shift our bones? Because of trauma, whether physical, mental, or emotional. Ultimately, we can have back problems because of mental and emotional issues too, not just physical injury. Our back muscles contract when we have a feeling of danger or the urge to move away from something. They ease up when we have a feeling of safety or desire to move towards something or connect with it. Over time, constantly feeling in danger (chronic stress telling our bodies that we are unsafe) keeps our muscles contracted until we are locked into spasm. Again, I find it important to combine chiropractic with resistance stretching like RFST or Lori Zeltwanger's Advance Release Therapy to break up or rearrange old fascia, as well as release emotional patterns.

The most helpful chiropractors I've been to combine nutrition with balancing the nervous system. I wouldn't be without a good chiropractor, but I make sure that I work on processing my thoughts and feelings, so that I'm not expecting my chiropractor to do all the work without any help from me. Occasionally I go to my chiropractor, get adjusted, and my back immediately goes out again. I can always trace it to a thought or emotion that I was having. I've learned not to lock into fear around it. I find it almost always goes away within a few minutes if I hold the Emotional Stress Release points and the Kidney Meridian #27 points in the diagram in Chapter 15 while providing myself a supportive thought to replace the stressful one. If that ever happens to you, see if this combination helps you reset your spine too.

Cranial Sacral Therapy

I've found Cranial Sacral Therapy (CST) as done by an osteopathic physician to be of enormous help. The muscles contract in a way that can prevent proper flow of spinal fluid from the cranium to the sacrum and osteopaths can get things flowing again. My osteopath's suggestion of trying Bikram yoga to help reduce spinal stenosis symptoms was genius; it helped change my patterns of using my body.

In the years since I lived near an osteopathic physician who did this type of technique, I've occasionally tried CST and found it pleasant but useless for making change until finding a gem in Santa Barbara who wants to remain anonymous. Her secret? She applies a good deal more pressure than the standard CST treatments as taught by some well-known CST schools. How do I know it works? My C5 vertebrae was too far back ever since an old aikido injury and chiropractic treatments didn't resolve it, but in just a few sessions, it's headed back to where it belongs. Additionally, I had some facial asymmetry that turned out to be connected to that same injury that's also cleared up in just a few sessions. I alternate between cranial sacral treatments and chiropractic, so that what comes up in one is cleared in the other.

The bottom line is that the bones of the head are very mobile, and when they are prevented from moving due to injuries, that plays out into the rest of the vertebrae. It even was causing my atlas to shift out of alignment, causing stress on the brain stem. If you remember my neurological chiropractor's diagnosis in Chapter 2, my higher blood pressure on that right brain stem was more likely caused by the aikido injury jamming up the bones of my head as well as the vertebrae in my neck.

Feldenkrais

This is a wonderful system to retrain the body in how to move. We typically use our bodies in a non-optimal way at least some of the time. We are often unaware of certain parts of our body, yet constantly aware of other parts of ourselves. We can overuse our bodies in a way that causes degeneration. Feldenkrais gives us an opportunity to reset how we use our body. It allows our unconscious to find easier, more optimal ways to move. We should be able to move without holding our breath or needing to breathe. We should be able to move our eyes without moving our head or our body, without jerkiness or holding our breath. Feldenkrais can make this easy.

Feldenkrais offers two modalities: the first is a group class called Awareness Through Movement (ATM) which helps us become aware of movement patterns. We can feel results in as little as an hour. The second form of treatment Feldenkrais practitioners offer is called Functional Integration (FI.) These are one-on-one sessions to help clients make changes in patterns of movement, thinking, sensing, and feeling. I've found them simple yet profound, non-invasive, and energizing.

Some Feldenkrais practitioners are combining Functional Integration with energy work, which I have found to be helpful.

NuBax Trio and Gravity Boots

Reducing spinal tension is important. Our typical pattern with our brain stem response to chronic stress causes back spasms and cramping as fascia and muscles contract. Chronic stress increases spinal tension. Excess tension in the fascia and muscles along our spine drives our vertebrae together in an unhealthy way. It's an unconscious reaction to emotional tension and to our primitive freeze response.

This excess fascial and muscle tension causes a reduced

amount of blood flow in these critical areas. Bones, ligaments, tendons, muscle, and fascia all suffer from poor circulation. I believe it's a contributing factor to osteoarthritis and osteoporosis, in part because not enough nutrients are being brought into the area, and cellular debris is not being efficiently cleared away.

I've used the Nubax Trio, a type of portable stretching device available online, to help get relief. The advantage of a Nubax is that the user doesn't have to hang upside down. Instead, the device is on the floor and one kneels over it to get the stretch.

Some people I know swear by regular use of gravity boots to help loosen up their backs.

If you are constantly in back pain, ask a chiropractor, osteopath or doctor to advise you on using one of these devices. The spine could be too degenerated to safely use one. If you get the okay, go slowly. The back can go into spasm if you try to do too much too soon. Once again, it's the build-up of fascia that causes the muscles to be painfully contracted, so while gravity boots or a Nubax Trio are of benefit, resistance stretching, and myofascial release are also an important part of healing.

The Divided Mind

In the book *The Divided Mind* by Dr. John Sarno, he talks about what he has experienced in his work as a back doctor. Dr. Sarno has found that injured or degenerated spines are not painful once surgery has repaired the physical issue, if that's all that's going on. Most of the people he sees can be helped by treatment, but 10-15 percent cannot. Over the years, he's found that for these people, back pain is associated with the unconscious mind holding onto trauma and unprocessed anger. Highly sensitive people are continually stressed by their environments. They react more strongly to situations than others, and they take on other people's energy. They experience other people's emotional states as their own. As the years go by, they hold more and more and more tension in their bodies. They are much more stressed than the average person. He also found that highly sensitive people need a combination of psychotherapy and back treatment to end their back pain.

Sarno explains that this type of pain is a normal human response to feeling overwhelmed. Anyone can get to the same place by having enough trauma, even non-highly sensitive people. Studies have shown that only two days of interrupted REM sleep is enough to give people symptoms of fibromyalgia. I believe unconscious anger is worth addressing, because underneath that, I have found huge reservoirs of love. As we move through the emotions that are hard to face, like anger or fear, and take steps to activate the right brain, our acceptance of emotional states grows, leaving us more frequently in a state of non-judgment or peace.

If you are highly sensitive, remember it is not your fault. According to doctors, this is a genetic predisposition. People who are highly sensitive and who have experienced trauma either in childhood or as adults tend to have a lot of pain and health issues. There is a way back to health and happiness, and I'm here to tell you that I'm now consistently healthier and happier than I have ever been in my life.

Sleep Position

A word of caution about sleep position. Fascia grows day and night in response to thoughts, feelings, and injuries. It is intended to strengthen us where we are weak. It's a common problem as we age that we are stiff when we wake up and I think the problem is connected to being mostly still in bed and fascia growing during sleep in response to dreams. It makes sense to me to be careful with our sleep position. I make sure my head is properly supported by a pillow. When I sleep on my side, my body weight is resting squarely on the side of my shoulder, not on the back edge. Alignment is important to keep one's shoulders from rolling forward. Bringing the legs up too much causes issues with digestion. I find I sleep better and have better digestion if my knees are no more than a ninety-degree angle to my body. I also notice that when my shins make a ninety-degree angle with my thighs or greater (so my feet are further away from my body) that I am much calmer and sleep better. Perhaps this is because when the knees and shins are drawn up and in too much, this mimics the classic shape of trauma—the fetal position. I used to have one knee drawn in higher than the other, which is also a stressful position that I don't recommend. It throws the body out of alignment and overactivates the psoas. And if you have troublesome dreams, all the more reason to find a good psychologist.

Action steps:
Easy:
Try a Feldenkrais class. The Seeing Clearly Workshop, which helps unlink breathing and vision from movement, is available online at www.feldenkraisinstitute.com, which also provides classes and therapists in New York City. You can also find an instructor near you at www.feldenkrais.com, as well as CDs for sale to walk you through training.

Resistance stretching also addresses pain, fascial tension, and muscle imbalance, so I'd recommend a local gym or the book *Resistance Flexibility 1.0.*

Moderate:
Make an appointment with a chiropractor, osteopathic physician or Feldenkrais practitioner for a one-on-one session and commit to regular self-care with them. If you are looking for which type of chiropractor might be best for you, I have found Gonstead to be very helpful for scoliosis for people in my family. Gonstead chiropractors work on specific regions of the spine that are stuck. They aim to bring back normal mobility to those regions. Sometimes chiropractic can bring too much mobility to areas that don't need it, and Gonstead avoids that issue. I'd recommend them for specific problems like scoliosis. The Gonstead chiropractor that helped my family so much with scoliosis did not help my fibromyalgia. I know she is a gifted chiropractor, but none of her work decreased my pain, and she kept

telling me that I should have been better long since. I began seeing other chiropractors who have helped me so much more. I think that for people who are not as in touch with their emotions, who are more thought oriented, Gonstead is great, just like resistance stretching is a great entry point for thinking types. You can find a Gonstead chiropractor at gonstead.com. For people who are overly in touch with their emotions, or who have autoimmune issues, I'd suggest chiropractors who work with meridians and emotions, particularly ones who muscle test. You'll need to interview your local chiropractors to see who is willing to work with you this way. And if you interview cranial sacral therapists, you might find one who has the touch needed for lasting change.

Harder:

Dr. John Sarno's findings are another reason to start counseling with a psychologist who is trained in Focusing or as I mentioned before, with a Jungian analyst who uses dreams, active imagination, creative expression, and Sandplay therapy in the tradition of Carl Jung and Dora Kalff to honor the body's wisdom. See contact details in Chapter 20's action steps.

Attend a group program offered by my friend Chad Cryder, author of *Men are DAWGS and Women are CATS: A Field Guide for Human Relationships*, and *A Great Love*. Chad is at www.chadcryder.com.

Chapter 10
Muscle-Based Therapies Relief

Tai Chi and More

When I was a child, I lived in a little village outside of Taipei called Tien Mou for a little over four years. There were lots of U.S. military families who lived there, along with the locals. We did lots of fun things with the communities mixing together, like listening to the traveling Chinese Opera that would come to town, while eating dried octopus. Not my favorite Chinese snack. My favorite was the dried, salted plums that made the inside of my mouth feel all pruned up like your fingertips do when you stay in the bathtub too long. About one block away was an institute where people did Tai Chi every morning behind a high masonry wall. We could only catch tantalizing glimpses of the Tai Chi from the front gate as we drove by, until the day my dad took us for a hike up Dog's Head Mountain and then down the other side, straight onto the institute's grounds. We walked along a path that took us next to dozens of people doing Tai Chi in unison, a sight that still takes my breath away.

Trauma Release Process: Tremoring 101

David Berceli is a psychologist who travels the world giving people who've gone through unspeakable trauma the tools they need to heal. He's helped victims of the Bosnian War, the Rwandan Genocide, and the 2004 Indian Ocean tsunami disaster, among others. What he's learned to help them heal can help the rest of us heal.

He first stumbled across the problem when he was in Bosnia,

where he noticed that babies were shaking in reaction to bomb blasts, but that the older children didn't shake as much. The older the children, the less they shook. The adults didn't show any reaction at all. It turns out they didn't want their children to know they were scared. In theory, this is admirable, but by not shaking, they were locking trauma in their bodies and teaching their children how to lock trauma in their own bodies. Older children were showing how "grownup" they were by hiding that response.

We also try to hide our stress or shock reaction in social situations and at work as a way of maintaining social status (and employment…) It's never too late to release trauma and it's something you can work on at home.

The Psoas
David Berceli's book talks about exercising just to the point of muscle fatigue and then allowing the muscles to tremor. He specifically talks about the psoas muscles and the muscles extending into the quadriceps and the inner thighs. Something he didn't mention that was very helpful to me was to put my hands against the headboard of my bed and press until my neck, shoulder and arm muscles fatigued and started to tremor. This released a lot of my fascial tension.

After completing the trauma release process, I had much less tension. I think it has contributed to my growing feeling of peace and calm. Occasionally I will have some tremoring after intense exercise, but it is nothing like the process in the initial years.

Muscles in spasm produce lactic acid, and I believe the combination with dense fascia traps much of the lactic acid in place. Anytime you have trigger points on your body or chronic pain in your back from muscle spasm, it's likely because there is a buildup of dense fascia, which makes the muscles too shortened. The fascia is locking the muscles in place and is doing most of the muscles' work. Once the fascia is released, I've found the muscle is quite weak. At that point, I need to rebuild my muscle strength. I now expect it as part of the process. I get excited when I experience this, because I know I'm making progress in healing. Fascia release happens at different levels. Fascia is constantly being formed, so it's a work-in-process to head towards reduced fascial tension, not a one-shot deal.

Getting Muscles Functioning Correctly

When fascia is released, it allows the muscle to move, proper blood flow gets going and lactic acid gets released. When I first started hot yoga, I would hit a point in a class where I would feel nauseated. I realized it was an overload of lactic acid, which is processed by the liver, and I needed to back off how much stretch I was doing so that my liver could adjust.

While working on the trauma release process I got to the point where the tremors weren't noticeable if others were to look at me. Once that happened, I started adding it into my hot yoga practice. I'd spend an extra few minutes at the end of the session as we were lying flat on our backs in Savasana to let the tremors subside.

If you try releasing muscle-based tension and find tremoring makes you too uncomfortable or anxious, get assistance before continuing. At times, this and all the other release therapies have made me feel uncomfortable or overwhelmed. Seeing a psychologist was a great help to me as I went through the healing process.

Qigong and TaiChi

Part of what happens in fibromyalgia is a hypersensitivity to physical sensation, so I can feel the energy in the meridians moving through my body. The most helpful of the Asian therapies I have found that moves the most energy for me are Qigong and Tai Chi.

Qigong is a wonderful system of body movement. I had a teacher who helped me clear my entire system, bringing in fresh energy and finding out which meridian pathways were currently blocked. What a wonderful gift. Qigong masters can get us into quite an in-depth connection to our body during a class. In Santa Barbara, I've been lucky to take classes with Master Li Jungfen, who teaches worldwide through shengzhen.org.

Tai Chi is also wonderful for moving chi (another term for energy) in the body. Like Qigong, it is also helpful with moving lymph through the body and helping us connect to our body.

Before I started these alternative methods of healing, I used to get at least two or three migraines a month. Vision therapy helped to reduce both the frequency and severity of my migraines. The process of meditation and taking classes in Qigong and Tai Chi helped me understand how much holding I was still doing. In addition, learning Touch for Health and PanHarmonic Healing, which I'll go in depth on in Chapter 15, has given me tools to release energy rather than hold it in my body. Being able to move energy through these different methods so I do not hold it and develop a migraine has been invaluable.

Resistance Stretching
As mentioned before, I have found RFST to be an effective form of stretching with resistance. I mention it here because the workout it provides allows tremoring too. Again, the meridian pathways reach through a lot of different muscles. Blockage along these channels can cause pain in the muscles they are paired with, which leads to an inflammatory pathway. Working with self-stretches, assisted and/or trainer stretching, I get an increased sensation of energy flow, lightness and ease of being. Activating muscles while stretching allows fascia to release and muscles to elongate.

Massage
Massage has also been a big help for me. The benefits from it are that trigger points can be calmed and the muscles that are in constant overuse for weeks, months or years get a chance to get rid of some of the lactic acid buildup. Massage that focuses on fascia can help allow the muscles to release rather than being chronically contracted. Chronic contraction is both inflammatory and painful. Massage also improves circulation.

I enjoy massages that are meridian based, though others can

find it overwhelming. I like Thai massage because it combines massage with meridian-based stretching. I found that during Thai massage I tended to have a lot of tremoring, which releases tension, stretches fascia, and brings about healthier blood flow. I also find meridian-based Chinese massage very helpful.

Rolfing was an amazing process of releasing fascia and allowing me to utilize my body better. Dense fascia had bound my shoulder blades to my back ribs and locked my hips out of alignment. My right collarbone didn't move properly, so my lungs couldn't expand fully. Despite what I'd heard about the discomfort of Rolfing, my Rolfer, Torrey Trover, was intent on keeping me comfortable. My first Rolfing session was an overview which included some visceral massage, which releases fascia from around the internal organs. That day, I learned firsthand from Rolfing how emotions get locked in the body, frozen in time. As the fascia was released, I re-experienced the emotion from a basketball being slammed in my stomach when I was eight. By paying attention to the feelings of both body sensation and emotional responses, I could process and release that trauma.

The Bowen Technique is a form of fascia therapy that I've found to be incredibly helpful. It's very simple, yet effective and it doesn't hurt as its being done. Kathryn Pieron is my Bowen body worker in Santa Barbara. The best way I can describe the sensation is that the body feels a bit like a string instrument getting its strings plucked–I felt all sorts of emotional messages getting released as different muscle groups got their fascia rolled. This was the biggest, most immediate shift I felt since trying Svaroopa yoga, so I was excited by the possibilities. Keep in mind for people with fibromyalgia or chronic fatigue that the process could seem sensorially overwhelming without a proper understanding. You might feel a bit headachy, but if you pay attention to all the sensations and emotions that come up without judging them, this technique can create a big shift. It took about twenty-four hours to process my first Bowen treatment, and once I got through it, I felt I'd reached a new level of reduced tension. The following treatments have been equally helpful and easy to handle. Be sure to hydrate as directed by your masseuse and your doctor.

Chi Nei Tsang & Transformational Abdominal Massage

Chi Nei Tsang is a type of Chinese massage that is an applied form of Qigong. Chi Nei Tsang believes that, in essence, emotions are organs and organs are emotions. This type of massage helps to clear the abdomen of unprocessed emotional charges. It helps people change how they manage life from the inside, so they can experience more energy, better physical health and greater joy. I have found it to be wonderfully therapeutic. More info can be found in the action steps at the end of the chapter.

Proprioceptive-Deep Tendon Reflex

P-DTR is a modality that helps to identify and reset areas of the body where an injury memory is stored, along with resetting the impacted neuroreceptors. It was created by orthopedic surgeon Dr. Jose Palomar. Dr Palomar is a pioneer in the research and development of therapeutic interventions to reset receptor dysfunctions. Basically, his theory is that part of what happens to us after an injury is that nerve receptors are stuck in active mode, and he's done research in how to reset them.

I've had this done and it is amazing; it's like turning back the clock to before the injury happened. One example was the time I went in and had some P-DTR done for pain in my upper back and midback. The next day I went to yoga and did a move I'd never been able to do in seven years of hot yoga. Because of an injury years before, I'd never had the strength or balance needed to lift one leg during side plank, but that day and ever since, I've been able to. P-DTR is not to be missed.

Action steps:
Easy:
If you have not been severely traumatized, read David Berceli's book, *The Revolutionary Trauma Release Process: Transcend Your Toughest Times* and begin to work through the exercises. (If you have been severely traumatized, please read the Harder section below.)

Moderate:
Find a masseuse to help support your work in calming your trigger points or accumulated held stress.

Try a Rolfing massage—and if you find someone who works well with you, try "the Ten", a series of ten massages designed to maximize releasing fascia-holding throughout your body in a balanced way. Find a professional near you at rolf.org. See Torrey Trover if you're in Santa Barbara. She can be reached at torrey.trover@gmail.com.

Find a bodyworker who uses Bowen Technique. You can find a practitioner through americanbowen.academy in the United States. If you're in Santa Barbara, I recommend Kathryn Pieron. Kathryn can be reached at kpieron@gmail.com.

Try working with a visceral masseuse or someone who does Chi Nei Tsang massage. You can find a masseuse who specializes in it at https://www.chineitsang.com

Find a bodyworker who uses P-DTR. Look for someone near you on the P-DTR website at www.pdtr-global.com.

Harder:
If you have been severely traumatized, find a good psychologist who can help you heal, then with your psychologist's blessing, begin to work through Berceli's book, or find someone who does Somatic Experiencing (SE) as developed by Peter Levine, author of *Waking the Tiger*. SE comes highly recommended, but I have yet to try it myself because I found the healing I needed earlier in my journey. In researching it for the book, I came across Irene Lyon, who has a

program to help heal the nervous system that combines Feldenkrais with SE, among other things. The program has an active community and offers 3 free videos that are right on point. If this sounds interesting, check out the videos and see if it sounds like it's your path. She can be reached at irenelyon.com.

Try classes in Qigong, Tai Chi or Jin Shin Do to see what works best for you.

If any of the processes in this chapter seem emotionally overwhelming when you try them, again, please find a psychologist who specializes in Focusing or one who does Jungian analysis incorporating dreams, active imagination, creative expression, and Sandplay. Contact details for Sandplay and Jungian analysts are in the Action steps of Chapter 20.

Chapter 11
More Myofascial Help

It's Not Your Back, It's Your Stress Level

Back in 2008 my sister and her family came to visit us in New York. I just loved having her visit; it really helped calm me down. We decided to take a yoga class together one Sunday morning but the simple act of walking out the door and closing it behind me threw my back out. We went anyway and it locked in the problem, which lasted for days. Back then, anything could set my back off. Sometimes I would sneeze, and my back would go out. Even thinking in bed was enough provocation for my back to go out. After my divorce I could not lift a three-pound weight over my head without it going out. Now I can do an entire iron yoga class hefting three- and four-pound weights overhead without a problem. My back is so much stronger these days... It's been a combination of reducing my stress levels and these wonderful therapies that have allowed it to happen. It could happen for you too!

Advanced Release Therapy, an advance on MFR

John Barnes is a physical therapist who is a leading expert in myofascial release (MFR.) He has centers in Sedona, Arizona and Malvern, Pennsylvania. Because he's trained over a hundred thousand healthcare professionals (mostly PTs and masseuses) in his methods, it should not be hard to find someone in your area who is experienced in this method to help you. That said, as I mentioned before, I prefer the work of one of his former practitioners, Lori Zeltwanger, who's added in a critical mind-body component and formed her own program called Advanced Release Therapy.

The core idea of Advanced Release Therapy and MFR is that fascia is moldable and can change shape. That sounded like a good way to work on my fascial tension, so I booked an appointment in Ventura, California with a local expert in this method, a masseuse named Cindy Rowland Wilson trained by both Lori and John. The first treatment was soothing and calming. As she walked me through the treatment, she encouraged me to feel into my body as she held my ankles. She asked me to feel where it was tight and imagine that it was softening or melting. I visualized melting candle wax and warm taffy being pulled and after a few minutes, I could feel the region softening and becoming more mobile. She then continued to my arms, gently moving them, and letting them release, again asking me for internal visualization help. It occurred to me to begin Focusing (see Chapter 20 for details) as part of the process, which I found to be a great pairing. Cindy explained that she only did a gentle release, to give me a taste of the method. She encouraged me to do a specific type of stretching at home and suggested some books for further explanation. She said a full treatment often makes those with fibromyalgia feel like they've taken two steps forward and one step back. She suggested thinking of it as a process of healing, not a cure-in-a-day. After trying the technique at home and seeing great results, I've added it to my daily routine.

Releasing Fascial Constrictions for Improved Lymphatic Flow
Among other things that Cindy has taught me, ART's form of MFR addresses fascial constrictions in the breasts. I never thought I'd use that technique, but it's been helpful because at times I feel breast constriction when I sleep on my stomach. Using the release technique alleviates the discomfort. Because it feels less restricted, I think it's possible that the breast tissue is likely getting better blood and lymph flow. This seems like a good thing to me, so I thought I'd suggest it as a tool to ask your ART/MFR therapist about, should you feel

constrictions.

Restorative Foam Roller Classes

Another way of helping to clear excess fascia is through a foam roller. These types of classes are getting much more known and popular around the country. I've found them very helpful to correct range of motion issues and painful knots in my muscles and recommend them. It's even helpful to improve sleep.

The Orbi Therapy Ball

Another useful tip that Cindy gave me was the importance of using an Orbi therapy ball to help release fascia (you can find it online at theorbi.com) or make one by putting two racquetballs into a tube sock, tying it tightly and cutting off any excess material once you're satisfied with it. I don't think there's anything I've tried that's been more important than working with the Orbi daily. I would not have known how to correctly use one without first going to an ART or MFR specialist for at least a few sessions. If I wake up in the night, I reach for the Orbi and start working on the points that have the most tension. It helps me to fall back to sleep more quickly, and over time it's helped significantly reduce my high fascial tension.

Keep in mind that muscles that are relaxed should feel soft. If you touch a relaxed muscle and it feels gristly, hard or tender, it's likely to have dense fascia in it.

In the months since I began this treatment, I've also seen Lisa West in Ventura, a PT who filled in when Cindy was away. Lisa is another skilled healer who's working on a book based on her experience as a therapist and I've counted myself lucky to be in her care, too.

The Difference between ART/MFR and RFST

ART/MFR is perfect for people who are not inclined to exertion. Resistance stretching and RFST require an effort at physicality and it's easier for people who are in shape. That said, RFST breaks up excess fascia and ART/MFR have us live with our excess fascia, albeit reshaped. ART/ MFR helps us reshape it so it no longer binds, but it remains (free of restrictions.) ART allows us to process the emotions while reshaping the fascia. I think there's a place for both types of treatments, and I'm glad to have access to both.

My first workshop in ART/MFR was with Lori Zeltwanger. She offers a 5-day immersion retreat twice a year, one in California, the other in Florida. It was a wonderful experience both for newbies like me as well as the therapists who attended.

Cindy recommended an excellent book called *Comprehensive Myofascial Self-Treatment*, by Joyce Karnis. In the book, Karnis discusses the dura, the deepest layer of the fascial system. The dural tube is a thick sheath that surrounds the brain and spinal cord all the way down to the tailbone. Karnis says common conditions that can be improved with treatment of the dural system include headaches, neck pain, back and tailbone pain, brain fog, decreased concentration and memory, depression, anxiety, muscle tone, tremors, numbness, and tingling. That piqued my interest because it's a laundry list of fibromyalgia symptoms.

Dural Tube Stretching
Eventually, my skill level at receiving treatment was good enough that when Cindy did a dural tube (also called a dural sheath) stretch, I could let go. She did the neck release on page 68 of Karnis's book, holding my head up for me. Over the next few weeks, I followed up with extended plow position poses in my hot yoga class and I've felt the sheath releasing more and more. It is helping to reset how jammed my upper cervical bones are into my brainstem. My chiropractor has joked that my C1 vertebra was so tight that it was on its way to my ears. I think whiplash or multiple falls leads to dural sheath tightness, which leads to fibromyalgia—and that the dural sheath being so tight disturbs sleep and puts too much stress on the neck vertebrae, jamming them into the brain stem. C1, also known as the Atlas, is connected to nerves that control the blood supply to the head,

pituitary gland, scalp, bones of the face, brain, inner ear, middle ear, and sympathetic nervous system. Possible symptoms of a misalignment of C1 include headaches, nervousness, insomnia, head colds, high blood pressure, migraines, nervous breakdowns, amnesia, chronic tiredness, and dizziness. The dural sheath can also be impacted by whiplash and falls on the tailbone. There are exercises to release that too. I'd like to suggest that along with developing the mind/body connection as outlined in this book, that once the initial spinal injury is healed, patients be encouraged to start doing dural sheath release exercises with an ART/MFR specialist to help avoid developing fibromyalgia. Check with your chiropractor and doctor, ART/MFR specialist or physical therapist first.

Holistic Pulsing (I know, what a name! but it works)
I first came across Holistic Pulsing (HP) at the weeklong Focusing Summer Institute I attended in 2016 where a teacher named Marieke Hoeve from Holland taught it to our group. HP is more commonly known in Europe and New Zealand and is done by practitioners who specialize in it.

During treatment, practitioners use gentle rocking to see where the body does not move freely. They spend time in those congested areas to help free tension and balance the body.

Holistic Pulsing feels like the gentle rocking I did as a child when I tried to soothe myself to sleep. It's an easy skill to learn and a great one to have in your toolkit. It immediately helped me sleep more soundly. We learned how to work with different areas of the body each day, but the highlight came at the end of the week, when Marieke taught us to combine it with Focusing (see Chapter 20.)

I mentioned Focusing in an earlier chapter and it combines well with multiple modalities. Combining it with Holistic Pulsing immediately led to tremoring release in my pelvic floor muscles. Many of us hold excess tension in our pelvic floor without ever being aware of it. (More details about the pelvic floor below.)

The Pelvic Floor

The pelvic floor is a set of muscles at the base of the abdomen, attached to the pelvis. These muscles need to be strong to have proper bladder and bowel control among other things.

Overall, one in four women will have pelvic floor problems during their lifetime. The risk increases with age. By age 80, almost half of all women will have experienced a pelvic floor disorder. Men have a lower risk but can also have pelvic floor problems.

I struggled with pelvic floor tension for more than five years before getting correctly diagnosed. Many factors can cause pelvic floor problems. For me, it was a combination of falling off a wall at age seven, a bike at age seventeen, the whiplash car accident at thirty-nine and then becoming a spin biking enthusiast in my forties. Instructors often don't correct for poor form, nor do they do proper stretching to release the pelvic floor after a class. It's common for women who have had Cesarean sections to have a problem because weakened abdominal muscles make it very difficult to hold the correct form through the course of a spin bike workout. Over time, this leads to excessive use of pelvic floor muscles and tightening of both muscles and fascia. Women who deliver vaginally have increased risk for pelvic floor problems, too. Men are likely to develop problems from heavy lifting, or from having pelvic surgery for prostate cancer.

Pelvic Floor Dysfunction

Pelvic floor dysfunction can be missed because it mimics so many other problems. My gynecologist was sure I needed estrogen cream when I really needed pelvic floor therapy. I couldn't identify the pain I was having, only that it was a stinging and burning kind of pain that turned out to be caused by muscle spasms. Stress in my life made the muscle spasms worse. Even more confusing for me, I would go to the pelvic floor therapist for treatment, then encounter a stressful experience at home and in less than five minutes I'd feel the stress undo the benefits of the treatment. I needed a combination of reduced stress *and* pelvic floor therapy to heal this region.

Accidents and Falls Add Up

For either gender, being in an accident that unseats the spine from its pelvic base can contribute to the problem, whether it's multiple falls, like people with cerebral palsy often suffer from, or a fall from a bike or a car accident. My physical therapist, Dr. Betty Gao of Westchester Physical Therapy, explained that the pelvis has several notches in it to keep the spine seated in the event of a heavy fall. The spine can slip and reseat itself, but once the spine is even minimally off center, the muscles on the opposite side at the base must contract to keep the vertebra vertical. The next vertebra will be impacted in the other direction as opposing muscles try to keep it from continuing too far in the direction of the vertebra below it, and so on and on.

According to Dr. Gao, these muscles are constantly in spasm, releasing lactic acid and prostaglandins among other chemicals. Once the prostaglandin levels become high enough, it goes systemic (circulating throughout the body) and the body starts to attack itself. That's one way fibromyalgia begins.

What I've learned from RFST and from ART/MFR, as well as Focusing, is that the fascia we create from our thoughts and feelings about sex, about any sexual trauma, or about past sexual partners can stay with us until we do the ART/MFR or RFST work to release it. In particular, the fascia around the psoas, our fight-or-flight response muscle that pulls us into a fetal position, connects to the pelvic floor fascia, so I believe it could potentially impact the ability to achieve erection in men (perhaps by interfering with blood flow) or orgasm in women (which requires the ability of muscles to release and work in tandem.)

Women, Fascia and Orgasm

Women need to have low enough fascial tension so that their muscles can tense further in order to have an orgasm. If resting fascial tone is too high, women (and most likely men too) have difficulty having an orgasm. There are a lot of conflicting messages for women around sex in our society, which can generate a lot of inner conflict and tension.

Fascia and scar tissue build up because of accidents, thoughts, feelings, and trauma. It's possible to treat the health issues that come up through a variety of ways, which I've listed below under the action steps at the end of this chapter.

If this is an issue, please remember that this is a process. The first step is becoming aware, and that's huge. I hope you feel encouraged now that you know more about where to focus your energies in order to heal.

Action steps:
Easy:
Try Holistic Pulsing to reduce pelvic floor tension.

Google YouTube videos for demonstrations of Holistic Pulsing.

Read *Gentle Miracles: Holistic Pulsing* by Tovi Browning.

Femfusionfitness has an easy half hour video of pelvic floor stretches: http://femfusionfitness.com/pelvic-release-stretches/

Moderate:
Try RFST and ART/MFR to reduce fascia and fascial tension.

Read Bob Cooley's *Resistance Flexibility 1.0* and John Barnes' *Healing Ancient Wounds*.

Find a pelvic floor therapist who uses ART or MFR.

Take steps to reduce the stress levels in your life. Meditation and yoga are good choices, as is marriage counseling or changing jobs.

Find a restorative foam roller class near you.

Harder:
Try a workshop with Lori Zeltwanger. You can find out more info at her website advancedreleasetherapy.com.

Consider John Barnes' centers in Arizona or Pennsylvania. More at myofascialrelease.com.

Look into Holistic Pulsing training and attend a training program. Most of what I've found is available through Holland, the UK, and New Zealand. You can reach Marieke Hoeve at mariekehoeve@upcmail.nl.

Find a resistance trainer near you or consider working with an RFST trainer at geniusofflexibility.com.

Dr. Betty Gao can be reached at her private physical therapy practice in Sleepy Hollow, NY. The office number is 914-909-6970.

Wednesday:

Stop Reliving Emotions

Chapter 12
Emotions Made Easy

Discovering the Power of Letting go of Denial

When I was at my lowest point physically and emotionally, I realized something. Ever since I was twelve, I used to visualize alternative endings to how my day went: what I could have said differently, what I wished people had said to me, things to worry about, all the If Onlys; that kind of thing. I had learned that the brain stem and emotional brain respond to visualizations in exactly the same way as to real life because they don't understand the difference. So, my adrenals were producing cortisol if I was reliving something scary or thinking of something to be on the watch about or visualizing what to do in the event of an emergency. But even more important, when I was visualizing alternative endings, I was soothing myself. I was denying the reality I'd experienced. I was preventing myself from sitting in the emotions of the day and learning from them, so I could prevent the situation from happening again. When I realized this, I immediately stopped visualizing about the past at bedtime. I used meditation techniques to calm myself down enough to sleep. I also found that daily journaling using Julia Cameron's Morning Pages exercises from her book, *The Artist's Way* improved the quality of my sleep.

What Emotions Are For

Our emotions are a survival mechanism to help process often bewildering environmental and social cues to maximize our chance of survival—both physically and socially. The emotional brain is an add-on to the brain stem, but the two regions don't always work well together.

Brain Stem Response

Having an emotional brain is an evolutionary advantage, but there is a problem with it: the brain stem cannot tell the difference between an actual event and an imagined one. All those times we imagined being a hero or got angry and stewed about the way we were treated at school or work, reinventing our response over and over again in our minds, our brain stem was pumping out adrenaline as if it were real. When we relive a traumatic or shaming event that happened to us, our brain stem pumps out the adrenaline needed as if it were happening all over again.

That adrenaline is made in a factory (our body) that has limited resources. When we overproduce adrenaline, we have fewer resources to produce other necessary neurotransmitters. In addition, producing too much adrenaline creates an inflammatory process and chronic inflammation leads to disease. So how do we cope with emotions?

Ninety Second Rule

According to neurologist/researcher Dr. Jill Bolte Taylor, emotions are a chemical response process that only last ninety seconds. Any further emotional reaction comes from a person choosing to stay in that emotional loop. In other words, emotions "only" last for ninety seconds—if you understand how to step out of the emotional loop, by accepting them so they can be processed, learned from, and released.

Those ninety seconds can ramp up into something so excruciating that some people will resort to anything: drugs, alcohol, you name it, to avoid it because those emotions keep coming back. It's not a conscious decision. Our unconscious brain stem is terrified. It's a pattern that starts in childhood and continues into adulthood. Avoiding emotion stores it and begins an inflammatory pathway. I've read that the actual biochemical process of getting rid of the emotional chemicals from our system can take up to 20 minutes. In my life, I was so scared of emotions like fear, anger, and sadness that I avoided them all, rationalized them away, and got sick.

Lots of people use sports or hobbies in healthy ways to process emotions. They tune into the flow they feel from engaging in them and release stress that way. Sports like surfing, playing golf or tennis come to mind, as do hobbies like gardening, collecting model trains, and knitting. A Cardiff University survey found that 81% of respondents with depression claimed that knitting made them happier. These are all wonderful ways to process emotion. They're also an opportunity to add tension to ourselves by being competitive about it or forcing a fit with an activity (perhaps because of family or peer pressure) when it's not really our cup of tea. Be sure to choose something that brings you joy.

My Best Pathways to Process Emotion
There are lots of pathways I've found to make me braver, so I can cope with emotion. The first one is meditation. I am not talking about the kind of meditation where I gaze at my navel and start chanting. There are completely left-brain ways to do meditation. I've combined the best practices I've learned into a meditation practice which processes emotions out of the body. Once I had the tools to release my emotions, it was a heck of a lot easier to confront them and allow my chronic stress to begin to release.

Separating From my Thoughts and Feelings
Meditation made me realize that there is a part of me that was not caught up in my emotional experience and I could call on it to help me choose another path. The part of me that was not caught up in my emotional experience was my right brain's state of mind. I can access it during times of trauma or stress. While both the right and left hemisphere's produce positive and negative emotions, the right-brain state is always peaceful because the right brain doesn't judge them.

113

Listening to Dr. Jill Bolte Taylor's TED Talk, *My Stroke of Insight* and reading her book helped me understand better about the right-brain state.

It can be cathartic to vent emotions, but my emotional self is not always the kindest or smartest part of myself. I would do better to call on that other peaceful part of myself to calmly take over in times of stress.

Meditation helps to strengthen the awareness and connection to that other self which resides in the prefrontal cortex. When our brain stem or emotional brain sends threat messages, we have a small window of time to choose our response. Once we respond with these more primitive areas, we get caught up in the emotion of the situation and can no longer easily access our prefrontal cortex. Our default survival mechanism makes us shift into using our more ancient brain systems.

By meditating, I'm allowing my brain to become better able to discern between a true emergency and situations where it's safe to stay in my prefrontal cortex. Ultimately our highest and best human selves lay in the prefrontal cortex, fully in touch with our compassionate emotions while acknowledging our own needs.

We want to spend more time in that kind of head space. Meditation reduces inflammation because it stimulates the parasympathetic nervous system when we are in this state. A world full of people doing their best to achieve mastery in the practice of meditation would truly be a beautiful place.

Primary Storage is in Our Brain, Secondary Storage is in our Body

The second pathway I found to help make me braver in dealing with emotions was to realize that I needed to feel the emotions in my body for them to be processed and released, and that there was a way I could do this that hurt less than just waiting for emotions to hit me unprepared. I had a big backlog of unprocessed emotions, but I figured that if I took on clearing a little of my suppressed emotions every day, I'd be reducing that inflammatory neurochemical stockpile. That meant literally noticing where emotions started and where they moved to within my body. I noticed muscle twitches and energy movement as well as feelings.

Seven Ways to Help Process Emotions

There are seven effective ways I've found to help process emotions. The first is with specialized kinesiology (see chapter 15), the second is with Focusing (see chapter 20), the third is MFR, the fourth is RFST, the fifth is yoga, the sixth is holistic pulsing, and the seventh is dance. I was completely closed to trying anything to do with specialized kinesiology for the first forty-nine years of my life. I only became open to it because of being sick enough, and that was only after trying everything else first. The other six things are much more mainstream, so if you have a similar mindset against trying alternative health remedies, try the others first.

When I was at my sickest, I realized I had become so avoidant of emotions that I rarely felt any. Instead, I felt varying amounts of pain, numbness and tingling when I got upset; it depended on my stress levels just how bad the symptoms were. It took a lot of effort to learn to tune into my body for the fleeting sensations I was still capable of. Our emotional brain sends out neuropeptides into our body and they lodge in specific regions. We even have expressions for this: "He's got a lot of gall." "She vented her spleen." "I didn't have the stomach for it." Folk wisdom understood there was a connection between these organs and certain emotions.

Emotions are Part of a Cycle

There is another downside to avoiding emotions. Eventually blocking the negative ones meant I blocked the positive ones too, because they are part of a cycle. This was first realized by traditional Chinese medicine. In my case, because I rejected anger, I couldn't feel joy. I had reduced the energy available to run on the fire element—those nerves that run through the heart, small intestine, pericardium, thyroid, adrenals, and their related muscles. This in turn interrupted flow through the rest of the meridian system.

We each have our emotional signature, depending on which emotions we were allowed to express when we were growing up. Within each family we were assigned a role which often had to do with our birth order. That emotional signature is a mix of blocked meridian pathways, where we've resisted the neuropeptides' messages, and opened meridian pathways, where we've allowed their messages.

Calming Our Emotional Mind
I think we need to learn both how to calm our emotional mind and to fully feel our held emotions in order to reach optimal health. If we ignore or avoid feeling our emotions, they persist. Because of how scared our brain stem can get, many people act as if bad emotions are "it" in a game of hide and go seek, as if all we have to do is run away to win the game. In addition to optimal health, calming the emotional mind allows us to maximize our executive function.

When scary, strong emotions show up, I think of it as getting blasted by hot or cold water unexpectedly while in a shower. We can figure out how to adjust the shower head and try to find a safe corner to stand in, but eventually a crisis hits that means the water blasts stronger than we've ever experienced. There's nowhere to go in the shower that isn't getting hit. During hard times, the tub seems to get deeper and deeper until we are swimming in it because most people don't know how to access the drain. It gets exhausting when lots of bad stuff happens at once and all we're doing is treading water without rest.

At times like these we feel like we are drowning in emotions. We can get so exhausted, so tired, and be in so much pain that we just want it to end. That is when some people think about killing themselves, when they've lost hope and just cannot take all the fear, anger, shame, and loss. Life feels too exhausting to continue.

There are solutions. There always have been, we just need find them and learn how to let those emotions drain off—-which is what I call processing. Committing to positive self-talk is important. When my boys were babies, every morning I would take them downstairs and hold them up to the windows of the front door. As they looked out, I would say, "It's a brand-new day. Every day is a brand-new day, filled with hope and new possibilities." As much as I was mothering them in a positive way, I was parenting myself too, focusing on the positives in my life, rather than the exhaustion from lack of sleep to care for them in the night, the worries about my health, the unraveling of my marriage. What kind of positive self-talk can you add to your life?

Emotions Contain Information that Increase Odds of Our Survival

Nothing is wasted by the emotional brain. Since emotional neuropeptides carry information that helps increase our odds of survival and are stored in our bodies for processing later, I think of us as having primary memory storage in our brain and a backup system for storage in our body.

There are situations when it is not possible to feel and express our emotions fully in real time, like in school or at work. But it's important to process emotions later, no matter how much time has passed. It gives us a chance to reset and calm down, so we're not so triggered the next time we go to school or work.

Unless They are Processed Negative Emotions Add up Over Time

Whether we have come to toxic emotional storage through major trauma or through the thousands of slights of daily life, they add up in the same way when they are ignored or avoided. Unprocessed neurochemicals are lodged in our body until our bodies are overflowing with them. Either way will cause the same pathway of disease to begin, it's just a matter of how early in our life they'll show up.

For me, the easiest and most complete emotional reset

happens through specialized kinesiology (more details in Chapter 15) because I can do it anywhere—in bed, or in the car. The second easiest is meditation because again, I can do parts of it anywhere, anytime. The third easiest is MFR because I can do that in bed too if I wake up. The fourth is RFST because I have to get out of bed to avoid disturbing my husband. You'll have your own unique preferences.

Insights from a Veggie Stand

I went to a Touch for Health class down in L.A. about five years ago. On Saturday after lunch, the walk back to the classroom took us by a farmers' market. A big chalk sign proclaimed, "A lot of our pain is really just coming from our own thoughts." I wanted to stop right there and spend an hour talking to the man and find out how he had come to the same conclusions as I had, but he was busy selling vegetables and class was starting, and I didn't want to miss out. What a wonderful thing though, getting insights on how to live a better life for both mind and body at a local farmers' market.

Questioning Our Thoughts

I was raised believing that others' actions were responsible for how I felt. I didn't understand that my life experiences created a pattern for how I would react to other people's actions. That meant I had responsibility for how I reacted. As Jack Canfield says in *The Success Principles*, 'you must take 100% responsibility for your life, no excuses, blaming or complaining.' Someone once said, 'holding onto resentment is like drinking poison and expecting the other person to die.' I could learn to forgive because I could see how another person with a different history might have a different reaction. It's important to forgive for our own benefit—since resentment is also an inflammatory emotion. If someone is mistreating us, it's also important that we take steps to protect ourselves, since abuse will also cause an inflammatory response. Best is if we forgive and get out of situations like that.

Sometimes others mistreat us because they get energy from

the ill-will they provoke in others. Perhaps it's because they learned that negative attention is better than no attention at all. Regardless of why, it's damaging to ourselves to respond in kind, especially if we are sick. I've found it's best to disengage and think neutral thoughts until I can move on with my day.

I was also raised to need everyone's approval and if I didn't get it, I was crushed. I didn't understand that even the nicest people have people who are critical of them. As Canfield states in *The Success Principles*, 'it's none of our business what other people think of us.' If we make it our business, it becomes toxic to our health. I've learned the hard way to act out of love and if other people misunderstand me and won't change their opinion of me, at least I've tried my best.

Questioning my thoughts and feelings has been an important tool for me to stop being a victim and start being an advocate for myself. It also helps reduce the repetitive thinking and resultant emotional whirlwind I experience, which lowers the stress and inflammation in the brain stem and emotional part of my brain. As I mentioned in Chapter 8, another tool for emotions that won't release is to hand them off in prayer. You don't have to believe in God; just try it and you might find that you can benefit from it too. Chalk it up to the powers of the human brain if you're an atheist.

Action steps:
Easy:
Find a meditation program you like; see my suggestions from Chapter 5.

Read *The Success Principles* and choose a few items at a time to work on.

Moderate:
Take a meditation class that combines writing to heal exercises with Bön breathwork to tire the body and process and release the energy of

emotions. I offer that combination in my programs; others may too.

Find an MFR practitioner near you at myofascialrelease.com and get a treatment.

Find a resistance stretching program at your local gym, or if there aren't any near you, buy *Resistance Flexibility 1.0* or try out the videos available at thegeniusofflexibility.com.

Buy a *Touch for Health: The Complete Edition* manual (the original version of specialized kinesiology for home use) and read it.

Find a yoga program you enjoy and go to extra classes when you're particularly stressed.

Try a dance class that makes you feel happy and attend classes regularly.

Harder:

Take a class with Lori Zeltwanger at Advanced Release Therapy. More at www.AdvancedReleaseTherapy.com.

Take a class in Touch for Health, Brain Gym ®, or PanHarmonic Healing, where you'll learn how to do muscle testing and give acupressure treatments and energy balances for yourself, family and friends. As of 2020, I am teaching classes online in all these subjects and I'd love to introduce you to them. Eventually I'll be offering in-person classes again too. More information at www.RightBrainUniversity.com.

Chapter 13
Beyond Processing Emotions

Finding Bliss in Negative Emotions

There's a little secret I discovered after learning meditation, mindfulness, specialized kinesiology (see chapter 15) and Focusing (see chapter 20.) Often when I connect to my feelings every morning and welcome them even if they're negative, after about 5-10 minutes of being with it, I find myself in bliss. It doesn't matter how crappy the feelings are. I can start off fearful, angry, depressed and end up in joy.

It took me a while to realize that only once emotions are truly welcomed, can they be fully felt and processed. Once that happens, our mind and body are at peace with each other, and peace equals bliss. That's the right brain non-judgmental state I'm connecting to. For many years I was hiding from the ability to feel bliss. How sad is that? At least I've learned the secret now. There's a caveat to this: if our feelings are painful, we can dissociate when we are first learning to connect with our emotions. It's an unconscious process, meaning we don't know we are doing it; our unconscious takes over to protect us. Dissociating, which means detaching from and trying to avoid the emotional experience we are having, can also make us feel calmer and sleepy. Dissociating is a common coping mechanism. I think of a little dissociating as being a tool because there is only so much emotional and mental pain human beings can handle at a time. How useful is it to know that when your mind/body have had enough, they will deflect the pain from you? Because then with your toolkit you can choose to work on the pain a little at a time until you are comfortable trusting that it won't get overwhelming.

Meditation, Mindfulness and Specialized Kinesiology's use of Acupressure

I am grateful for meditation and mindfulness because they gave me tools to separate from my emotional state and learn that there was a part of me that was always okay and could be reset to calm, even when I was suffering from an emotional storm. Ultimately meditation and mindfulness are only a part of the toolkit. If I have an urgent emotional message from my body, I can move into Focusing to get to an understanding of what my body is trying to express. Or else I can use acupressure points from specialized kinesiology (Chapter 15) to process it. I've found that I don't consciously need to know everything that the body and unconscious are processing—the big stuff always makes itself known. The rest of it is processed and learned from by my body/mind so I can have access to it later if it needs to become conscious.

Questioning Your Thoughts

Tools like these are handy in life, so that we can catch ourselves when we separate from being happy and joyful. One of the downfalls of our culture is the tendency to think we'll be happy when some goal is met, like once we finish college or get a high-paying job, buy a house, or have children, or retire. It's been clear from research done on this that achieving goals has little lasting impact on our happiness. That's because when we achieve our goals, we develop a new normal and our grasping mental state wants more. As Marci Shimoff says in her book *Happy for No Reason*, "question your thoughts, because your thoughts aren't always true. Judging, worrying, overthinking, dwelling on the bad, and focusing on the negative stimulates areas of the brain involved in depression and anxiety. If instead, we think positively, accept, and trust the good in our lives and savor it, it's calming to our brain." After reading her book, I made it a point to change my mindset. I focus on happiness now. Gratitude is what I turn to whenever I start down a negative path. I remember to forgive rather than continue with an overthinking spree. It's not an easy change because, as I've said before, human beings are judgment machines. Our brains are hardwired for judgment when we're stressed. Even when not stressed, many of us habitually revert to unconscious patterns handed down from our parents and their parents rather than thinking for ourselves. Having the tools to cope with the emotions that come up when we question our default response is vital for clear thinking. So is remembering our intention of heading towards positivity. The more chronically stressed we are, the more ill we are, the more important it is to make the change.

Progress, not Perfection

I'm human, so all I'm capable of is progress, not perfection. Even so, these attempts at progress that I make daily have helped change my life. Here's an example from my life; perhaps you can think of something recent in your life that you could try this type of response on:

I had an appointment for a Thursday afternoon with a specialist in Los Angeles to see if I needed a root canal. I live a two-hour drive away. The charger prongs on my cell phone were broken, so I bought a wireless charger for the drive down until I could get my phone replaced. I got to LA with 30% battery power from using the phone to navigate; something was wrong with the wireless charger, too. I charged the phone the entire time I was in LA, but didn't realize the Near Field Communications setting was off, preventing it from charging properly. I had an emergency root canal and left the office for home in the dark during rush hour in LA with 13% battery power. I think a lot of women might relate to feeling vulnerable in a situation like that. The GPS led me in a direction I didn't recognize. I caught myself thinking thoughts like, "this is the worst!" "oh my gosh, this is so dangerous!" before catching myself and remembering that times like that are where I'm supposed to be finding my happiness. My first cynical thought was, "yeah right, but this is an impossible situation!" I knew I had to turn my thinking around. I reminded myself that since I didn't know the outcome, I couldn't know how dangerous it truly was. It was dangerous only if I got stranded without GPS, and only then if I got unlucky about where I got stranded. Most people are helpful and kind. Until the worst happens, it might be dangerous, but it might not be. I know it's better for my brain and my health if I can keep myself from going to the worst possible scenario, so I turned off survival mode by starting to be grateful for what I had: I was warm, had a reliable car and a full tank of gas.

Once I started thinking that way, rational thoughts started showing up. I realized how lucky I was, because I only needed the power to last until I got to the 405 freeway—I could find my own way home from there. It also occurred to me that if I ran out of power, the charger seemed to work if I kept moving the phone around to restart it, so I could park and idle the car if necessary until I had enough charge. Thinking those thoughts quickly got me out of high-alert mode and into adventure mode. Not long afterwards, I realized I'd shifted into feeling happy. I made it to the 405 just fine.

Being hypervigilant to danger and treating hypervigilance as reality can create epigenetic changes to our cells that make us live in chronic stress. Being mindful that there are choices in how you think and that you can redirect yourself to healthier brain chemistry has been the key to going beyond merely reacting to thoughts and emotions for me. If you're interested, think of ways this could work in your life.

Taoist Calligraphy

Taoist Calligraphy is a recent way I've found to practice meditation and mindfulness. More serious students may be taught with ink, but an easy way for beginners to learn is to use absorbent, quick-drying cloth mats with waterproof backing. These roll up for storage when not in use. These mats are an easy way to bring calligraphy into a daily practice. By moving slowly and mindfully while practicing, it is possible to feel the energy springing up within oneself, which is connection to your Higher power, Source, God, the Universe, the Tao; whatever your name for that is. It's a rather amazing experience that is very calming and soothing. Allowing energy flow throughout the body is healthy for us. Our thoughts often restrict it, as does avoiding feelings. I highly recommend it.

Action steps:
Easy:
Find meditation and mindfulness programs you like; see my suggestions from Chapter 5.

Moderate:
Read Eugene Gendlin's book *Focusing*. Read Bebe Simon's *How I Teach Focusing: Discovering the Gift of Your Inner Wisdom*. Attend a training program in Focusing. Find a Focusing partner through focusing.org.

   Find a teacher of Taoist calligraphy in your area.

Harder:
Take a course in Touch for Health, Brain Gym®, or PanHarmonic Healing, where you'll learn how to do muscle testing and give energy balances for yourself, family, and friends. Again, I am teaching classes online in all these subjects and I'd love to introduce you to them. More information at www.RightBrainUniversity.com.

   Find a therapist who uses Focusing to help give you insight into your inner guidance at www.focusing.org.

Chapter 14
Acupuncture

Acupuncture in My Life

It was at the suggestion of a former sister-in-law of mine that I started making an eight-hour round-trip drive once a month to see an acupuncturist who had successfully helped many couples suffering from infertility.

I didn't mind the drive, since it took me straight into the Green Mountain region of Vermont for a weekend getaway with my in-laws. It definitely helped me get pregnant—as a support for donor egg through in vitro fertilization (IVF)—and successfully carry my twins to term. I have wondered if I would have needed IVF at all, had I gone to an acupuncturist first.

Many people hesitate to try acupuncture because they don't like needles, but once I tried a treatment and felt how relaxing it was, I got over having needles put in. There were too many benefits to it to let that hold me back. I've made it a regular part of my health program ever since.

The Benefits of Acupuncture

There's been a lot of research showing the benefits of acupuncture. It's been clinically shown to reduce pain, improve sleep and digestion, as well as one's general sense of well-being. It's also been shown to help nausea, migraine headache, anxiety, depression, insomnia, and infertility. It's been proven to help allergic rhinitis and hay fever, dysentery, menstrual cramps, facial pain, and

Temporomandibular Disorders (TMD), hypertension, hypotension, knee pain, low back pain, morning sickness, vomiting, rheumatoid arthritis, sciatica, postoperative pain, stroke, and sprains.

I've also used acupuncture to help improve digestion and immune function. I feel it's been an important part of my healing.

I learned about Five Elements Acupuncture in the past year. It uses specific points to help release where we hold emotion in the body. These points are called Windows to the Sky. Practitioners who treat using this method give sessions which support work being done with a psychologist.

My practitioner asks what is going on in my life and how I've been, both regarding health and pain, but also emotionally. I tell him the condensed version of what is going on in my psychologist sessions, dreams and specialized kinesiology sessions and he bases his treatment on that. I've found it very helpful to use this type of acupuncture. The other type of treatment which he does that helps with pain is cupping—heating the air inside specially designed bottles and running them along my back. I end up with some bruising at times, but it helps locked fascia to release, which also helps make me feel more mobile.

Mary Tingaud has a go-to reputation in town for hard-to-help cases, including mine. In addition, there are lots of babies in town that wouldn't be around without her help, and she also does thermography.

I've also been helped by Pamela Grant, an acupuncturist who is also a Shengzen Qigong teacher in Santa Barbara. She does a lymphatic drainage treatment that works wonders.

As an aside for sufferers of infertility, be sure to read Chapter 23, particularly the section on oxalates, and consider joining the Trying Low Oxalates group. I have seen some women in the group who are struggling with infertility find that going on a low oxalate diet leads to getting pregnant.

Action steps:

Easy: find a good local acupuncturist. The following are professional associations through which you can find a good referral: the National Certification Commission for Acupuncture and Oriental Medicine is at nccaom.org, the American Acupuncture Council is online at acupuncturecouncil.com, and the California State Oriental Medicine Association is at csomaonline.org.

Moderate: find a 5 Elements practitioner if needed.

Harder: If you're ever in Santa Barbara for one of my programs, I highly recommend three acupuncturists in town. Mary Tingaud is at marytingaud.com. CCOM, which is run by Mark Sherwood and Nicki Doner Sherwood, can be reached at yourccom.com. Pamela Grant is at pamela-grant.com.

Chapter 15
Specialized Kinesiology

Omega Institute and Neuroplasticity

I was first introduced to specialized kinesiology in 2013 at a conference I attended on Neuroplasticity at Omega Institute in Rhinebeck, New York. Omega has a beautiful tree-filled campus on a hillside about five miles from the Hudson River. I enjoyed the keynote speakers each night such as Dr. Jill Bolte Taylor. One of the speakers was a specialized kinesiologist who was also an educational kinesiologist by the name of Paula Oleska. After her talk, I speed-walked as fast as I could to Omega's bookstore to hunt for a book she recommended, *Touch for Health: The Complete Edition.* Another lucky lady and I bought the last two books as a long line formed hoping that they had more in stock in the back. I scanned the thick book, wondering how on earth I was supposed to learn how to use it. All I knew at the time was that I wanted to work with Paula when I got back home to Sleepy Hollow, New York, and I did for a year, until I moved back to Santa Barbara, California. Working with Paula changed my life. I had no idea that someday I'd be taking the same classes as she did to become a specialized kinesiologist and educational kinesiologist or speak at a conference with her in the audience. It's amazing to see where life has taken me now that I've eased up on the reins.

The Benefits of Specialized Kinesiology

The same type of acupressure treatment that chiropractors use to help our muscles function better, Applied Kinesiology, is also available in a simplified home version for everyday people to help reduce pain and stress levels. Small studies have shown that Applied Kinesiology is beneficial, though most medical doctors consider it highly suspect. I'm not making any claims about the health benefits of specialized kinesiology, but from personal experience, I know it has been crucial in giving me tools to reduce my stress and pain as well as helping me keep a level emotional state. I think being in less stress and pain is likely to be beneficial to my health in the long run, but that's just my opinion.

In case this topic has you rolling your eyes, I understand. Before I got sick, I had never heard of specialized kinesiology, but if I had I would have laughed at people who tried it. I was so closed-minded and intolerant that I probably would have thought of them as pathetic. Talk about having to eat crow. Here's how much I value it now: if I had no other tool to keep calm, I could live a comfortable life with only specialized kinesiology. This is not the best match for cerebral types who live life in their heads, since they are not connected enough to their bodies to tune in to and recognize the changes. For them, I'd recommend beginning with resistance stretching or rolfing. You don't need to feel any connection to your body to realize the benefits you get from resistance stretching and rolfing. Rather, I think of specialized kinesiology as being a perfect tool for people who are *overly* connected to their body; the highly sensitive types who are constantly struggling with strong body sensations, whether that's physical pain or emotional ups-and-downs.

I'm really excited to introduce you to this exercise below. It's helped a lot of people change their lives. My clients all love it.

First, it's important to have a safe space to return to in case you ever feel overwhelmed during the exercise. Think of a time in your life when you felt safe and loved. Visualize yourself there now. Maybe it was out in nature, maybe it was in someone's presence.

Now notice the feeling a few inches below your navel at the center of your body. We'll call that your core. How does that feel? Does it feel grounded? Light? Pleasantly warm? Peaceful? Keep the feeling in your core as you step away from the literal memory of the experience and into the sensation of it. That is your safe space within you. Remember it for later.

An Easy Demonstration with the Five Elements
Follow along with this simple demonstration, and I'll explain how you can use it at home. Close your eyes for a moment and connect with a spot where you feel pain in your body. How painful is it on a scale of 0 to 10? Write that number down. Next, think about the most emotionally charged situation that is currently troubling you. How strongly are you impacted by it on a scale of 0 to 10? Write that down too. It's important to write these numbers down because we tend to forget how badly we were feeling once we start feeling better.

Reverse Five Elements Exercise
Next, use the diagrams on the next few pages to do the following five exercises. Repeat each movement three times, paying attention to the sensations in your body as you engage your muscles. The idea behind these exercises is that they shift energy in the body and allow the body to move out of fight or flight, so we can better access our prefrontal cortex. You might notice that it's hard or a little uncomfortable to make one or more of the movements at first, yet it eases up as you go through the exercises. That is allowing energy to move in areas it might not normally go.

I find these types of movements below, which are based on muscle tests that chiropractors use, to be helpful for reducing pain in specific areas, such as the back, even if I don't have time to do all five of these exercises. You might want to memorize your favorites so that you can use them as needed. You can do these movements on your own, without anyone's help—the hands shown are for guidance only.

LIVER	::	WOOD
MERIDIAN		ELEMENT

RHOMBOIDS

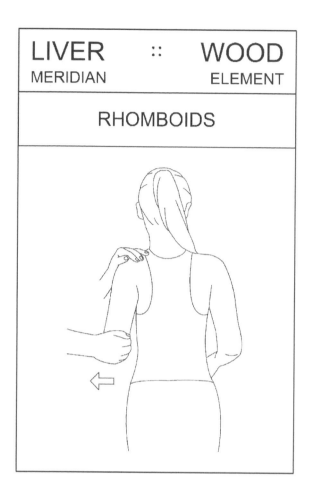

Bring your elbows to your waist. Squeeze your shoulder blades together firmly towards your spine. Move your left elbow 4" away from your body. Rotate your elbow up in line with shoulder level. Return to starting and repeat two more times. Repeat on your right side.

BLADDER :: WATER
MERIDIAN   ELEMENT

SACROSPINALIS

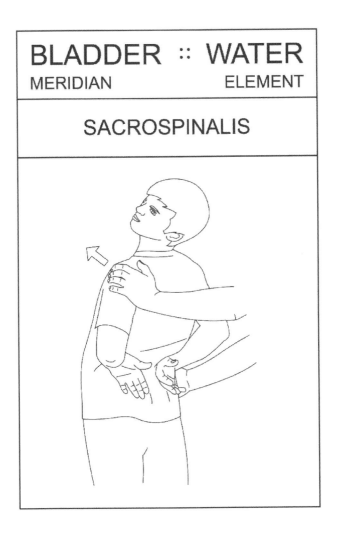

Look over your left shoulder. Move your left shoulder forward 5" in the direction of the arrow and then back to the starting position three times. Remember to breathe normally. Repeat on your right side.

LUNG :: METAL
MERIDIAN | ELEMENT

ANTERIOR SERRATUS

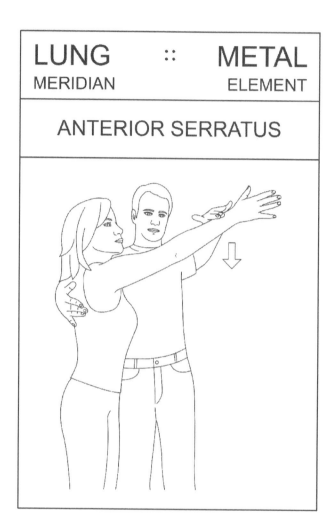

Bring your right arm above your head. Extend your right shoulder forward. Move your hand up and down 6" like you are shaking hands with a giant three times. Repeat on your left side.

STOMACH :: EARTH
MERIDIAN   ELEMENT

PECTORALIS MAJOR
CLAVICULAR

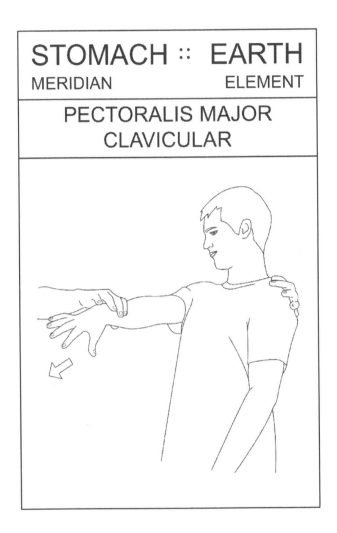

Bring your right hand, thumb down, out in front of you at the midline of your body, shoulder height. Bring it down at a 45-degree angle towards your right hip as if you are swimming. Return to the starting point and repeat two more times. Repeat on your left side.

HEART :: FIRE

MERIDIAN   ELEMENT

SUBSCAPULARIS

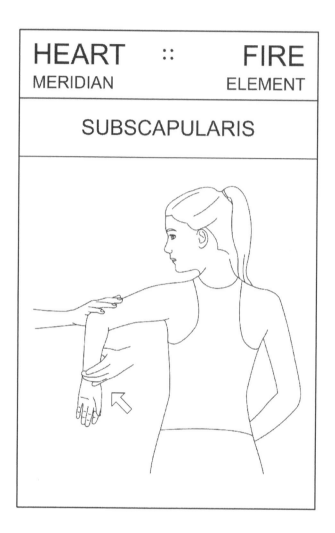

Bring your left arm up 6", elbow at shoulder height and hand down, like a scarecrow. Bring your hand up while keeping your elbow in place. Return to starting and repeat two more times. Repeat on your right side.

Noticing Your Body

Once you do these five exercises, be sure to check in with the pain in your body. Now how painful is that spot on a scale of 0 to 10? Did you get some relief? Has anything shifted for you emotionally on a scale of 0 to 10? These exercises are useful after a hard day's work to help shed the tension of the day, or in the morning if you dread going to work. You might try them on your children before school or homework. These muscle movements are adapted from *Touch for Health: The Complete Edition,* used with Matthew Thie's permission. If you find them helpful, imagine what movements specifically targeted to your own body's needs could do.

Another Reverse Five Elements Exercise

Here's a version you can do in public without anyone knowing.

Do the same setup as before where you think of a problem that's bothering you now or something that you've never been able to let go of and give it a number between 0 and 10 with 10 being the worst it could be.

Next, think of the color green (or look at it if you have trouble visualizing it.) Take a deep breath in. Think of the sound of shouting. Let your breath go.

Think of the color blue and take a deep breath. Think of the sound of groaning. Exhale.

Next, think of the color white and take in a deep breath. Think of the sound of weeping. Let go of your breath.

Think of the color yellow and take a deep breath. Think of the sound of singing. Exhale.

Think of the color red and take a deep breath. Think of the sound of laughing and let go of your breath.

Check in with yourself afterwards to see if any pain has lessened or emotional tension has released. Compare your before and after numbers. Most people notice at least a fifty percent improvement in their scores.

You can use the Safe Space exercise before you sleep every night. It will help you sleep better. Practicing this over time will help you stay calmer during an argument or other stressful situation.

ESR with K27 Points

Another helpful exercise for stress relief is to rate your pain and emotional distress on a scale of 0 to 10 and write that down. Next, follow the diagram on the next page. Place the thumb and index finger of one hand on your forehead at the points marked ESR (which stands for Emotional Stress Release) in the diagram below. Take the other hand and place your thumb and index finger in the notches below your collarbones marked as K27. These are at the end of the kidney meridian. If you're finding the right notches, they'll likely have tender bumps. Take a deep breath and relax. Tell yourself that you're safe and that all is well. Hold for about ten breaths or until you have the urge to sigh.

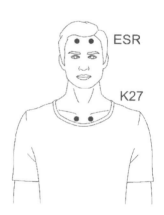

Hold the ESR points with the thumb and index finger of one hand. Hold the K27 points with the thumb and index finger of the other hand. Close your eyes. Breathe slowly, in for four counts and out for four counts. Keep on until you notice that you give a deep sigh.

Holding Points

Rate your pain and emotional distress again. Have they improved? This combination of points is from PanHarmonic Healing (PHH) and I've found it incredibly helpful for me to reset to calm. This is just a small taste of PHH. There is much more that PHH can do to help us be more comfortable in our bodies.

Setting a goal statement in a session and looking for where the body feels discomfort or pain as well as limitations of range of movement when walking is an important component of educating the unconscious. More information in action steps.

Holding points on the body is an example of specialized kinesiology (SK.) These are a form of acupressure. These examples can be used to help lighten your mood, lessen your pain levels, and increase your energy. I do some sort of SK on myself every day. A side benefit of specialized kinesiology has been that as I get the emotional holding patterns out of the way, I feel more connected to my soul and aligned with my higher power. I've been told that some recovering addicts/alcoholics find it helpful to use specialized kinesiology as part of their toolkit for maintaining their sobriety. Specialized kinesiology may be helpful for other issues. Recent studies have shown that some people with borderline personality disorder may be misdiagnosed and instead need treatment for PTSD. Studies also show that children who are diagnosed with depression or ADHD could really be suffering from trauma. Perhaps this is why specialized kinesiology is of benefit, since I've found it helps release emotional trauma.

Can You Sense an Argument?

Have you ever felt the impact from the dark cloud of an argument when walking into a room? Our bodies generate a weak electromagnetic signal when we think or feel or move. That weak electromagnetic signal is a part of non-verbal communication. Some people are very sensitive to this type of communication, particularly introverts. This electromagnetic signal extends around our bodies.

Thoughts are energy, emotions are energy. The stronger the thoughts and emotions, the more energy they generate. Our beliefs about ourselves impact our bodies, and others' beliefs and energies impact us as well.

Healthy Emotional Etiquette

When we interact with people, even indirectly, our mirror neurons are engaged. We get a taste of their emotional state. Have you ever had a conversation with someone where you vent about a problem and feel better afterwards? You were discharging emotional energy. Have you ever had a conversation with someone where they vent about a problem and you feel terrible afterwards? They discharged their emotional energy onto you. It takes a skilled, mindful listener to create a safe space for someone to vent while not taking on the negative energy themselves. Some people never learn how to process their emotions; they look to other people to discharge on. It's important that our friends learn how to reciprocate, whether they are introverts or extroverts.

Part of my definition of introverts is that they are people who, often unknowingly, take on the unconscious concerns and emotions in the form of energy of other people. Part of my definition of extroverts is that they are people who can unknowingly hand off some of their concerns and emotions in the form of energy onto other people. An awareness of this issue is vital to keep us in good health. If we are sick, we need to protect ourselves from people who won't stop handing off energy without reciprocating. They may be unaware of the effect they have on introverts, but that makes them no less difficult to be around. Introverts also need to learn how to shield themselves from the energy drain so that they can be comfortable around others. Extreme introversion or extroversion is not healthy—we all need balance in our lives. Our tendency is often hardwired in us as a reaction to early childhood trauma. We'd do best to be flexible--situationally able to accommodate the need for introversion to recharge and extroversion to succeed in groups or a business meeting.

Developing Boundaries

People with illnesses like fibromyalgia and chronic fatigue tend not to have boundaries. This is because in their childhood they constantly took the emotional temperature of their environment to stay safe. They looked to the outside at other people's emotional state rather than to their own emotional state for guidance. The same thing holds true for them in adulthood because it's an unconscious process. After a lifetime of giving, this can lead to becoming ill. Those who are sick often have surrounded themselves with family or friends who do not reciprocate or who keep them in a state of fear, so they don't have to deal with their own fear.

Even after years of work, I still struggled to maintain proper energetic boundaries until a few years ago, when I took a class from Merle Yost, and then joined his monthly training program. I am very grateful for his program, *Unspoken Boundaries*, which finally gave me the tools I needed to protect myself fully. Merle offers online group programs at this point, but I was lucky to work with him in person with a group of psychologists and healers. The tools he taught have made all the difference to me. He's a psychologist and a gifted intuitive, which makes him an incredibly skilled teacher.

Recovering from Dissociation

As discussed earlier, Touch for Health, Brain Gym ® / Edu-K and PanHarmonic Healing are types of specialized kinesiology and educational kinesiology that can be invaluable in unlocking emotions and trauma stored in the body. These are all offshoots of Applied Kinesiology. Some people can feel energy moving in their body and some people can't, but most come away from a session with a sense of relaxation and catharsis, reduced pain and an increased sense of well-being.

When I first started working with a specialized kinesiologist, I used to get very sleepy when some of the acupressure points were held. This sleepiness is a form of dissociating just like what can happen when we are first learning to Focus (see Chapter 20 for more information about Focusing.) I worked on becoming more present in the sessions over time, trying to stay with the sensation rather than caving into the sleepiness. I think of specialized kinesiology as a tool just like in Focusing, because after a while, I could choose to work on the emotional pain a little at a time until I got comfortable feeling almost any emotion. At first, I was so shut down that there were certain emotions I couldn't feel at all, even if I tried. Over time, though, I could learn how to pay attention to the sensations, however fleeting they were. Eventually those sensations lasted longer, until I could allow them in. After a long time, I could allow them to flow. There is nothing like the feeling of being rid of something that you've been holding for a long time. It's liberating. I practiced on myself every day to try to keep the momentum up and to learn how to be okay with whatever message my body was trying to give me.

Applied Kinesiology
Applied Kinesiology was created when a chiropractor, Dr. George Goodheart, started exploring the overlap between Traditional Chinese Medicine and the forty-two muscle tests that chiropractors use. As chiropractors began using Applied Kinesiology on patients, their patients learned bits and pieces and began to try to use it on themselves. One chiropractor who studied with Goodheart, Dr. John Thie, developed it into a lay process for regular people to be able to use for themselves and their families. He wrote a manual called *Touch for Health* and developed trainings so that anyone could learn how to release stress and tension for oneself, friends, and family in a way to help support health and wellness in-between doctor and chiropractor visits.

The *Touch for Health* manual explains how the pain we feel in one muscle is often because its partner (called the opposing muscle) is underactive. The first muscle does too much of the opposing muscle's work for it. If we can get the energy to flow to the muscle that is not being used, it reduces the strain on the muscle that is causing the pain. The problem is that we tend to have patterns of muscle use that we can trace back to our childhood. For example, if we weren't allowed to express our anger, the muscles in the liver and gallbladder meridians might not be firing well. If we weren't allowed to express our fear, the muscles connected to the kidney and bladder meridians might not be working correctly. If fear was the only emotion we were allowed to express, the kidney and bladder meridians may be overused. Touch for Health can help us release those patterns and start developing healthier new ones.

Touch for Health Sessions
A Touch for Health session educates you about how to use this system for yourself. You create a session goal, which is a positive affirmation for yourself. You notice the level of physical and emotional pain you're in. The instructor uses a fourteen, twenty-eight or forty-two muscle test which is based on the forty-two-muscle test that chiropractors use to see which meridians are blocked. They then use Traditional Chinese Medicine acupressure points and other techniques to unblock the meridians. Once the energy is flowing again, they check with you to see if the pain is gone. It often is. If not, they use additional techniques from the Touch for Health manual to help reduce it further. Then they retest the muscles, which should be firing normally, and work on any additional areas if they are still not firing well. You're given some everyday techniques to help increase your comfort. You leave feeling refreshed, calmer and in less pain. Touch for Health sessions are particularly helpful using a technique called a Reactive Muscle Balance. This type of balance assists in resetting spasming muscles. It's also effective in helping other types of pain.

When I wanted to learn how to help spread the word about specialized kinesiology, I started by learning Touch for Health. It has such strong connections to chiropractic that it will seem the most familiar to people. By tuning in regularly to our bodies, we are more aware of when we need to see a health professional, allowing us to get help sooner.

Storing Emotions

As mentioned earlier, the mind is incredibly efficient, storing specific emotions along specific muscles and organs so they are easy to find again and learn from later until they are accepted, processed, and released. Specialized kinesiologists can help us access these pathways through the training that they have had. We learn how to process and release emotions through use of acupressure and other tools.

Brain Gym ®

A very helpful offshoot of Touch for Health is called Brain Gym®. Brain Gym® is considered educational kinesiology. It is a part of Breakthroughs International's programs. Brain Gym® helps synchronize the body to allow learning. Brain Gym® was developed by an educational professional, Paul Dennison, who was trained in Touch for Health. He had learning disabilities, and developed a program to help himself, which in turn has helped tens of thousands of others to learn more easily. Brain Gym® has been used by teachers since 1986 to help our children use their eyes better, pay attention in class, and otherwise wake up the brain to learn without stress or strain. Adults can be helped by Brain Gym® too. Adults typically have behavior patterns developed during childhood which no longer serve them yet are stuck in place. Brain Gym® can help adults shed the past and move forward in order to achieve our life goals. They've been vitally important to my healing, so much so that I've become a Brain Gym® instructor, so that I can teach them as part of my healing and wellness programs at Right Brain University. While there are no double-blind studies on Brain Gym®'s helpfulness, I can tell you that in my personal experience it has harnessed my brain's neuroplasticity to allow growth and change in my life. I also feel so much calmer after using it.

PanHarmonic Healing

As I mentioned earlier, I've also gotten a lot of help from a type of specialized kinesiology called PanHarmonic Healing (PHH), developed by Santa Barbara chiropractor Dr. Valerie Girard. I went to weekly sessions with an educational kinesiologist, Julie Newendorp, who was trained in part by Dr. Girard. Once I got to a certain point in my work with Julie, she suggested I take Dr. Girard's training, so I could help myself between sessions. It has been a game changer. I've found it easy to learn how to use this system to have tools whenever uncomfortable feelings come up. Of all the types of specialized kinesiology I've tried, it's the one I find easiest to work on myself with, and the one I've needed the most. It has a comprehensive system to deal with a lot of emotional energies. Other kinesiologies do wonderful things for me too but require a practitioner for me to get the best from them. Since it's helped me so much, I've become an instructor in this modality too; so far, I'm the only one besides Dr. Girard herself.

Why You Should Use This Tool

PanHarmonic Healing isn't just useful for feeling peace and joy and reducing PTSD. I have had incredible success helping people improve test scores and pass the bar by using this tool. What are the implications for us all? That by avoiding emotion, we are dumbing ourselves down. First, by being in fight, flight, or freeze, we aren't thinking with our whole brain, only the dominant half. As I've mentioned, it's a survival mechanism so we can escape predators. Second, we are not thinking so much as reacting with our brain stem and emotional brain when we are in fight, flight, or freeze. Executive level thought is where we want to be for optimal brain power. I have read that one third of us have at least one traumatic event happen by the time we are eighteen. After the year we have all had thanks to Covid, we are kidding ourselves that we are operating at optimal brain power without resetting with PanHarmonic Healing.

Developing PanHarmonic Healing's Emotional Reach
After becoming an instructor in PHH and teaching the original material on emotions connected to twenty points on the body, it became clear to me that there were additional points. Dr. Girard had located eighty additional points on the body but was too busy to develop the material further. She asked me to map out their emotional meanings. I have spent the past five years recording the meanings I discovered in my own sessions as well as from my work with clients. I'm now offering advanced classes in these additional points. I've also developed an additional sixteen points and found their meaning, in addition to developing further work in PHH that is beyond the scope of this book to discuss.

Examples of Simple PHH Combinations
How do you know which emotional hold to use when? By learning muscle testing, which is a part of my introductory PanHarmonic Healing classes. You might think that muscle testing is too hard, but I can show you ways to improve your ability to get answers you are confident in.

Here are some PHH acupressure holds that you can use to help yourself feel better in the time it takes to take three breaths and go into the energy of what you're feeling:

148

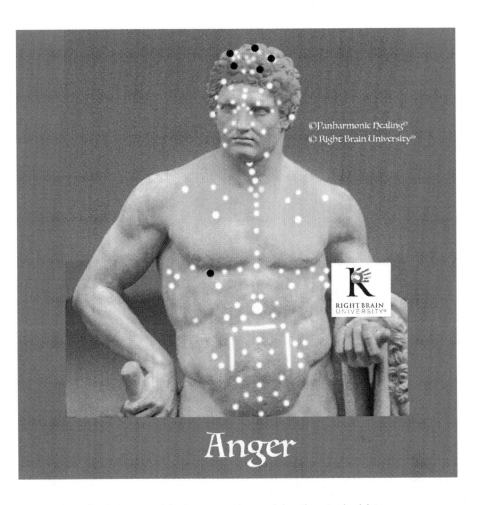

Anger

When you feel anger, this is a good combination to hold to process and release the emotion.

Make a circle of the five fingers of your left hand and place them on the crown of your head. Take the index and middle fingers of your right hand and place them together on the ribcage under the right breast on the second furthest dot from the center of the body.

Feel into your body and notice all the sensations. Go into the energy of what you're feeling. Take three deep breaths.

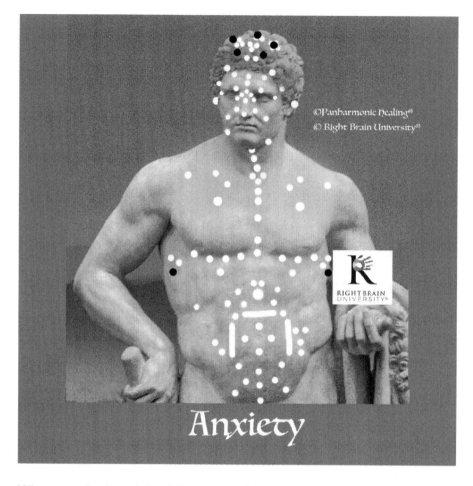

When you feel anxiety, this is a good combination to hold to process and release the emotion.

Make a circle of the five fingers of your left hand and place them on the crown of your head. Take the index and middle fingers of your right hand and place them together on the ribcage under the right armpit at the point shown.

Feel into your body and notice all the sensations. Go into the energy of what you're feeling. Take three deep breaths. Repeat on the other side.

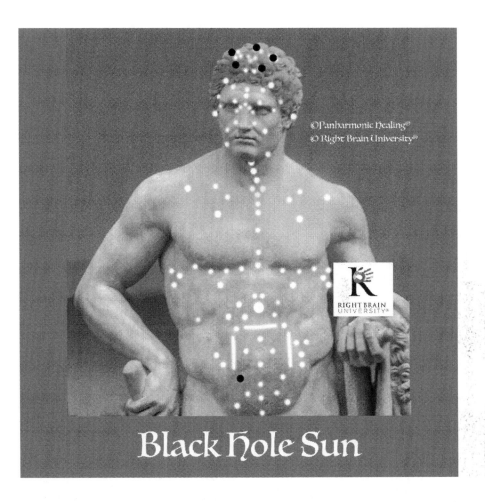

Black Ḥole Sun

When you feel the crushing pressure of a black hole throughout your body often without an identifiable feeling, this is a good combination to hold to process and release the emotion.

Make a circle of the five fingers of your left hand and place them on the crown of your head. Take the index and middle fingers of your right hand and place them together halfway between your belly button and the right hip bone.

Feel into your body and notice all the sensations. Go into the energy of what you're feeling. Take three deep breaths.

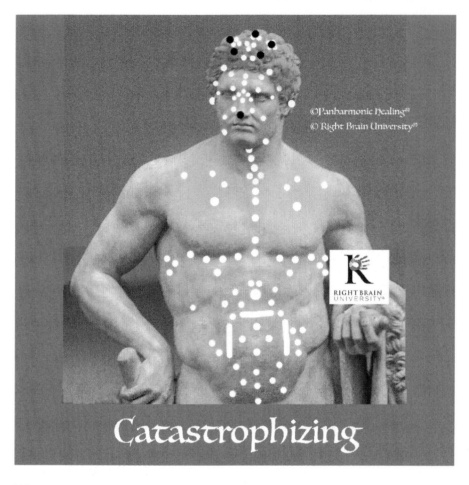

Catastrophizing

When you can't stop thinking of the worst outcome with every little problem, hold these points.

Make a circle of the five fingers of your left hand and place them on the crown of your head. Take the index and middle fingers of your right hand and place them on the tip of your nose.

Feel into your body and notice all the sensations. Go into the energy of what you're feeling. Take 3 deep breaths.

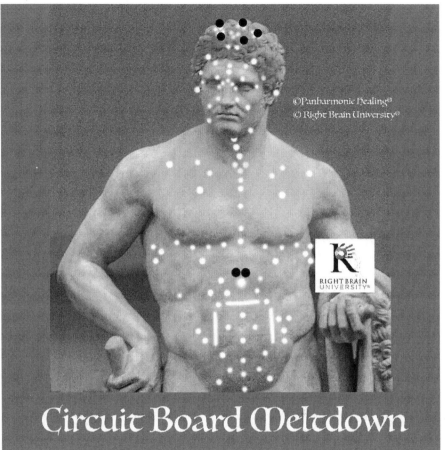

Circuit Board Meltdown

When you feel like you are utterly fried, this is a good combination to hold to process and release the emotion.

Make a circle of the five fingers of your left hand and place them on the crown of your head. Take the index and middle fingers of your right hand and place them on the soft part of the upper abdomen on either side of the midline.

Feel into your body and notice all the sensations. Go into the energy of what you're feeling. Take three deep breaths.

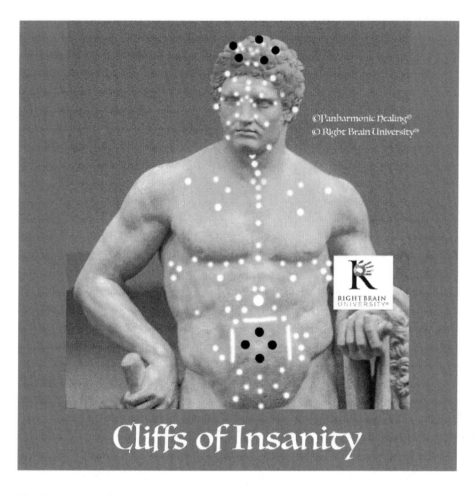

Cliffs of Insanity

No disrespect intended–I have spent more time than I'd care to remember clinging to the edge of these cliffs and wanted to share this simple path back to solid ground as part of the rest of your mental health help. When you feel like you are in danger of losing your mind, this is a good combination to hold to process and release the emotion.

Make a circle of the five fingers of your left hand and place them on the crown of your head. Take the thumb and first three fingers of your right hand and place them one inch out around your navel. Feel into your body and notice all the sensations. Go into the energy of what you're feeling. Take three deep breaths.

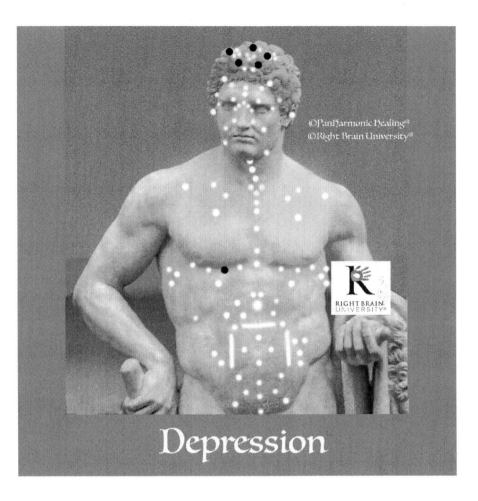

Depression

In PanHarmonic Healing, we think of depression as being anger turned inward, upon oneself. When your anger has turned inward and unleashed depression, this is a good combination to hold to process and release the emotion.

Make a circle of the five fingers of your left hand and place them on the crown of your head. Take the index and middle fingers of your right hand and place them on the right side of your breast, on the second black dot from the center.

Feel into your body and notice all the sensations. Go into the energy of what you're feeling. Take three deep breaths.

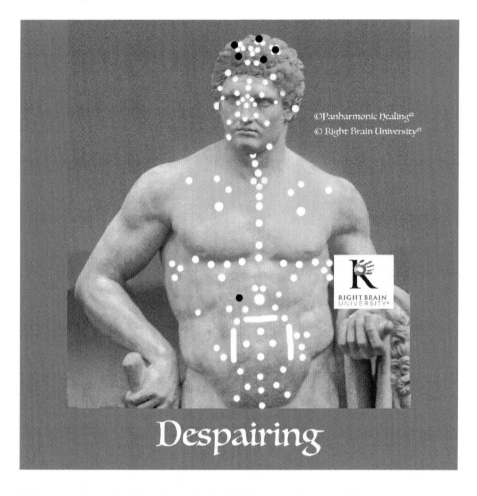

Despairing

When you are feeling despair, hold these points.

Make a circle of the five fingers of your left hand and place them on the crown of your head. Place the index and middle fingers of your right hand on the red dot on your abdomen.

Feel into your body and notice all the sensations. Go into the energy of what you're feeling. Take 3 deep breaths.

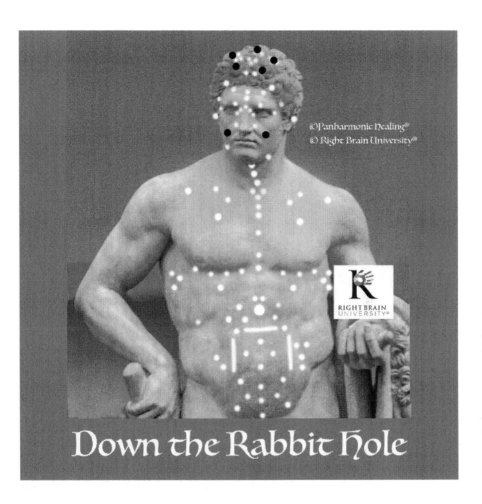

Down the Rabbit Hole

When you feel like your thoughts are driving you down an emotional rabbit hole, this is a good combination to hold to process and release the emotion.

Make a circle of the five fingers of your left hand and place them on the crown of your head. Place the thumb of your right hand one inch to the outside of the bottom of your nose and place your index and middle finger together on the opposite side.

Feel into your body and notice all the sensations. Go into the energy of the feeling. Take three deep breaths.

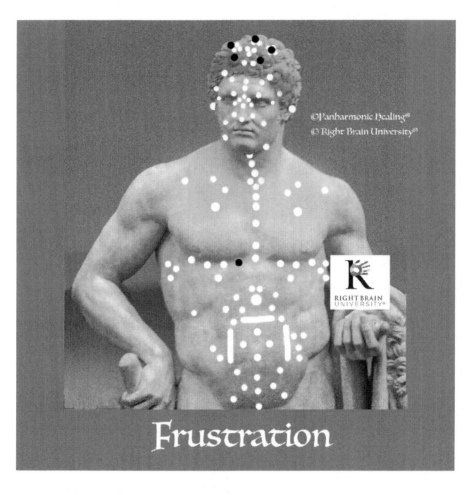

Frustration

When you feel frustration, this is a good combination to hold to process and release the emotion.

Make a circle of the five fingers of your left hand and place them on the crown of your head. Take the index and middle fingers of your right hand and place them together on the ribcage under the right breast on the black dot closest to the center of the body.

Feel into your body and notice all the sensations. Go into the energy of what you're feeling. Take three deep breaths.

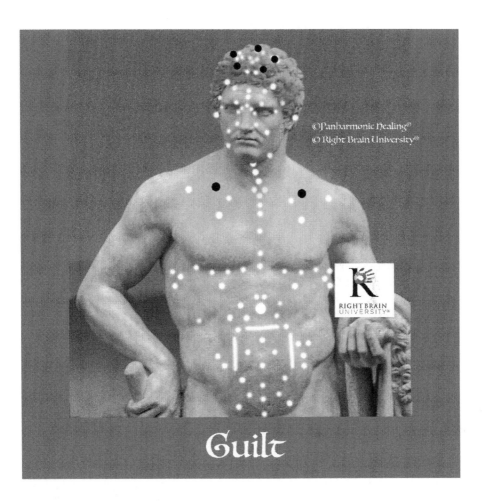

Guilt

When you feel you've done something wrong or not lived up to an expectation and you've done all you can do to right the situation, this is a good combination to hold to process and learn from the emotion.

Make a circle of the five fingers of your left hand and place them on the crown of your head. Take the index and middle fingers of your right hand and place them beneath the right collarbone at the midpoint. It's often tender.

Feel into your body and notice all the sensations. Go into the energy of what you're feeling. Take three deep breaths. Repeat on the left side.

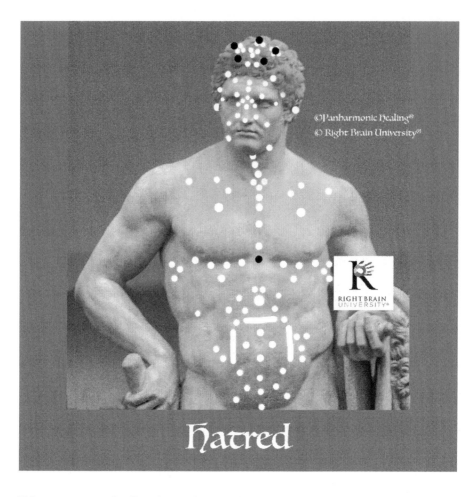

Ħatred

When you are feeling hatred, hold these points to release and integrate the emotion.

Make a circle of the five fingers of your left hand and place them on the crown of your head. Take your right hand and place the index and middle fingers on the black dot at the breastbone.

Feel into your body and notice all the sensations. Go into the energy of what you're feeling. Take 3 deep breaths.

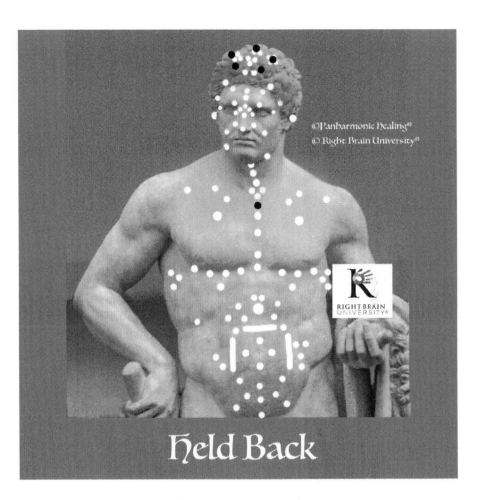

Held Back

When you feel held back, hold these points.

Make a circle of the five fingers of your left hand and place them on the crown of your head. Take your index and middle fingers of your right hand on the black dot at the upper chest.

Feel into your body and notice all the sensations. Go into the energy of what you're feeling. Take 3 deep breaths.

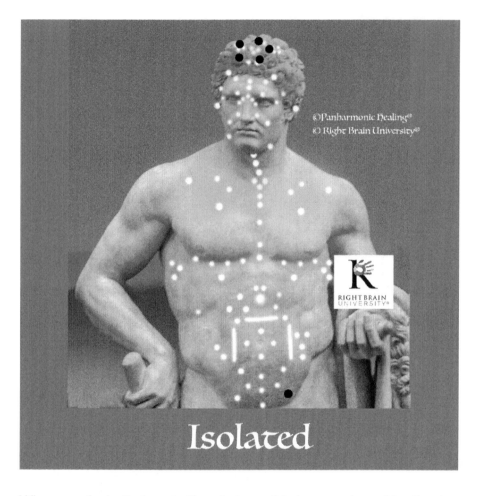

Isolated

When you feel utterly cut off and alone, this is a good combination to hold to process and release the emotion.

Make a circle of the five fingers of your left hand and place them on the crown of your head. Take the index and middle fingers of your right hand and place them together onto the soft lower left part of your abdomen, nestled in the pelvis.

Feel into your body and notice all the sensations. Go into the energy of what you're feeling. Take three deep breaths.

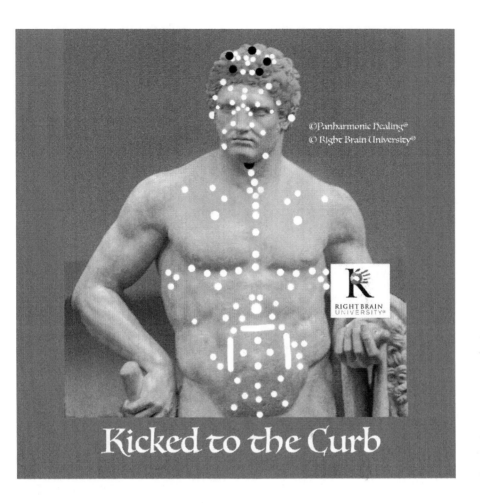

Kicked to the Curb

When someone treats you as if you were garbage, use these points to help reset to calm. Help your body learn the lesson, so it can let go of the feelings.

Make a circle of the five fingers of your left hand and place them on the crown of your head. Take the index and middle fingers of your right hand and place them at the top of your throat above your Adam's apple where it intersects with the underside of your chin. Close your eyes as you hold these points.

Feel into your body and notice all the sensations. Go into the energy of what you're feeling. Take three deep breaths.

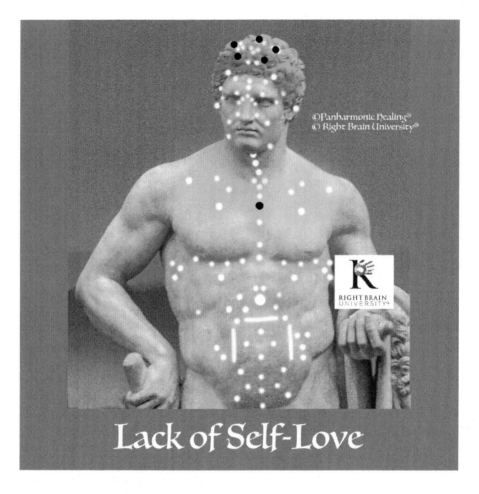

Lack of Self-Love

When you suffer from a lack of self-love, this is a good combination to hold to process and release the emotion.

Make a circle of the five fingers of your left hand and place them on the crown of your head. Take the index and middle fingers of your right hand and place them on the high point in the upper middle of your chest.

Feel into your body and notice all the sensations. Go into the energy of what you're feeling. Take three deep breaths.

164

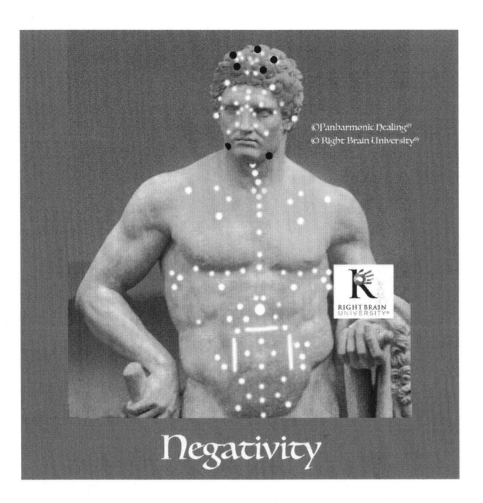

negativity

When you feel negativity, this is a good combination to hold to process, and release the emotion.

Make a circle of the five fingers of your left hand and place them on the crown of your head. Turn your right hand upside down and place the index and middle fingers on one side of your jaw and thumb on the other at the black dots.

Feel into your body and notice all the sensations. Go into the energy of what you're feeling. Take three deep breaths.

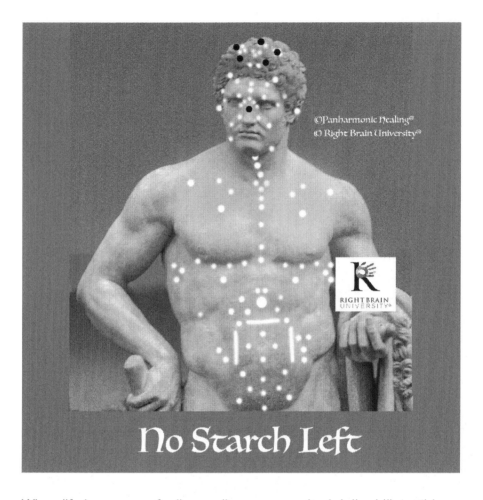

No Starch Left

When life leaves you feeling as limp as a washed dollar bill, try this combination.

Make a circle of the five fingers of your left hand and place them on the crown of your head. Take the index and middle fingers of your right hand and place them on your nose where cartilage meets bone.

Feel into your body and notice all the sensations. Go into the energy of what you're feeling. Take 3 deep breaths.

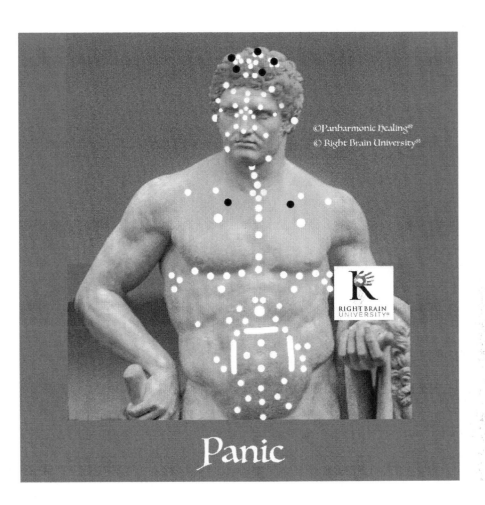

Panic

When you are feeling panicked, hold these points.

Make a circle of the five fingers of your left hand and place them on the crown of your head. Take your right hand and place the thumb on the right red dot and place the index and middle fingers on the left red dot.

Feel into your body and notice all the sensations. Go into the energy of what you're feeling. Take 3 deep breaths.

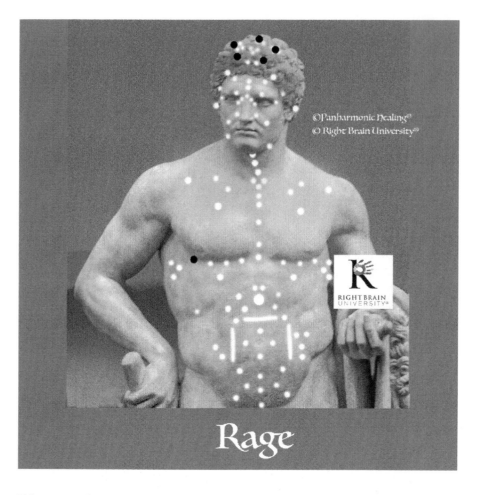

Rage

When you feel rage, this is a good combination to hold to process and release the emotion.

Make a circle of the five fingers of your left hand and place them on the crown of your head. Take the index and middle fingers of your right hand and place them together on the ribcage under the right breast on the dot furthest out from the center of the body.

Feel into your body and notice all the sensations. Go into the energy of what you're feeling. Take three deep breaths.

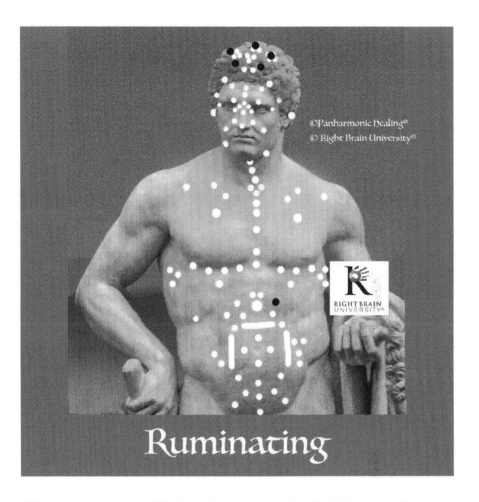

Ruminating

When you can't stop thinking about something, hold these points.

Make a circle of the five fingers of your left hand and place them on the crown of your head. Place the index and middle fingers of your right hand on the black dot on your upper left abdomen.

Feel into your body and notice all the sensations. Go into the energy of what you're feeling. Take 3 deep breaths.

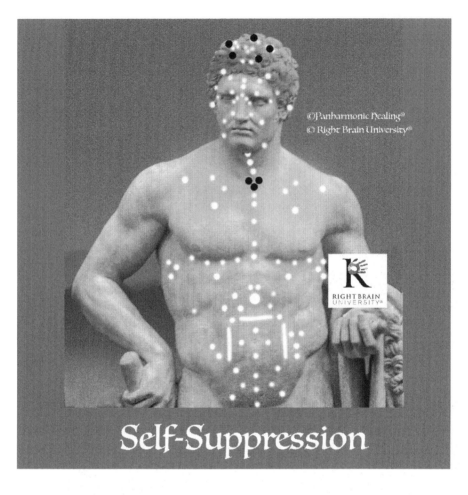

Self-Suppression

When you feel like you're holding yourself back this is a good combination to hold to process and release the feeling.

Make a circle of the five fingers of your left hand and place them on the crown of your head. Take the index, middle, and third fingers of your right hand and place them together at the notch at the base of your throat.

Feel into your body and notice all the sensations. Go into the energy of the feeling. Take three deep breaths.

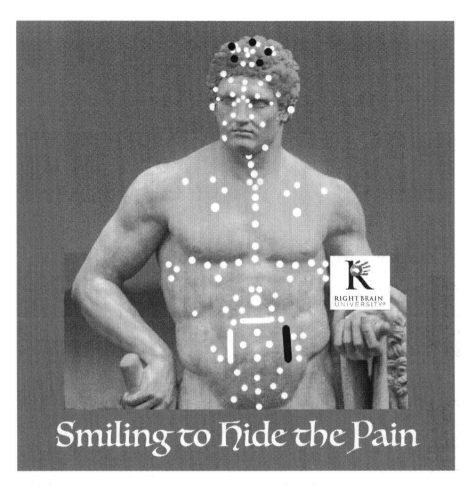

Smiling to Hide the Pain

When your smile is pasted on and you hurt like hell inside, this is a good combination to hold to process and release the emotion.

Make a circle of the five fingers of your left hand and place them on the crown of your head. Take the pinky side of your right hand and place it on the left side of your abdomen, fingers pointed down.

Feel into your body and notice all the sensations. Go into the energy of what you're feeling. Take three deep breaths.

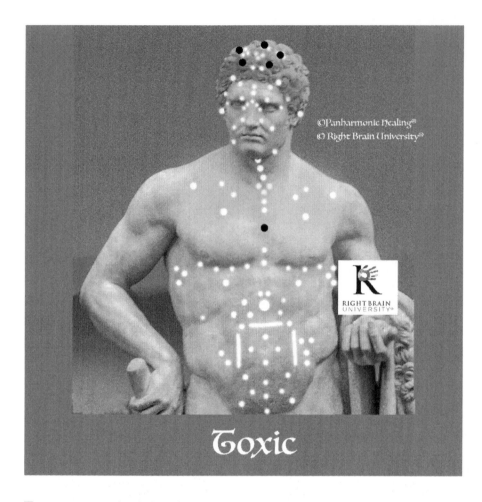

Toxic

To process and release feeling toxic, make a circle of the five fingers of your left hand and place them on the crown of your head.

Take the index and middle fingers of your right hand and place them on your chest at the black dot.

Feel into your body and notice all the sensations. Go into the energy of what you're feeling. Take 3 deep breaths.

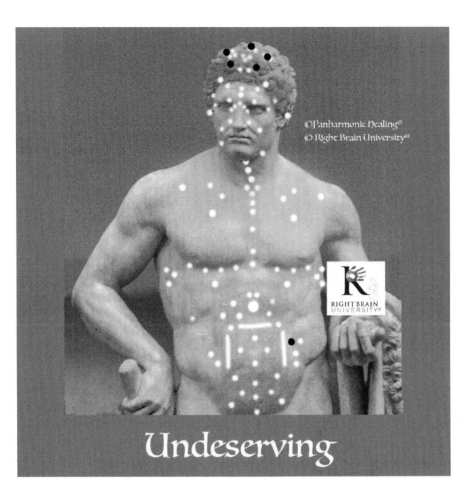

Undeserving

When you don't believe in yourself, you can't help make good things happen. Let go of the belief that you don't deserve better with this combination to process and release the emotion.

Make a circle of the five fingers of your left hand and place them on the crown of your head. Take the index and middle fingers of your right hand and place them together on the soft spot below the diaphragm on the upper left side of your abdomen.

Feel into your body and notice all the sensations. Go into the energy of what you're feeling. Take 3 deep breaths.

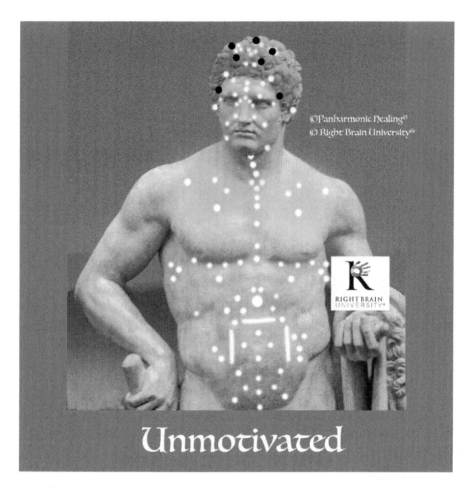

Unmotivated

Wish you had a good way to find motivation? Process and release the emotions that are holding you back.

Make a circle of the five fingers of your left hand and place them on the crown of your head. Take the index and middle fingers of your right hand and place them on the right side of your temple, on the black dot.

Feel into your body and notice all the sensations. Go into the energy of what you're feeling. Take three deep breaths. Repeat on the left side.

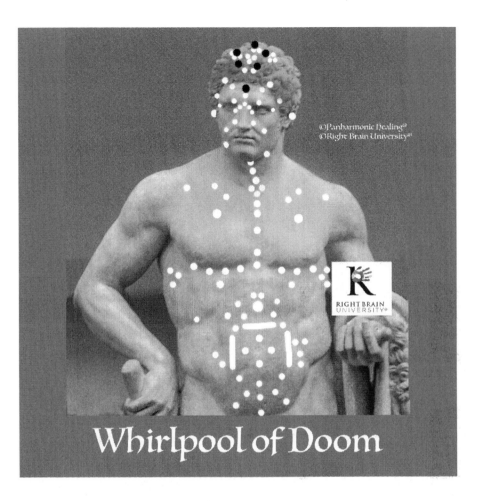

RIGHT BRAIN
UNIVERSITY®

Whirlpool of Doom

When you feel yourself being sucked down into the abyss, this is a good combination to hold to process and release the emotion.

Make a circle of the five fingers of your left hand and place them on the crown of your head. Take the index and middle fingers of your right hand and place them together in the middle of your forehead at the black dot.

Feel into your body and notice all the sensations. Go into the energy of the feeling. Take three deep breaths.

More Free Tools with PHH

For those of you who'd like to learn a bit more about PHH before committing to taking a class, email me with "More PHH Tools" in the subject line and I'll send you a link to three different categories of emotions. There's more than one type of anger, there's more than one type of sadness, there's more than one type of guilt—as a matter of fact, PHH can clear almost two dozen types of each emotion.

The emotions in the photos above are all unexpressed emotions. By that, I mean unexpressed anger, unexpressed isolation, unexpressed panic, unexpressed feeling toxic, or unexpressed feeling undeserving.

Let's give you an example of another emotional category. Another very common emotional category is called attached emotions. Attached emotions are emotions we get some sort of benefit from; it could be a conscious or an unconscious benefit or both. Getting a benefit from feeling a certain way can make it very hard to change. Usually this is something that developed in childhood that no longer serves us. An example might be that in a dysfunctional family, you were asked to take sides by your parents. Say you chose your mother's side. You might have lots of attached anger about your father that is being held because it was needed for your survival as a young child to ensure your mother loved and cared for you constantly. As an adult, though, you don't want to hold onto emotions because they are inflammatory, and inflammation can lead to disease. You want to be able to learn from emotions both consciously and unconsciously and then let the body process them as they release.

Look back at the previous emotions; see how they all have five black dots on the top of the head? That means they are all unexpressed emotions. Instead, with the example of attached circuit board meltdown below, there are now two points to hold on the forehead combined with the abdominal points. Each of the emotions above can now be paired with the two dots on the forehead instead of the five black dots on the top of the head to help you process and integrate attached anger, attached anxiety, attached guilt, attached isolation, attached panic, etc.

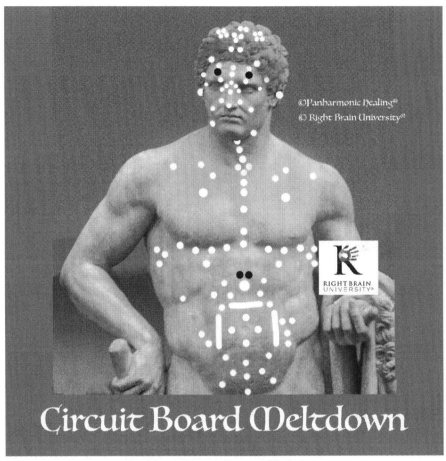

Circuit Board Meltdown

Attached Circuit Board Meltdown

The Emotional Language of PHH
The points shown in the diagrams above have up to seven emotions connected to them at this writing. What does that mean? There is an emotional language of the body that develops from being fluent in the use of this system. With twenty-three emotional programs easily muscle-tested for to combine with one hundred fifteen emotions, it's an infinite combination that the superconscious can use to communicate with us and help us spend more time in our cortex.

More time in our cortex means an easier life, both at home, school, or work. And for those of us interested in raising our vibration, it does that too.

Self-help vs. Session Work

Why learn PanHarmonic Healing for yourself? Because life happens 24/7 and lots of sessions can get expensive.

Why go to a specialized kinesiologist rather than do work on yourself? Because more can get done when someone other than ourselves is holding space for an energetic upgrade. We are limited by our own karma when we work on ourselves. I also find that the unconscious is willing to allow more emotional release when there is someone who can interpret the information and guide us.

Additionally, specialized kinesiologists are trained in muscle testing and are usually trained in more than one modality, so we can test for what's needed and help you get the quickest results. And on top of that, we've helped hundreds or thousands of people through sessions, so we've got a wealth of experience to explain what comes up in a session. We are fluent in a way that will take years for you to master. As a teacher, I am happy to provide shortcuts in class to help you master this work as quickly as you can, but it is something that takes time and practice. I have found learning PanHarmonic Healing's emotional work to be as important for communicating with myself as knowing English is for communicating with other human beings, and I think you will too.

Expressing Feelings

Going to psychotherapy in my twenties was helpful, but it unintentionally gave me tools to only deal with the mind. I started rationalizing away my feelings, rather than tuning into them. I explained away others' hurtful actions, so that my empathy was only for other people, which meant my own feelings were never honored. Now I know I must express my feelings and once they're heard and acknowledged, even if it's only within myself or via journaling, they can change. They are only set in stone when they're not expressed.

A specialized kinesiology session consists of taking stock of what's been happening and what emotions have come up during the week. You might take notes during the week of what you want to accomplish in a session (what major events happened to you that week, how you felt about them, how your life goals are going, and anything important that came up during your psychotherapy session) and discuss this with your specialized kinesiologist when you first start the session. Your own body is the guide. It has priorities on what emotional holdings it needs to process and release via acupressure, and which order it wants to process them in. Your body heals itself. The practitioner is only there to help you access its wisdom until you learn enough to access its wisdom on your own. At the start of a session, the client sits and discusses their goals for the session. Once that's established, the practitioner begins muscle testing to see where nerve energy is blocked. The practitioner can work with the client over the internet or in person. If it's in person, a practitioner may prefer to muscle test the client or to muscle test themselves to get answers for the client. Some clients like to sit through the session, while others prefer to lie on a massage table. This is not massage; the client is always fully clothed and in charge of how the session proceeds. Over time, the work leads to you being able to stay in a higher vibration for longer and longer until you shift to the next highest level. Continued work continues to raise your vibration.

Combining Kinesiologies

Any of these kinesiologies are great on their own, however a combination session offering multiple modalities lets you head in whichever direction your body needs. For example, a combination of Touch for Health, Brain Gym®, and PanHarmonic Healing lets the specialized kinesiologist see where energy is blocked in the body, allows old patterns to be released, and healthy new ones to be integrated. Often the process releases stuck energy from the present which is linked to something in the past. The client leaves the session with a sense of calm, increased capacity for executive function, and a new tool for how to release emotions on their own timing. It's easy from the start to quickly learn tools to clear any shock or trauma from interacting with the world.

Tools to Feel Safe

For the lucky ones who can feel energy moving, these sessions give a feeling of safety. They can feel energy draining away as a cold or warm feeling, as numbness or tingling, or as muscle twitches, which in my experience is a part of the feelings getting processed. Even if they can't feel the energy moving, once the points are released, the emotion stops. It might bring on a strong emotion at first while the points are being held, but the client is in control of that because they set the pace of the session. Knowing the feeling goes away once the release is completed can encourage them to hang in there, both during sessions with their specialized kinesiologist as well as with work they do on themselves at home.

Developing Personal Power

We often start to panic when we have a bad feeling. I sure used to. Typically, we shut down the connection to our body and try to think about or do something else, often to the point of reaching for a bottle or a pill. If we don't like being out of control, we might shrink our life smaller until finally we are afraid to try anything.

Once I started seeing a specialized kinesiologist and learning tools for home use, my new pattern was to work on myself every day whenever bad feelings came up. Using these tools left me with a feeling of calm and helped me gain a bit of personal power to be able to reset my old patterns.

Specialized kinesiology gives us invaluable tools to know when we're experiencing our own emotions and when we're being influenced by other's emotions, as well as helping us to clear emotions. As I mentioned before, we all have emotions 24/7--they don't just happen at the specialized kinesiologist's office. Sometimes we can't connect to emotions consciously, but they are still being produced on an unconscious level. Learning these techniques can allow us to stop reliving the past, heal on both the conscious and unconscious level, and start enjoying our lives to the fullest.

We Are All More Interconnected Than We Know

As I mentioned earlier, introverts become very good at picking up others' emotional states to stay safe. As you learn specialized kinesiology and how to clear your energy, you'll likely become more aware of what is impacting your body. The next time you're feeling fine one minute and the next minute you're in throbbing pain, you'll have the tools to know if it's your emotion or if you've picked up someone else's energy.

I've found we are more vulnerable to getting sick when we are around other people who are projecting negative energy. We can also feel more pain around some people's energy too. If someone is in pain or crisis, an empath picks up that energy and it is reflected in the empath's body. My specialized kinesiologist encouraged me to learn more about the body's energy systems, including how to heal auras and how to strengthen one's hara. The hara is the area of the belly that Japanese martial arts were developed to strengthen. It's connecting to the energy from the gut brain which is connected to chi beyond us. If you've ever seen a demonstration where black belt masters can make themselves too heavy to lift, this is the energy they draw from.

The Body's Energy System

I noticed that sometimes after being around certain people I'd come away feeling physically terrible. Sometimes it'd be my back or neck going out, sometimes it'd be a sense of general fatigue. Occasionally, if I was eating a meal with a person who seemed angry, upset or irritable, I'd get sick immediately. For example, one time I had a coughing fit and huge reaction to a food that normally doesn't affect me. Within a minute my health took a nosedive, beyond what could be explained by how fast germs multiply. Every time that happened, during my next balance, my kinesiologist would test my aura and it'd be ripped open. The skeptic in me got all the proof I needed because I don't make enough endorphins to hide pain. I am overly sensitive to all sensations, so I could feel it as she re-knit my aura each time.

Re-knitting the Aura

A practitioner re-knits an aura by moving their hands over the energy field between 1-3 inches away from the client's body. They use muscle testing to make sure the aura is strong again. Re-knitting made me aware of having a wound which I hadn't known existed. It gave me the soothing feeling that the equivalent of ointment and a Band-Aid had been put on that wound. I felt a sensation of there being some boundary to me beyond my body that started to get filled up again each time it got re-knit. This was the first time I realized that part of what I thought of as being sick was really about that energy layer being breached. It made me realize I needed to learn more about auras and other levels of our energy body.

Connecting to The Field

For most people, taking classes in these specialized kinesiologies or going to sessions to process pain or emotions will be all they ever want to accomplish and all they ever need to have a happier, healthier life. For those on a spiritual path, though, it seems specialized kinesiology can connect us to a deeper wisdom and a higher path. Much of what causes pain in this world is caused by people overly invested in their ego-selves, who have no skills to cope with strong emotion. That describes me, before I started to heal. I have found that specialized kinesiology allows me to connect to my higher self. It allows the ego-self to be set aside, at least for the space of a session, to undo whatever negative programming from the past is currently up for healing, to reset to calm, and tap into a greater good and one's highest life direction. If you've heard of or seen the popular movie *The Secret,* which teaches about the law of attraction, the emotional clearing taught in PanHarmonic Healing can be used to assist people to stay in touch with Divine Will by helping to keep the ego in check. In this way, the right-brain state can help us remain connected to that which is greater than us. People can also use it to allow themselves to reset when they are upset, so they remain in a higher level of thinking and connection.

The other benefit of PanHarmonic Healing combined with other kinesiologies is that processing and releasing emotions allows us to develop more and more ability to help others heal. I had no connection at all to any ability to do energy work. I was stuck in trauma and had no interest in alternative healing my entire life until I got sick. Learning acupressure and practicing it diligently to help myself feel better led to me being able to not need to use touch anymore, so that I became a healer who can work with people around the world. Imagine a world where anyone can learn these tools to heal rather than striking out in anger or fear.

The Hundred Monkey Principle
In much the same way as the hundred-monkey principle works (that once a hundred monkeys on one side of an island learn a skill, the monkeys on the other side of the island with no contact also develop the skill) there appears to be a deeper interconnectedness to consciousness than our culture currently recognizes. It is said that the more people there are on a spiritual path, the more awake and aware the cultures of our planet will be. To use the same term as Lynne McTaggart uses in her book *The Field*, it is thought that the development of these kinesiologies could be meant to help our ascension as a species. These methods all allow us to spend more time in our highest-level human brain–the cortex and prefrontal cortex. That's the way I think of ascension; the ability to spend less and less time in the brain stem and emotional brain response, and instead to enjoy the best parts of ourselves accessed through the cortex and prefrontal cortex. I do my part to help people with ascension: I teach Touch for Health, Brain Gym®, and PanHarmonic Healing levels 1 & 2, along with the advanced emotional healing classes I developed

(PanHarmonic Healing levels 3-6) as well as working with groups and private clients. The contact information for my teachers and my kinesiologists are also in the action steps listed below. I hope I'm a good example of how much help they are with supporting traumatized people to heal.

Has the Author Lost Her Mind?

I'm sure some of you are wondering this, so I'll address it directly. Here was my logic: I spent the first forty-two years of my life asleep, and it led to autoimmune disease. As I began to wake up and question my thoughts, my beliefs, and my life, I realized that I could not control my feelings and that denying my feelings had made me sick. I'd run my life completely through my mind, that is to say, my ego-self, and it had led me to illness. It seemed clear to me that some of my beliefs had to be wrong, as well as some of my thoughts and patterns of behavior.

When I had a specialized kinesiology session, I could go beyond anxiety and fear, beyond anger, to feel interconnected and whole within 60-90 minutes. It was the opportunity to reset from stress; much the same feeling as having a perfect, stress-free, deep sleep with comforting dreams. But when we are stressed, how impossible it is to get that type of reset through sleep! We often have interrupted, fractured sleep.

The conscious mind is only about five to ten percent of our whole brain. There is so much said in our culture about listening to our gut and following our intuition. It seems that our intuition is connected to our superconscious, to the greater part of our mind and body. It also seems to be interconnected in some way to others and to that which some call God, the Higher Self or The Universe. Why not give that gut instinct a chance to guide me, I reasoned? Certainly, my tiny rational mind had screwed up royally. My programming was faulty. I was overly fearful about everything. My body was exhausted. Perhaps there was a better guidance system on board that I could tap into while I was in that connected state. And so, I began to take baby steps into that reality.

It was daunting, because surrendering control when one has been captain of one's ship for a lifetime feels at times like an extremely bad idea. And yet, over time, I could see that it led me to a healthier state. It led to empathy for myself when needed and empathy toward others when needed. To undoing a lifetime of self-sabotaging patterns and developing healthy self-love. Away from inflammatory thought spirals and emotional shipwrecks and towards clarity. It led to greater ability for my rational mind to be a calm parenting influence on my scared inner children and greater ability to lead those inner children to reconnect and heal. And that's why I recommend specialized kinesiology to those on a spiritual path as well as for those who have chronic illness. I highly recommend psychotherapy at the same time to provide a framework for your mind and body to have the easiest time rebuilding from past trauma. More on that in Chapter 20.

Additional techniques

I have also found something called Ask and Receive as well as Emotional Freedom Technique (EFT) helpful in supporting trauma release, though for me they are far less specific and far less helpful than PanHarmonic Healing, Touch for Health, and Brain Gym®. You can find more about these techniques below.

Action steps:
Easy:
Try Ask and Receive at askandreceive.org.

Learn more about EFT at thetappingsolution.com or read Nick Ortner's book *The Tapping Solution: A Revolutionary Method for Stress-Free Living* or Jack Canfield's *Tapping into Ultimate Success.*

If you're open to it, keep up a positive frame of mind with Notes from the Universe. They are free. Sign up at tut.com.

Learn some simple acupressure with me in my free YouTube

videos. For the link to my YouTube account, go to my website's home page and scroll down to the bottom of the page at ww.rightbrainuniversity.com. Click on the YouTube symbol.

Moderate:

You can find information on when I'll be teaching Touch for Health, PanHarmonic Healing, and Brain Gym® online at www.rightbrainuniversity.com. You can also find other Touch for Health instructors at touchforhealth.us, and other Brain Gym® instructors at breakthroughsinternational.org.

Matthew Thie is the son of John Thie and is the co-author of the *Touch for Health: Complete Edition* manual. He offers group classes in Los Angeles and around the world. He's a wonderful instructor. You can find him at Touch4health.com.

If you are looking for a Touch for Health reactive muscle balance, look for someone who is certified as Touch for Health Proficient, a Touch for Health instructor or consultant. These three types of Touch for Health practitioners are certified in giving a 42-muscle balance, which I've found to be a necessary part of a reactive muscle balance. It requires a double session to do this type of balance, but I've found it to be well worth it.

Sign up for a class in PanHarmonic Healing. You can look at my website, www.rightbrainuniversity.com, to see when I offer classes. Dr. Valerie Girard is still in practice and can be reached at dr.valeriegirard@gmail.com.

Julie Newendorp is the founder and president of the Nurturing Parent Center. She doesn't teach, but she's a gifted healer, and a great resource for us all. Her website is nurturingparentcenter.com.

Harder:

Sign up for an online class with my aura and hara teacher, Talitha Wall, at talithawall.com.

Paula Oleska's website is naturalintelligencesystems.com.

Do you struggle with test anxiety or with work performance during stressful situations? Do you have a hard time letting go of stress? Using Brain Gym®, PanHarmonic Healing, primary reflex integration, and Touch for Health, I have helped people pass the California State bar exam, get a 34 on the ACT, get a 173 on the LSAT (which was in the 99th percentile for the October 2020 exam), pass the LMFT, do better at work, and increase enjoyment of life. I help high school and college students perform better on everyday tests, too.

I also help people with weight loss through releasing and reducing stress, emotions, and automatic patterns. More information at www.rightbrainuniversity.com.

Take a boundary workshop with Merle Yost at www.merleyost.com. Ask him if it's possible to take his classes as the original seven-hour long version, which is what I benefited from. These provide so much more than the shorter sessions.

Thursday:

Develop Parasympathetic Breathing, Exercise, Vision, and Thoughts

Chapter 16
Breath Is More Than Just Getting Air Into Us

Spin Bike Queen

After picking up hot yoga again, I tried spin biking and absolutely fell in love with it. It was an incredible workout and absolutely exhausting. I love doing exercise in a group, where I am pushed and encouraged to keep up with everyone. I have always had to breathe through my mouth my whole life, because of congestion. Spin biking left me exhausted afterwards and panting. Yet after taking classes in breathing, I was able to retrain myself to comfortably breathe through my nose the entire workout, and not have my heart work so hard. Breathing this way also reduced congestion and seemed to correspond to another increase in my ability to avoid colds and bronchitis.

Breath is Also About How We Breathe—Using the Parasympathetic vs. Sympathetic Nervous Systems

As I mentioned in Chapter 3, our autonomic nervous system (ANS) is divided into three types: sympathetic (SNS), parasympathetic (PNS) and enteric (ENS). The ANS regulates all our internal organs and glands unconsciously. That means that the right brain is in charge of processing it, which is yet another reason we need a well-developed right brain.

Sympathetic = Fight or Flight = Inflammatory

I would have thought the sympathetic nervous systems, the SNS, would be our best friend because the name reminds me of sympathy, but this is the pathway that causes inflammation. It produces the fight-or-flight response to help keep us alive in times of immediate danger and is also the system that causes the problem with chronic stress.

Another important duty of the SNS is to stay active at a low level to help maintain a constant immune response in our bodies to support life.

Breathing Stressed Means Feeling Stressed

When we breathe through our mouths, we are inadvertently signaling our bodies that there may be danger. The next time you feel angry or stressed, notice if you are breathing through your mouth. If so, bring your breath back to breathing calmly through your nose. This is why yoga and meditation both primarily use nose breathing.

The Parasympathetic Nervous System is Calming

The parasympathetic nervous system (PNS), the liver, the kidneys and the brain also work with the SNS to help us maintain a constant state to support life. The PNS is calming and reduces inflammation. It's in charge whenever we rest or digest. When we breathe through our noses, we feel calmer because we are activating the PNS.

Breathing Styles are Passed Down from Parents to Children

Stressed parents pass down their stressed breathing habits to their children as children mimic their parents' behavior. How we breathe can either activate our SNS or PNS. For long term health, we want our breathing to keep us in a steady, calming, healthy non-inflammatory state.

We want to breathe in a way that keeps our PNS active as much as possible. Our body knows how to immediately shift to SNS in a stressful situation. Back when I got migraines frequently, I used to catch myself "not breathing enough." I thought maybe I was oxygen-deprived, and perhaps that's why I kept getting so many migraines, so I'd start speeding up my breathing. I learned the hard way that breathing is not supposed to be under conscious control. I was accidentally increasing the amount of inflammation in my sinuses and bronchia.

Making the Switch from Mouth to Nose Breathing

The SNS can take care of itself, but many of us need to learn how to activate PNS breathing. This goes beyond simply breathing through your nose whenever possible. I had no idea that this could be a stressful process until I tried it. For people like me who are more emotional and anxious, it can be a big transition to learn how to switch over. If you want to try this, I'd suggest going slow. Keep it positive by thanking yourself for trying to change rather than getting frustrated if it's not easy for you. Realize your breathing does not have to change overnight or even in a month or two. You are heading toward better health simply by trying to learn this.

Children Who Have Trouble with Nose Breathing

Dental decay caused by mouth breathing at night is a common problem with kids and adults who have nasal congestion. We can reduce our children's risk of cavities as well as our own by making sure we all can breathe through our noses at night.

Issues with Asthma, Allergies and Snoring

On my journey, I came across the Buteyko breathing method developed by a Russian scientist, Constantin Buteyko.

Buteyko realized that our body needs a higher concentration of carbon dioxide than what is currently in our atmosphere. If we over-breathe (take in too much air) such as when we have a cold, cough a lot, or are emotionally stressed, our body will create inflammation around our airways to prevent loss of carbon dioxide.

Over-Breathing Can Set up a Cycle of Inflammation, Asthma and/or Allergies

This means people who are emotionally stressed tend toward asthma. Buteyko believed the same pathway happens with allergies as well, where over-breathing leads to inflammation which is often connected to a specific allergen as an emotional trigger. All of this is played out on a completely unconscious level.

The Buteyko Method has had a great deal of success in helping severe asthmatics reduce or even eliminate their need for rescue inhalers. My favorite Buteyko Method trainer is Tess Graham, the mother of children with chronic asthma who were cured through breath retraining. Helping others has become her life's mission, and she's a lovely human being. Her program is based on and authorized by the late Professor Constantine Buteyko. Tess is an Australian-based physiotherapist with a degree in the Buteyko Breathing Method direct from Moscow, and a clinical practice in breath retraining. She has two books, *Relief from Snoring and Sleep Apnea*, and *Relief from Anxiety and Panic* as well as an online program.

There's a breath retraining program in Woodstock, NY that I struggled with because it moved a bit too fast for me. If you remember to follow your gut instincts in making a choice, I'm sure you'll do well with either program. Contact details for both are in the action steps.

Switching to Nose Breathing at Night

My experience has taught me that dealing with underlying emotional issues can lead to a reduction in the inflammation in my airways. Switching from mouth breathing to nose breathing, so that the parasympathetic nervous system is more active, helps to calm things down.

Even though I was a mouth breather from childhood, it turned out I could change. It's easiest to transition first during the day to breathing through the nose. People may have emotional issues with this transition. I sure did. Clients are encouraged to breathe less, which can feel suffocating at first if they try too hard. I found it helped to take it very slowly. I thought of each breath through the nose as a victory and any time I reverted to mouth-breathing, I was patient and supportive of how hard it is to change.

After a certain point with the New York Buteyko method, they recommend a small piece of scotch tape over the mouth as a reminder not to mouth-breathe at night. Putting tape on my mouth made me feel panicky but going to sleep with my hand on my lips worked as a good enough reminder for easing into it slowly. Especially for people who have had bronchitis to the point where they can barely breathe at night, any restriction at night can bring up that feeling of suffocation.

Now the only time I mouth breathe is when I have a cold, which I rarely have. I have gone from needing antibiotics six to eight times a year to not having been on antibiotics in years. For the past five years, I've been able to ward off most illnesses at the start with hydrogen peroxide in my ears as soon as I feel something coming on. I wouldn't recommend this if you tend to get ear infections, but for me, it's been a huge help to keep the lymph nodes in the neck clear and functioning.

Breathing and Fascia

Many of us have fascial restrictions through our rib cages and diaphragm. Usually this is a silent problem, although perhaps you feel breathless at times. You might have gotten checked out by your doctor without any problem being noted. You could have noticed you have a problem with how fully your rib cage and diaphragm can move if you try doing exercises lying down on one of those big fifty-inch diameter green balls. If you haven't, try lying down backwards on one. Do you feel breathless? How big a breath can you take? If you feel like you're unable to take a normal breath, it might be that your ribcage is bound up with fascia. When I first started working with my physical therapist, she had me work on a big green exercise ball. I was unable to move my ribs more than a half inch while lying on my back on it, so I couldn't breathe in properly while using it. If you notice the same problem, it's a good reason to seek out someone who does John Barnes MFR, a Rolfer, or a physical therapist.

Intercostal Release

I created and developed a process to be able to expand my ribs, so that my intercostal muscles would release. I would breathe in as far as I could, then pause and try to make my ribcage expand just a tiny bit more, taking care not to hold my breath, as that can raise blood pressure. I only practiced for 2 minutes a day. This is because how much in vs. out breath we take is a delicate process. It can impact the alkalinity of our blood and I wanted to be gentle on my system.

Over time, I could stretch further and further. After about six months I felt and heard a huge popping sound within my ribcage, which was fascia releasing. It didn't hurt at all. From that point on, it has allowed much more movement in my ribcage. I think the fascia constriction itself causes something we could call 'positional fear' or 'held fear' rather than fear caused in reaction to something happening currently in life. After releasing the fascia around the muscles in my ribcage and abdomen, freedom of movement has helped reduce emotional constriction. On average, I feel far less fear than I did before. Ask your doctor or physical therapist before you do this if you'd like to try it.

Action steps:
Easy:
Increase the amount of time you breathe through your nose. Notice how much you breathe through your mouth when you talk and try to use your nose to breathe instead.

If you catch yourself taking a deep breath without having exerted yourself, try to find the thoughts or feelings that triggered it. Release them through Focusing (see chapter 20) and/or PanHarmonic Healing.

Soothe your breathing and let it calm back down.

Moderate:
If you have problems with allergies, asthma, snoring or sleep apnea read Tess Graham's books or try her program at

www.breatheability.com. The NY Buteyko Method can be found at www.breathingcenter.com.

Try resistance stretching near you, or Bob Cooley's book *Resistance Flexibility 1.0: Becoming Flexible in All Ways.*

Harder:

Work one-on-one with someone who does John Barnes MFR at myofascialrelease.com, or a local resistance stretching trainer or with an RFST trainer at thegeniusofflexibility.com to target your ribcage.

Try working with someone who does Chinese Chi Ne Tsang abdominal massage.

Chapter 17
Improving How We Exercise

Sprint 8 for Better Fitness Levels

Twenty years ago, my family and I visited my first husband's cousin Dale for Thanksgiving, taking Amtrak from New York City to Atlanta because our two-year-old twin boys were crazy for trains. Eighteen hours each way on a train with twin toddlers turned out to be a v-e-r-y bad idea for the grownups, though the twins had a blast.

Cousin Dale had been ranked as one of the country's top three triathletes back in the early 1980s. He'd long since retired, his body struggling with all the overuse he'd put it through. He shared with us that he'd finally found something that made all the difference to him: a book that allowed him to exercise smart in only fifteen minutes with quality exercise rather than exercising in quantity, which his body could no longer handle. That book was *Ready, Set, Go Synergy Fitness* by Phil Campbell. When we got home, I bought the book and started doing Phil's Sprint 8 workout twice a week. It helped me stay just active enough even during my worst health, so that I never was completely bedridden. One of the things he recommends is breathing through the nose when working out.

Nose Breathing for Better Fitness Levels

Also suggested by Dr. Douillard in his book *Body, Mind, and Sport*, I've found nose breathing to be helpful to this day when I exercise. Modifying breathing to the parasympathetic state has been shown to reduce our risk of injury, since fight, flight or freeze puts us into our highest state of muscle, tendon, and ligament tension. I'm not the only one who has found that it improves endurance levels if you breathe through your nose rather than your mouth. Lastly, in my experience, it also reduces sinus and lung congestion. My mild asthma went away.

When I first started experimenting with nose breathing in my spin bike workouts at the gym, I could only nose breathe for about twenty seconds before being so exhausted I would have to resume mouth breathing. I couldn't imagine ever being able to make the change. But after a few months of transition and building endurance I could do the entire forty-five-minute workout while breathing through my nose. As I mentioned, I felt better, fitter, and stronger.

If this sounds interesting, I'd recommend getting a doctor's clearance first. I think it's easiest to make the transition slowly, starting with trying it as you're walking around throughout your day. Once that starts feeling normal, move on to exercise. When you begin to exercise, breathe through your nose. If you feel like you need to breathe through your mouth, slow down your pace to see if you can keep from mouth breathing.

The book Spring 8 advocates high-intensity aerobic exercise because it is beneficial for increasing fast-twitch muscle fiber. Fast-twitch muscle fibers fatigue quickly but are used in bursts of movements like jumping or sprinting. If all we do is jog, all we're building is our slow-twitch muscle fiber. Slow-twitch muscle fibers can work for a long time without getting tired. They are used for long-distance activities that require endurance. Fast-twitch muscle accounts for about half of our muscle mass. It's used for rapid movements like sprinting. Children naturally keep their fast-twitch muscle in top tone because they don't pace themselves. Instead, they run til they're exhausted and then they stop until they catch their breath and then they go at top speed again. We can learn from what they do.

This type of workout works well no matter what level of fitness you are at. Warming up for 3 minutes, sprinting for 30 seconds at whatever method of exercise you've chosen, then recovering for 1 1/2 minutes by walking in between. Keep that up for eight sprint cycles, then cool down for 2 minutes. If you're out of shape, modify the number of sprints you try. Just warm up, sprint once, then cool down if that is what you need to start. This type of exercise is beneficial for metabolism, especially as we age. I suggest reading the books mentioned above for more details.

The Benefits of Interval Training and Distance Running
A study by Mayo Clinic researchers recently published in *Cell Metabolism* showed that activity levels within genes changed with interval training in ways that are believed to influence the ability of mitochondria to produce energy for muscle cells, as compared to moderate exercisers or weightlifters. The changes impacted 274 genes in the younger participants, compared with 170 genes in moderate exercisers and only 74 for the weightlifters, but in the older study participants, almost 400 genes worked differently, compared to 33 for weightlifters and only 19 for the moderate exercisers.

While interval sprints are helpful for metabolism and mitochondria, it's not been found to be particularly beneficial for the brain. A study published in the *Journal of Physiology* recently by researchers at the University of Jyvaskyla in Finland working with rats, showed that the most beneficial form of exercise for the brain is distance running. It's believed that sustained aerobic exercise produces more BDNF (brain-derived neurotrophic factor) which regulates neurogenesis, the formation of new brain neurons in the hippocampus. In studies with animals, exercise on running wheels or treadmills has been shown to double or triple the number of new neurons compared to the brains of animals that remain sedentary. News like that has me dusting off my running shoes for both interval training and distance running. I also have started using jump rope to do interval training and am seeing quick metabolic benefits. It's also myelinating the brain through repetitive movement, so it's a win-win.

Do You Really Hate to Exercise?

If you think you hate to exercise, you might be wrong. I used to hate it until I realized what I hated is how I thought about myself when I exercised. Maybe you hate how you feel about yourself when you exercise too, or maybe you talk negatively to yourself when you exercise. Maybe kids made fun of your sports ability when you were young. Other people can undermine and sabotage us about exercise. They might not like us changing, even if they seem to encourage it. Actions speak louder than words, though, so look at their actions. We might not have much control over how others talk to us, but we are always in control over how we talk to ourselves. It will take time before we get good at catching our thoughts. If we keep practicing trying to pay attention to them, we can succeed. Same thing with what people said to us when we were children—it's possible to get rid of negative programming through meditation, specialized kinesiology, and therapy. Try these methods out and see how they all work well together.

Setting Boundaries

If you've got saboteurs in your life, set boundaries. Renegotiate your relationships. Are your friends supportive? When you want to join a gym or yoga studio or buy exercise equipment, do you get a lecture from your significant other about how frequently you need to use the membership or the equipment? That can make you associate the gym and the equipment with feeling shamed. Try to explain to them how that undermines the very thing they are concerned about, because who wants to replay the shame tape every time you exercise? Ask them for support rather than lectures—maybe by giving you a high-five every time you go to the gym or getting a kiss every time you get off the exercise bike. Think of ideas specific to you that might help you build positive, loving associations with exercise. There's nothing like being one's own best friend and coach to get the best out of ourselves.

Action Steps:
Easy:
Start listening to how you talk to yourself about exercise. Change it up if you're talking negatively to yourself. Get your doctor's blessing and begin a modest exercise program if you aren't already physically active. Read Phil Campbell's book, *Ready Set, Go Synergy Fitness.*

Moderate:
Read John Douillard's book, *Body, Mind, Sport*, which has a very helpful Ayurvedic slant on exercise and breathing.

Harder:
Work with a trainer who does resistance stretching. It's helped my family and me to free muscles that were gummed up with fascia and retraining them to work properly, so we can exercise better. It's also dramatically helped improve scoliosis for my family members. Look for help at your local gym and if none is available, try Bob Cooley's book *Resistance Flexibility 1.0: Becoming Flexible in All Ways.*

Chapter 18
Vision Therapy

What's Up With Your Vision?

How many things do we not know are wrong with how we see? When I was a kid, I used to entertain my friends by crossing my eyes, which made them wiggle back and forth. Little did I know then that this was a sign that my eyes didn't team together well. I also had problems with divergence insufficiency from childhood, which made me see double images at a distance when tired. I thought that was normal because it was all I'd ever known.

Seeing 3-D

I still remember the first time I saw in 3-D. I was forty-two years old, and I'd just gotten my first pair of prism glasses. I got in the car and put them on for the drive home. I drove about three blocks before suddenly everything went from normal to looking like someone had pulled the tabs in a children's pop-up picture book. I swear, if no one had been behind me, I would have caused an accident. My eyes were on the trees and the buildings and all the incredible space between things. My foot forgot that it had a job to do. My jaw dropped open. I must have slowed down to ten miles an hour before it even registered.

Once an optometrist prescribes glasses like these, the visual changes won't stick without vision therapy. The brain is used to processing vision in a certain way and once it's acclimated to the prisms, it will revert to its old patterns. I went to a vision therapy session every week for a year. Each week, I learned a new developmental vision exercise and was given daily exercises to do. Vision therapy and prism glasses dramatically reduced my anxiety levels and eliminated my migraines. It can even be useful for people with 20/20 vision, because sometimes people waste a lot of brainpower on suppressing vision from one eye in order to have 20/20 vision. An optometrist with training in vision therapy can catch that and correct it.

Can You See in 3-D?

Have you ever gone to a 3-D movie and been unable to enjoy the special effects everyone is oohing and aahing over? According to optometrists, as many as twenty percent of the population might not be able to fully see in three dimensions. People (like me) often don't realize they have an issue, or that the problem is bigger than getting a headache at a 3-D movie: it can impact our academic ability as well as our driving ability. It can make us more likely to trip and fall, and it can make us terrible at sports or only able to excel in specific kinds of sports.

The hard work of visual processing was a migraine trigger for me. Literally not knowing where I was in space created anxiety, although I didn't realize what the cause of the anxiety was until after treatment. Once I had prism glasses and finished vision therapy, driving was no longer stressful. Even jogging and walking had been causing me tension, but not anymore. If you have anxiety issues, you might want to consider seeing a vision therapist.

Master Those Primary Reflexes

Perfect 3-D vision requires mastery of three primary reflexes: the Landau, the Asymmetric Tonic Neck Reflex, and the Pavlov Orientation. As mentioned before, primary reflexes are patterns of movement that are programmed into our brain to help us develop in utero and beyond, but they should be progressively mastered and no longer active by the age of three. Trauma can reactivate primary reflexes at any time in life.

These three primary reflexes prime the brain both for seeing and processing visual information automatically. The ideal visual field is like the MasterCard symbol: if each eye's visual field is represented as a circle, then both eyes together should see two circles with a bit of an overlap. This allows for the easiest conversion into a three-dimensional image. Too much overlap creates problems for the brain to process, as does too little overlap or no overlap at all. Problems with the amount of overlap makes the brain process vision with the cortex as a double-check rather than processing automatically. This reduces how much ability we have for executive thought.

Visual processing takes 80% of our brain's energy, so it's critical that it is automatic. We have two types of visual systems that our brain automatically switches between: peripheral and central vision. This can be thought of as global vs. focal or seeing the world vs. reading a book. Ideal vision would mean that the eyes lead the brain rather than the brain leading the eyes. In an ideal world, we wouldn't stay in either global or focal for any length of time; instead, we would shift between them naturally so as not to overwork any particular set of eye muscles.

Brain Compensations

When we don't master the three primary reflexes mentioned above, one strategy is for our brain to take the 2-D images from each eye and flip between them, so it can construct a guesstimate of what 3-D is like. If we are flipping between 2-D images, we tend to hold our breath when moving rather than being able to move and breathe at the same time, because breath-holding reduces the amount of information to process. People with this issue are in a constant state of internal tension. Their baseline internal state is set to 'overwhelmed' and they don't even know it because it's all they've ever known. As stated above, they can't optimize the use of their cortex, since their cortex is being used to second-guess their vision to keep them safe in the world.

They are likely to try to keep their head as steady as possible because it is so much harder to process data when there is a big change in the horizontal plane. People with this problem tend to be more cautious with movement, and they are less athletic and physically interactive with the world than they are capable of being.

As I mentioned earlier, even if we have mastered the primary reflexes, anyone who has been traumatized is likely to have reactivated primary reflexes, which can take away from our automatic vision. These reflexes can be reintegrated using specialized kinesiology, which would be of help in vision therapy.

These kinds of visual issues can cause problems in academic ability. People without automatic vision carry much more stress from their delayed processing capacity. They work harder in school and at work for poorer results. It takes energy to sort out the information from our environment that our brain is taking in as we work on a task—energy that could be better used to get our schoolwork done faster, better and with less strain if only our vision was automatic.

You can get help with primary reflex integration from me or through Julie Newendorp's Nurturing Parent Center, among other places. More details are listed at the end of this chapter in the action steps.

Why I Go to a Vision Therapist
I had always gone to regular eye doctors, all of whom gave me stronger and stronger prescriptions over the course of my life. Unfortunately, I had too little overlap for my brain to make 3-D images automatically, only I never knew it. Children with ADHD have three times the rate of convergence and divergence insufficiency than their typically developing peers. Eye issues like these are also more common in the autistic spectrum community. Fortunately, thanks to a friend, I came across the office of Dr. Mel Kaplan, the founder of the Center for Visual Management in New York. A Doctor of Optometry, Dr. Kaplan had worked as a clinical instructor of behavioral sciences at New York Medical College and has published

a body of research on ambient lenses and their role in helping people who struggle with learning, emotional or autistic spectrum disorders. He's written two books about vision: *Seeing Through New Eyes*, and *The Secrets in Their Eyes: Transforming the Lives of People with Cognitive, Emotional, Learning or Movement Disabilities*. He's by far the best vision therapist I've been to.

Distance Divergence Insufficiency

Regular eye doctors recognize the problem of near point convergence and know how to correct it, but they do not treat the distance issue because it mimics needing regular distance prescription lenses.

This is what distance divergence insufficiency looked like for me: imagine you go to a theater to see a play and after a half hour or so, your eyes tire and the images blur. If you stop struggling to focus, the image would double. You could think of it as having situational double vision, which was all I ever had known, so I thought it was normal.

When eye doctors increased the prescription, it just gave me headaches from eye strain. Yes, I could see better briefly while being tested, but since that wasn't the heart of the problem, the eye strain got continually worse. As the eye strain grew worse over the years, so did my anxiety levels until it was crippling me. As Dr. Kaplan explains in his book *Seeing Through New Eyes*, it was all connected.

Eye Strain or the Wrong Prescription?

By the time I was in my forties, I could only use my glasses for driving and even then, I would get headaches from the amount of correction that I had been given. I ended up with 20/200 vision. After working with Dr. Kaplan and his vision trainers, my vision improved until it ended up at 20/30 and my anxiety levels dropped significantly. For the first time, I could hold onto a train of thought or follow someone's logic in an argument and see where it broke down, all because I had more brain power freed up for executive thinking.

Too much time in either focal vision (using a computer or

reading a book) or global vision (searching the distance for a predator) causes stress in our systems. It is contracting to our bodies because when specific muscles in our eyes are used for too long without a break, it leads to spasm in muscles in the neck, shoulders and back. Contraction at its extreme causes pain. In our culture, we tend to spend too much time in focal vision from an early age, particularly now with computer and phone screens, along with teaching children to read at younger and younger ages. Being able to shift between global and focal vision is calming. When we are standing in nature, drinking it in, seeing the whole and feeling a part of it, it feels peaceful and soothing. We can think of too much time spent locked in one type of vision as activating the sympathetic nervous system and instead being able to shift between focal and global every twenty minutes or so as activating the parasympathetic nervous system.

Our Children with 2-D Vision Need Help
We need a balance between the two systems, but our society and our schooling overemphasize focal vision. As schoolwork gets more difficult in second, fourth and seventh grade, children with 2-D vision have a hard time keeping up. More are diagnosed at these times with learning disabilities, but most are not tested for primary reflex issues or convergence insufficiency. It's a lost opportunity to be helped by vision therapy or physical therapy and specialized kinesiology to integrate their primary reflexes.

If children were tested for having good 3-D vision and had issues corrected, they could more easily reach their full potential. To understand what goes on with 2-D vision, think of the brain's potential output like a river. A big part of the river for someone who sees 2-D is being diverted towards making a 3-D approximation of the world. With so much of our cortex's energy diverted this way, there are fewer resources for academic thinking in these children than for others who have automatic 3-D vision.

Imagine All Children Living up to Academic Potential

Children who are intelligent in other ways but who have this vision problem are not going to live up to their academic potential. They often go through their school years with the feeling of being stupid because they know they are capable of much more than they can produce. This carries over into adulthood.

Additionally, their brain is working so hard that it leads to them being overwhelmed. We all have emotional overreactions when there is too much data for our brains to process. The brain gets overloaded. It sends that overload to the amygdala, which reacts with strong emotion like anger or fear.

Have you ever had to focus on a visual problem, like reading an instruction booklet to assemble a new gadget, while at the same time facing auditory demands from children in need of attention? A prime example happens during the holiday season. Did you get frustrated? Sometimes parents can blow their top when under bombardment like this. It's an example of what happens when the brain gets overloaded.

The Effect of Stress on Vision

Stress can also reduce our ability to see clearly, as can strong emotion, like anger. For example, if our upper trapezius muscles are tight, it can blur our vision. Both stress and anger can tighten the upper trapezius. Many people who can get by as children and young adults lose their visual processing ability as they age. They start falling asleep when they try to read because they no longer have enough energy.

This reduces our lifetime productivity and enjoyment. People give up on school or don't try to return to school when they are smart enough to succeed and only their vision is holding them back. The worst thing is that brilliant people might spend their lives feeling dumb, while the rest of us lose out on benefitting from their talents.

It is often the smartest babies who figure out how to cheat the primary reflex system instead of following the prescribed movements. Stressed babies don't complete the primary reflex system properly either.

Visual Imbalance Causes Emotional and Physical Tension
Vision therapy helped me process emotions. I was unaware how much emotional and physical tension my eyes were causing me. After I got prism glasses and did therapy, my emotional tension dropped dramatically. Prism glasses allowed me to see objects where they really were in space, so my brain didn't have to make corrections. Once I knew where I was located in the world, I felt more comfortable and had less physical tension. I was then able to process more information because my brain wasn't so occupied with keeping me safe in the world. Now I know more immediately how I feel. Before vision therapy, I needed to think constantly so that I could figure out how I felt. My poor brain was like a hamster on a wheel— compelled to exercise to the point of exhaustion. It was much too busy trying to keep me physically and emotionally safe. What a relief to finally have some peace of mind.

Over the course of my life, I had become increasingly frozen by my visual processing issues. Since getting new glasses and doing vision therapy I have written a novel and two screenplays as well as this book, learned how to do public speaking, coped with divorce, downsizing, and a cross-country move. I credit Dr. Kaplan and his vision therapy for allowing me to be open to new ways of seeing and thinking.

Monovision Contacts Lenses and Glasses
Monovision contact lenses and glasses have become a popular option for presbyopia, but they compromise depth perception and intermediate vision. Depth perception is a critical skill. A further complication of monovision contact lenses is that the resulting visual changes can cause some areas of the brain and body to receive too much blood, while others get too little. The brain is still trying to create 3-D vision, which reduces the amount of capacity for executive function. Given how hard I've worked to attain 3-D vision, and that

I've been told by a neurologist that my fibromyalgia symptoms are connected to an imbalance between hemispheres, I'd never use monovision products and can't recommend them to anyone.

Action Steps:
Easy:
For everyone, I'd suggest trying to increase the amount of global vision you get daily. Going to the beach or taking a walk in nature is a way of engaging your global vision. So is going outside and watching clouds pass by as you look for shapes in them. It's a vital part of reducing stress.

Moderate:
If you're having trouble with chronic anxiety, depression, and health issues, *even if you have 20/20 vision,* you might want to give vision therapy a try. Look for someone through the College of Optometrists in Visual Development online at covd.org. Get prism glasses if needed and do vision training.

Learn Touch for Health to give you resources to reduce muscle tension—in particular, targeting the upper trapezius muscles helped both reduce chronic shoulder pain and improve my vision.

Harder:
Find someone who does Brain Gym ® who can integrate primary reflexes. Julie Newendorp, founder of the Nurturing Parent Center in Santa Barbara does, as do I. It's a great support for vision therapy. I can be reached at elizabeth@rightbrainuniversity.com and you can reach Julie at julie@nurturingparentcenter.com.

You can find out more information on primary reflexes through Svetlana Masgutova's book *MNRI Dynamic and Postural Reflex Pattern Integration* available at masgutovamethod.com. She also has her own network of trained therapists to help with primary reflex integration. More info at masgutovamethod.com.

Dr. Kaplan has doctors continuing his work at The Center for Visual Management in Tarrytown, NY, and acts as a consultant. You can contact the center at thecenterforvisualmanagement.com.

Chapter 19
Rhythm and Timing Therapies

Hula Hoops and Double Dutch

Back in the dinosaur age known as the 1970s when I grew up, we played games like Double Dutch, hula hoop, hopscotch, and jacks. Double Dutch required teamwork and was absolutely thrilling, the peak of which I experienced on one trip to Raymond, Washington. We were there visiting my grandparents on a summer that was slightly less rainy than usual. The scent of fir trees and moss was strong, mingling with that of smoke from pulp burning at the paper mill. The neighborhood kids made my sister and me a part of their tribe and we spent hours with them playing Double Dutch. Back then, children had time to spend on games like these, which used the big muscles in our bodies and developed that all-important myelin coating that allowed signal to travel more quickly and strongly through our bodies, because we were given so much less homework and had so much more boredom unless we played games together.

The Benefits of Rhythm and Timing Therapies

One of the most important things our brain does is coordinate timing: timing between all the different parts of the brain with the organs, timing between the left and right sides of the body and brain, timing for the immune system, for digestion and most important, to keep us safe in the world of motion. Therapies that help develop this region have the added benefit of also improving impulse control.

Rhythm and timing therapies help develop synaptic

connections with targeted exercises, ideally to a beat. They give the brain a chance to practice coordinating timing. Rhythm and timing therapies have been an important part of helping me recover from ADHD and its related anxiety and depression. The way the brain processes information is malleable. If you have any doubts, read the books *The Brain that Changes Itself* by Norman Doidge and *The Woman Who Changed Her Brain*, by Barbara Arrowsmith Young. I've gone a different route from Barbara Young's, but my route back to health as well as to grow beyond ADHD has been through stepping out of my old brain programming by reprogramming my brain. Bön/Buddhist meditation, yoga, MFR, RFST, therapy, vision therapy and specialized kinesiology have all been vital to the process.

Interactive Metronome
Another big help has been increasing my processing speed using Interactive Metronome (IM), a software program that uses a metronome beat to give the user feedback on how far off they are in attempting to keep time to a beat. Clients wear a trigger on their hand, use a floor trigger, or one in their shoe that provides feedback to the computer. This research-backed program grows synaptic connections as well as dendrites. Synapses and dendrites help neurons talk to each other. Movement while using IM lays down additional myelin onto the axonal portion of neurons. This helps signals travel up to five times faster than if a neuron has an incomplete myelin sheath. A strong myelin sheath also is protective to a neuron.

I got trained in Interactive Metronome to help clients before realizing how much it could help me too. Using IM has helped me reduce my ADHD symptoms. I've had a lifelong problem with organization, distractibility, attention, procrastination, anxiety, and depression. I had some success in the work world (I handled $70 million a year in import goods for a woman's clothing manufacturer) by putting all my brain power into my job. Once I had children, even as a stay-at-home mom, I couldn't cope with the chaos of organizing a household. I could barely keep my own head above water; having twins was beyond my ability. My anxiety and depression got worse, and an autoimmune illness flared up, fed in part by the anxiety and sleeplessness. IM has been a big help to being able to function again.

What's Fired Together is Wired Together

The premise of IM is that what is fired together is wired together. When you repeat an experience over and over, the brain then learns to trigger the same neurons each time.

At first, the IM I did for myself helped me with reaction time and my ability to maintain a conversation. I was one of those people with such a meandering thought process that I would regularly lose my original train of thought. It was humiliating, so I kept my mouth shut more and more. IM helped clear up my thinking.

After I finished vision therapy, I still had problems with reversing a car in a straight line. It was especially important that I improve because the house I lived in at the time had a narrow and steep driveway bordered by high retaining walls. In the wintertime, the driveway got ice and snow on it regularly. I needed to back out with precision, since ice could make the tires slip towards the retaining walls. I did another round of IM, where I specifically targeted peripheral visual response to the metronome beat for my weak left eye/right brain combo. It was incredibly hard because I basically almost couldn't do it. I had to ease my way in with some auditory input. Over time, it got easier and easier because I was growing synaptic connections that grew my ability to see peripherally. Now I'm able to reverse in a straight line with complete comfort and parallel parking has also dramatically improved.

The latest round of IM I did was about figuring out new ways to target what I think needs to be wired together better in my brain. One of the things I came up with is to do Interactive Metronome while filing bills. That means I'm growing my working memory (engaging the rules of filing) at the same time I'm practicing filing. I've been doing other working memory tasks and games while doing IM as well.

Because rhythm and timing are housed in the right prefrontal cortex and I know my right hemisphere is underdeveloped thanks to a neurologist, I am intentionally targeting the left side of my body with Interactive Metronome to further develop the right hemisphere.

Right Brain University® (RBU) & Rhythm and Reflex®
I founded Right Brain University® to teach people tools to process emotions rather than be at the mercy of them, as well as to spread the word about how to heal. I founded Rhythm and Reflex® to improve the executive function of clients who are struggling to make the most of their brain.

I've developed a program to try to improve the brain more deeply than with Interactive Metronome (IM) alone. IM has been proven to make synapses and myelinate them. I got to wondering if the results could be improved by putting the body and brain into balance using specialized kinesiology before a session. If it worked, it could mean that we were getting a better *quality* of synaptic connections, not just an increased *quantity* of synaptic connections.

I test to see if a client has any retained primary reflexes that are preventing their brain from optimally functioning and clear that first. Then I go through looking for any meridians that have nerve energy blocks and clear them. I look for movement issues in the different layers of the brain. The cortex handles left-right movement, the midbrain handles up-down movement, and the brain stem handles forward-backward movement. Any of these could be off, or a combination. I check whether the gait reflexes are automatic and whether the client has any stress associated with using his or her eyes and if there is any auditory intake stress.

My clients are having amazing success both with and without IM. One high school student who was struggling with the SAT Math prep test (completing only 40 out of 60 in timed tests and of those 40, little better than 50% were correct) did 11 sessions of Rhythm and Reflex-IM and got an 800 on his Math SAT. Another high school tennis player wanted to improve his tennis game. He came away happy with his improved reaction time, but also with a newfound ability to study longer on school subjects that bored him. I use this to help people who have been held back by their test-taking ability, as well as people who are looking to improve their visual processing speed.

I assist people who are looking to improve their executive function. I work with busy executives who want to maximize their ability to make the best decisions they can and go beyond the non-optimal emotional patterns that developed in childhood.

I'm also enjoying helping people with fibromyalgia and other autoimmune diseases to help reduce pain, increase energy, and improve quality of life using specialized kinesiology and IM. It's so rewarding to help others learn how to take steps to turn their lives around, wherever they are in their illness.

And I've also been helping people who want to lose weight, giving them tools to reduce stress and release emotion rather than getting hit by cravings. I've also been developing new forms of specialized kinesiology balances to help best serve my clients.

Yoga
Repetitive yoga practices like Core Power hot yoga or Svaroopa also develops myelin in the body and brain. With every movement, you are laying down myelin. Practicing the same routine two or three times a week is going to help keep neurons protected with myelin as well as challenge balance in a way that will maximize the brain's motor neuron development. Be sure to get your doctor's blessing before trying it.

Tibetan Bön/Buddhist Meditation
This type of meditation is sometimes called Tibetan Yoga. The outer Tsa-Lung uses a repetitive breath and movement pattern which also develops myelin in the body and brain over time. It is calming in its own right but because of the repetitive movement it's also a myelin-builder. It's much more than that, but for those looking to maximize

myelin production, it's good to include.

Outrigger Canoe Paddling

I've joined a weekly women's outrigger group in Santa Barbara and just love it. I get to spend time in nature, take in incredible views, and enjoy the company of my fellow paddlers afterwards too as we enjoy lunch together at a local restaurant. In addition to being a great workout, paddling is perfect for developing rhythm and timing: if we don't paddle in unison, we risk flipping the outrigger canoe. It's taken months for me to be able to change sides in rhythm with the other paddlers. It also grows myelin. If you live near the ocean or a lake, consider finding a paddling group near you.

Drum Circles

As mentioned in Chapter Six, drum circles have incredible health benefits. In addition to these health benefits, they also help increase myelin and improve rhythm and timing. Win-win-win. Read more about the benefits of drum circles in chapter six and join a drum circle today.

Other Ideas

Martial arts are another type of exercise that develops myelin because of repetitive movement. Japanese sword training, a part of Samurai training, is equally complex, precise, and repetitive. Think of anything you might do that contains an element of repetitive training and you can adapt it. Regular golf drills, tennis drills, and swimming drills all come to mind. These are powerful ways to keep the brain young.

Jump rope has become part of my new go-to routine. It's great for rhythm and timing. It develops a unique type of core strength—despite my hot yoga routine, I found it very hard and tiring at first. I started out doing interval training with it, jumping rope for thirty seconds and then resting and repeating for fifteen minutes. It wasn't easy because I wasn't coordinated enough. Over time, I've progressed to jumping rope for sixty seconds and in between sets holding a medicine ball while doing squats. I do six reps of jumping rope in fifteen minutes. I think it's great for helping to circulate lymph too. I like the fact that I enjoyed doing it as a kid, and after progressing at it I am doing well enough that I feel eager to do it rather than having it feel like a chore.

Action Steps:
Easy:
Read *The Brain That Changes Itself* by Norman Doidge and *The Woman Who Changed Her Brain*, by Barbara Arrowsmith Young.

Find a drum circle near you or if you are in Santa Barbara, try Sese Ntem's Ewe Drum Circle. The Ewe culture is about connection. Humans are a social species, and people with bigger social circles have
been shown to be healthier. This means introverts are at a health disadvantage. You can reach Sese at sese.ntem@gmail.com.

Find an outrigger canoe group or kayaking group. If you are in Santa Barbara, try Joyce Carlisle's outrigger canoe group. Joyce is a well-known personal trainer in town. You can reach her at joyce@stonehousefitness.com.

Moderate:
Look for a repetitive movement class like yoga, martial arts, or take your favorite sport and integrate a repetitive movement drill from it two to three times a week.

Buy a jump rope and get your doctor's blessing to use it. Go slow and be encouraging of your efforts.

Harder:
Try IM or its cheaper cousin Bal-A-Vis-X, a hand-eye coordination exercise program which develops rhythm and timing at a much slower pace than IM. Find an IM practitioner near you at interactivemetronome.com.

Find out more about Bal-A-Vis-X at bal-a-vis-x.com. It is designed to be used in school classrooms.

Consider vision therapy if you don't have perfect 3-D vision. The world should look like a children's picture pop-up book. If it doesn't, even if you have 20/20 vision, you might need help. Find a visual optometrist through the College of Optometrists in Visual Development online at covd.org.

You can find out more about my work with Rhythm and Reflex® at my website, rhythmandreflex.com. I help people of any age improve executive function, help ADD/ADHD, and increase processing speed, which gives more time to respond effectively to whatever comes up in life.

Chapter 20
Left-Brain Healing Therapies that Work

Getting Help from Psychology and More

When I was twelve, I missed so much school due to illness that I had to see a psychologist to prove that I wasn't milking it. I don't think he understood how terrifying it was to be a sickly kid trying to make up homework while feeling miserable, but he sure did turn my relationship with my sister around by getting it through my head that she loved me. My parents were constantly telling me that, but they had ulterior motives. Like many parents, they wanted her out of their hair so they could have free time, so I viewed their opinion with a great deal of suspicion. From that early age, I have had a great appreciation for therapists. Since my twenties, I have more often had a therapist than not had one and for the past ten years, I've seen a therapist regularly. I can't imagine not having one.

Therapy and Humanistic Psychology

It's a common human survival mechanism to separate from our feelings when we get traumatized. Even relatively minor things can be traumatic for young children, especially if they are highly sensitive. Traditional therapy is useful for giving us an understanding of our situation, but it's not uncommon that as much as psychoanalysis can help us, it can also end up giving us resources to further separate from our feelings. In my twenties and thirties, I certainly used the tools I learned in therapy this way. Understanding why other people were experiencing the world a certain way gave me an excuse to take their side over my own. Since emotions are a survival mechanism, we don't have that as an option. It's not about choosing sides. We must allow ourselves to experience emotions. Experiencing them doesn't mean acting on them. I've found that it's suppressing them that leads to a buildup and subsequent venting that make this seem to be a linked process, but it doesn't have to be.

In my experience, it's important to find a therapist who takes a holistic approach, who makes sure to stop you when you are expressing a feeling to ask where it is happening in your body, however annoying or threatening that might be to you, because in the long run, it is what will heal you. I remember being annoyed at my therapist at the time in Nyack, New York, Alan Levin, when he first introduced this to me. He kept asking me what I felt and where I felt it in my body. It seemed irrelevant at the time, and even annoying because I was so bad at it, yet it was the key to getting well.

The cure that therapy provides can only really happen once we find someone with whom we feel safe enough to do the work of feeling those feelings.

Feeling Emotions Heals Us
Avoiding the feelings led me to the path of chronic illness. Letting myself feel the feelings is what made me well. There is no way to get from being sick to being well without feeling the feelings on their way out. If you're reading this book and thinking of how someone else could benefit from it, know that there's no rushing anyone into this process. It's a big commitment to be brave in the face of anxiety or depression. Someone must be sick enough to have the motivation to make the change. It is difficult to learn how to express feelings, to follow their path in the body and not panic. It was even hard for me to figure out what was a thought and what was a feeling at first. They were jumbled together, and I had no idea when I was switching from one to the other.

Understanding the Normal Response to Trauma

The book, *Getting Unstuck: Unraveling the Knot of Depression, Attention and Trauma,* by Dr. Don Kerson was helpful. He explained that it was normal for people when traumatized or shamed to leave behind and separate from a part of oneself. In the end, most people will have many inner children inside that are abandoned and need to be reintegrated.

The fact that a psychiatrist was saying that this is a normal response to trauma, that there was a way out, and I could be helped was a game-changer for me. The biggest help was his exercise of visualizing the inner children I had left behind and reconnecting with them through a meditation process. We can visualize being in a safe place with these younger selves and comforting them. I practiced this regularly.

Constant Shaming for Being Human

As human beings, we all have fears, weaknesses, and self-doubts. Unfortunately, in our society men are often shamed in their childhoods and beyond for expressing their fears or for crying. Both parents and peers can be belittling. Employers can too. Being shamed in childhood can lead to unconscious suppression of these feelings, so deeply that men might not be aware of it. They can dissociate—have the feelings go unconscious—whenever uncomfortable feelings come up. Women face the same problems, for example, girls who are bold may face parental or teacher anger and peer shunning, again leading to unconscious suppression and dissociation. Depending on where or by whom we are raised, we can be shamed for being kind to people from different races, people who are overweight, or who have a disability. There's no end to whom it might not have been safe be kind to or identify with when we were children.

Suppressing Feelings Causes Inflammation

Suppressing feelings means whenever we have emotions, those messages that are not deemed acceptable are hidden from our awareness. This causes inflammation from accumulated neurochemicals that remain in the body until processed.

In more extreme cases of trauma, this could lead to domestic abuse or to hating people of the opposite sex because it wasn't safe to identify with a different gender, or people who have a physical or intellectual disability. As we head into an era where creativity is highly valued, we owe it to our boys and girls to teach them to accept a full range of emotional expression. It's best to develop our full capacity for tolerance, too. Without it we harm ourselves.

Our unconscious doesn't want to be punished, that's why it hides things from us. As soon as you create a safe space for your inner child, you'll be astonished at what starts to come up. Your body and mind want to process emotion and heal. All you have to do is learn how to safely get out of the way through processes like Dr. Kerson's visualizations, changing our negative self-talk, Focusing, John Barnes MFR, and the rest of these mind-body tools I've been talking about.

Eye Movement Desensitization and Reprocessing (EMDR)
EMDR is a great tool for helping release trauma. It should be tried first with a psychotherapist, after which you can practice at home once you receive the go-ahead. The process is for the eyes to move side to side while you think of a difficult visual memory.

The normal way that adults store memories is to separate the visual memory of the event from the actual event. For people with PTSD, this separation doesn't occur. Recollection of the event recreates it, and our reaction, as if the event were happening all over again. Since it is quite common for anyone to have PTSD as the result of breaking a bone, divorce, or job loss, many of us could benefit from EMDR.

Francine Shapiro, the creator of EMDR says you can also move your eyes on the diagonal instead of just left and right, which I've found to be much more helpful than side-to-side.

How EMDR Can Help

As an example of how EMDR can potentially help you, here's how I used it to help me: at one traumatic point in my life, my PTSD was reactivated. I stopped being able to sleep through the REM cycle, where we do most of our dreaming. I woke up in a panic every night with a confusing jumble of disjointed anxiety-provoking images in my head. I stopped dreaming in color and instead had black and white images and static, like on an old TV. I couldn't tell my therapist about my dreams because the more I tried to retain the fragmented jumble, the more they evaporated.

I found that if I focused on one image, I could retain it and think of it while I allowed myself to feel that panic. I paid attention to the feelings and whatever they did, however they changed and moved within me at the same time I did EMDR with diagonal eye movement. Diagonal eye movement worked much better for me that the typical left to right movement. I could feel a shift. I hoped that this would help me process what I needed to be working on so that I could start to sleep better. Sure enough, after a few months of doing it faithfully I started to have occasional flashes of color in my dreams and then over time, I started having regular dreams again, in color.

Focusing

Focusing is a form of healing therapy developed by Eugene Gendlin back in the 1970's. Focusing is learning how to attune to our emotions within our body, a formal practice of connecting with our body's own innate wisdom. It's looking for an internal awareness, a 'felt sense', asking ourselves how we are now, and welcoming however we are in the moment, no matter what feeling arises. According to Gendlin, a felt sense is a sense of unease or tension. It's something we distinctly feel but is not clear to us. It's often unpleasant, strange or curious to begin with.

We can work by ourselves or with a friend, but it is also possible to get training in how to focus and get paired with a partner through the Focusing Foundation. This is a relatively low-cost process for those with few resources who want good, solid results. There are also psychologists who combine therapy with Focusing for deep, lasting changes in our mental health and wellness. Focusing allows healing and teaches us how to tune in to our internal guidance within a safe environment provided by a therapist, ourselves or a Focusing partner. Focusing helps us to connect with our creativity as well as making sure our body's emotional messages are received.

Sometimes we know how we feel. These are not times for Focusing. Those times are perfect for welcoming the feelings anyway and allowing them to flow through us without judgment. When we have an unpleasant, strange, or curious sensation, where we don't know how we feel, that is the perfect time to start Focusing. The body is receiving neurochemical emotional signals that it will ignore until we pay attention to our inner sense and sensations. Once we pay attention, the signals begin in earnest. We pause, and we stay with the experience. From this, we can learn to understand consciously what we really want at an unconscious level. It can help us integrate body, mind, and spirit. Focusing can help us get more out of psychotherapy, and it can help us connect to our creativity. Tuning into all my emotions and body sensations non-judgmentally as Focusing teaches, has allowed me to get more out of many of the other therapies I've learned.

Jungian Sandplay Therapy

My current therapist is a Jungian Analyst who uses Sandplay therapy in the style of Carl Jung and Dora Kalff. Sandplay therapy is a way of connecting to the unconscious when we feel stuck and unable to communicate with it via dreams. I have found the use of the sand trays, one filled with wet sand, the other with dry sand, combined with use of miniature figures and symbolic objects to be helpful to connect with my unconscious. The Jungian interpretation of dreams and view on the collective unconscious has also been an important part of what I needed to get well. Jungians encourage their clients to get body work, as it helps release and heal both mind and body, the conscious and unconscious. I sure wish I'd come across Jungian therapy sooner. Their deep connection to dreams and the collective unconscious is invaluable. For anyone interested in Jungian analysis, I'd suggest finding a therapist who incorporates dreams, active imagination, creative expression and sandplay therapy in the tradition of Carl Jung and Dora Kalff. I think it's a vital part of the connecting to the unconscious and the higher self.

One of the most important tools that I learned from my therapist was how to stay present in the body during stress. When something happens that cues a survival pattern, we can immediately check out of higher brain mode in a split second. Jungians call that survival pattern a complex. If we practice paying attention to our breath—not trying to change it, just noticing it, paying attention to gravity cues like the feeling of one's body in a chair or the sensations in our feet as we stand on the ground, we can stay in our higher brain. We might not always succeed at keeping out of the survival pattern, but the more we practice, the more capable we become. This is because we are growing new pathways in our brain as a result of a different response to the stimulus. Eventually we don't get triggered into our old behavior anymore.

HeartSpeak

Another way into emotions that are stuck is a relatively new program called HeartSpeak. It combines specialized kinesiology with cognitive behavior help. Developed by Dr. Anne Jensen, a clinical researcher with a Masters in Evidence-based Health Care from Oxford University in the UK, she's also been working to show the efficacy of muscle-testing.

HeartSpeak reconnects a client to their emotional mind. It uses muscle testing to determine what needs to be cleared. The client gets detailed information about how to maximize clearing and is led through steps to release the held emotion. The client learns a new way of reacting to an emotion rather than just the same old way that leads into a downward spiral.

Toastmasters

Here's one that took me a long time to realize: I joined Toastmasters because I'm such an introvert that I knew it'd take a lot to be able to become a competent speaker. I've been a member for eight years as I write this, but it's only in the past year after serving as president of my local club that I realized what a good job Toastmasters has done in allowing me to continue to learn emotional self-regulation in a social situation. When I first joined Toastmasters, the moment the meeting ended I was on my way out the door. It took years for me to hang around and eventually to look forward to the time after the meeting to chat with my fellow members. I didn't understand that as a member who focused solely on my speaking ability. Focusing on the speaking also helped enormously with emotional self-regulation, but as I continued to heal, the next step was into leadership. I'd like to say I was bright enough to realize it, but the truth was that I was thrust into the position. After a year of being president, I realized I was ready for the next level at Toastmasters, so I volunteered to be an Area Director. I can't recommend Toastmasters highly enough. I went to my first meeting as someone so nervous that my voice was an octave higher than normal, heart racing, with all the saliva gone so that my upper lip got stuck above my teeth. Each time I went it got a little easier. I'm much more outgoing and happier in social situations, and I have Toastmasters to thank. Toastmasters is incredibly inexpensive and has great educational tools to learn how to advance in both speaking and leadership.

Action Steps:
Easy:
Read *Getting Unstuck: Unraveling the Knot of Depression, Attention and Trauma,* by Dr. Don Kerson.

Read *Homecoming: Reclaiming and Healing Your Inner Child* by John Bradshaw.

Join a local Toastmasters club near you. More information at toastmasters.org.

Moderate:

Learn how to Focus. I'll suggest reading *Focusing* by Eugene Gendlin or the book *How I Teach Focusing: Discovering the Gift of Your Inner Wisdom* by Bebe Simon.

Find a life coach and try a few sessions.

Find a HeartSpeak practitioner and schedule a session. I use HeartSpeak with my clients. Dr. Anne Jensen can be reached at www.heartspeak.com. There are over 300 practitioners in multiple countries as this book goes to press.

Harder:

Find a therapist you want to work with and start the process of healing. Try combining it with bodywork for the quickest results. Phone sessions allow you to completely connect to your body rather than be distracted by interacting with a therapist in person.

Find classes, other therapists, or a Focusing partner to work with through focusing.org.

Finding an analyst who also does sandplay is not easy. The International Association for Analytic Psychology—iaap.org—lists all certified analysts near you and you can interview them to make sure the body is a focus of theirs. Sandplay Therapists of America can be found at sandplay.org. The majority of sandplay therapists are not analysts, so be aware of that if it is important to you to work with an analyst. Analysts and therapists who have been trained in Marion Woodman's BodySoul process are another source of help. You can find them at mwoodmanfoundation.org.

Take Level 1 and 2 of HeartSpeak to get tools to help your family and friends or to become a practitioner.

Friday:

Improve Digestion and Nutrient Absorption

Chapter 21
Improving Digestion

I put the section of nutrition and digestion last because out of everything I've changed in my life, I've had the hardest time changing what I eat. I don't think that I am alone with this issue. We all need our comfort foods. While I generally ate a good diet, for years I also had sweets and snacks that I knew were bad for me because I was emotionally starved and needed the comfort and feeling of acceptance and love that they gave me. I also ate because there were emotions I couldn't face and eating distracted me from facing them. I'm much better now than I was, but I still notice the effect of stress on what, how much, and when I eat. I think it's a common human condition. As you read this section, remember to be encouraging to your inner child. It might feel overwhelming to look at the big picture I'm painting. Instead look for one small thing that resonates most with you if you feel you need to make digestive and nutritional changes. Making huge changes all at once seldom lasts. Taking small steps that build on each other over time is the way to create lasting change. And if you find your eyes glazing over from all the details, just turn to the action steps section for helpful ideas instead of finishing the chapter.

My Journey

I have had a huge struggle with digestion for most of my life. I used to lie on the cool marble floor of our house after supper when I was a little girl because it helped the stomachache I always got after eating.

I thought that was normal. I remember going on dates when I was a teenager, eating the requisite pizza and soda and feeling like a bomb had gone off in my stomach. I thought that was normal too.

I had a bad bout of food poisoning in 2006. It is common for food poisoning to lead to a condition called SIBO, Small Intestinal Bacterial Overgrowth, due to the valve between the small intestine and large intestine being stuck open. This is one common cause of Irritable Bowel Syndrome (IBS.) I suffered from IBS attacks for a year, making several trips to the emergency room before it was diagnosed by a gastroenterologist. Now that you have my history as a digestive tract sufferer, you know why I have spent a lot of time researching how to get better.

Why Timing of Water is Critical
Even if your digestion works well, you can make it better, though be sure to get your doctor's okay to try this. Drink 12 ounces of water 15 to 30 minutes before eating. This is a tip I learned from my Ayurvedic doctor, Dr. John Douillard, who told me that the stomach has a layer of tissue that acts as a pool of bicarbonate, a protective layer that ensures that stomach acid cannot burn a hole through the stomach.

Our brain has a biofeedback mechanism to tell if this tissue is properly hydrated or not. It needs to be fully hydrated to be protective. If it is not fully hydrated, the brain will dial down the stomach acid strength.

Stomach Acid to Bile Connection
We need stomach acid at full strength to break down the food into absorbable nutrients. Good quality bile is only possible with full strength stomach acid. Over time, if we have not done a good job about being hydrated, we do not have the bile quality needed. Bile and stomach acids are necessary, so we can digest and absorb building blocks for our body. Years of going without full strength stomach acid (either because we are poor water drinkers or because of taking too many antacids or acid blockers due to heartburn or acid

reflux), means we have been harming our health. We have nowhere near the stockpile of nutrients we need to stay healthy and keep any genetic disposition we have toward illness at bay.

Other Problems Caused by Not Drinking Enough Water
When we do not drink enough water, it also causes our bile to get thicker, which can lead to gallstones clogging up our gall bladder. Whenever we eat, bile gets released into the food that is about to enter our small intestine. The fattier the food is, the more bile gets released. Bile is alkaline and is meant to neutralize the acidity of the food/stomach acid mixture. It cannot do its job if it is too thick or if our gallbladder is clogged with gallstones.

For years I had low cholesterol, a combined HDL and LDL of 137. Cholesterol is needed by the body for proper function. Cholesterol is important for keeping skin healthy. I used to get horribly deep cracks in my skin particularly in winter because of inadequate cholesterol, but that's changed since working with Dr. Douillard because my cholesterol levels have normalized. We need cholesterol to produce hormones such as adrenaline, testosterone, and estrogen too, so if our cholesterol levels are too low, we may have low hormone levels.

I believe that our brain sends hunger signals until it senses it has the nutrients it needs. If the brain does not get what it needs, it is going to keep sending signals to eat. I certainly notice that when I eat nutrient-dense foods, I'm satisfied sooner. Also, if we do not chew our food thoroughly, our body can't digest it enough to provide us the nutrients we need. I try my best to chew thoroughly. I try to wait until I'm hungry to eat, but not too hungry, because then I'm in a hurry and eat too quickly. In rebuilding my health, I've found that when I eat pureed vegetable soups that I do not eat as big a meal as I do when I skip soups or don't puree them. The nutrients in pureed foods are more easily absorbed compared to hastily or incompletely chewed food.

The Negative Impact of Poor Digestion on the Immune System

Something else I learned from Dr. Douillard is that if we do not produce enough bile to neutralize stomach acid or if the bile is too thick, or there are too many gallstones, the food entering our small intestine will be too acidic. When this happens, the small intestine will produce mucus to protect itself.

The problem with having mucus in our small intestine is that 80% of our immune system is in the first part of our small intestine. It's in tissue called Gut Associated Lymphatic Tissue (GALT). GALT is the central command zone for our lymphatic system. GALT is supposed to pull off any toxins in our food. If it is covered with mucus however, there is no way that any toxins are being pulled off.

This means that if we have these kinds of digestive issues: making insufficient bile, a clogged gallbladder, or thickened bile, we are digesting toxins. It makes sense that anyone who suffers from bad digestion should start eating organic food to reduce their intake of toxins, if they are not already doing so.

You may feel abdominal discomfort after a fatty meal - this is often in the liver and gallbladder regions as the gallbladder struggles to release bile but can't because the ducts are clogged with thick bile or gallstones.

It is hard to get back to feeling good once your gallbladder is clogged or you have poor quality bile. An intestinal cleanse and gall bladder flush are helpful to relieve this. I do this yearly through Dr. Douillard's online program, although some people do this twice a year. Contact info is in the action steps at the end of this chapter.

The Impact of Chronic Stress on Digestion

Again, chronic stress means we are in a state of fight or flight or freeze. Under chronic stress, our brain is primed to use the brain stem and emotional parts of the dominant hemisphere of our brain, so we're not thinking as clearly and rationally as we could be. These regions were not meant to be used so constantly, which starts an inflammatory response within the brain.

Adrenals Win Out Over Digestion

Digestion is halted when we are in fight or flight. In this state, blood is sent to the legs and arms, so we can escape from a predator instead of to our digestive tract. The blood moves away from the digestive tract. Adrenaline needs to be made from cholesterol and that takes a lot of vitamin C to make. As a result, the digestive tract becomes undersupplied with vitamin C as well as B vitamins. If we were really running away from a predator our bodies would burn off the adrenaline, but since our boss and coworkers are not officially predators, the cholesterol that is used to make adrenaline gets coated onto our arteries. (If we had healthy amounts of lecithin in our bodies, the cholesterol could pass on through our arterial walls, so our body could make use of it, but we need adequate amounts of choline and inosotol, two B vitamins, to make lecithin.) Many of us have a genetic need for high amounts of some B vitamins, or a reduced ability to process B vitamins to their usable methylated state.

The Downward Spiral

Without the blood on hand we need to digest food, without the nutrients for a healthy digestive tract, with fascial tension so high that cells can't properly operate, we start a downward spiral in the health of our digestive tract.

The tissue is less healthy because it is not getting enough blood, vitamin C or B vitamins. If it is not healthy it cannot absorb nutrients as well as it should. If it is not getting enough water to stay optimally hydrated, food gets stuck in the digestive tract and does not move as fast as it should. That means bacteria can proliferate and attack the walls of the small and large intestines.

Pockets of infection can start up. Because of being on high alert and pumped up on adrenaline, our bodies never get the signal that it is time for a repair cycle. We need to be in a parasympathetic nervous system state (PNS) to not only digest but to repair our small and large intestines to remove and repair damaged cilia. Being in sympathetic nervous system (SNS) dominance means staying in an inflammatory, constantly degrading physical state. This can lead to leaky gut syndrome.

Excess use of NSAIDs (non-steroidal anti-inflammatories such as aspirin or ibuprofen) can cause leaky gut due to the spaces between the digestive tissue widening. Excessive use of antibiotics can cause both non-beneficial bacteria and yeast to thrive; it can also cause leaky gut. Lectins (a low-grade toxin used by plants to protect themselves from over-foraging) found in most plants can cause leaky gut and interfere with nutrient absorption. Lectins are also found in animals to help support immunological functions and assist in protein synthesis and delivery. Small amounts of lectins in the foods we eat are fine; it's when there are large quantities that they can prevent us from absorbing nutrients in our food. Traditionally, the most problematic foods were soaked or fermented to help inactivate the lectins. Lectins are most concentrated in foods like beans, (especially soy), grains (especially wheat), nuts, dairy, and the nightshade family (eggplant, tomatoes, potatoes, peppers, tomatillos) and GMO foods, where lectins can be spliced in to protect food from pests. Some people have found relief from autoimmune illness by avoiding high lectin foods, according to Joseph Cohen in *The Self-Hacked Secrets*.

Diets that are high in hard-to-digest foods like dairy or wheat can also tax the digestive tract if we are under chronic stress.

Peristalsis
Our digestive tract is quite athletic when we are healthy. The motion of the digestive tract is called peristalsis and the muscles used in peristalsis are stimulated by insoluble fiber. Over time, the lack of regularly eating high-fiber green leafy vegetables can catch up with us and our digestive tract can get flabby and out of shape.

If the digestive tract is struggling to recover from food poisoning or long-term neglect, sudden intake of large quantities of insoluble fiber like popcorn can set off a stomachache if not an outright IBS attack. If our digestive muscles are kept in good shape by regularly eating insoluble fiber, particularly leafy greens, and regularly taking probiotics, then these kinds of problems are unlikely to crop up.

Chronic Stress, Muscle Tension, and Fascial Tension

Muscle tension in the body can also impact digestion. In particular, fight-or-flight muscles like the psoas can cause tension through the abdomen and restrict proper movement of food through the digestive tract. Fascia can also bind the muscles around the digestive tract and keep them from moving properly. I think of this as another benefit of RFST, yoga, and meditation: improved digestion when fascial and muscle tension decrease. Fascial tension impacts us down to the cellular level because there is fascia around each cell.

Muscle tension can also be caused by too little magnesium. Again, this can happen over time from our digestion going wrong because of being in a sympathetic nervous system dominant state. This kind of muscle tension, together with the fascial tension that chronic stress causes, can be a driver of reduced blood flow and therefore reduced oxygenation for muscles, tendons, ligaments, joints, and bone. I believe it can lead to degenerative conditions like arthritis as well as playing a part in autoimmune disorders.

The Importance of Healthy Bacteria in Our GI Tract

There is a need to make sure that the digestive bacteria (called the microbiome) that we inherited is kept healthy and vibrant. More and more though, after multiple generations of antibiotic use in humans and livestock, the quality of the microbiome we inherit is not so great. It has been shown that good bacteria tend to die off when we are stressed. Freeloading bad bacteria are more vigorous, so they step in and take over.

It is important to reduce our stress load and identify if we experience intestinal gas and bloating. If we notice an increase in the quantity of intestinal gas, there are steps we can take to identify the culprits and get rid of them because they are starving us of vital nutrients. Taking over-the-counter medications and ignoring the general trend of our digestion leads to chronic ill health. I think we are at the mercy of our genetic weaknesses when we do not provide our bodies with the building blocks to stay healthy. It sends us down the pipeline into inflammation and ill health.

UCLA researchers have found that gut bacteria alter people's brain function. Other research has found that a type of bacteria called Lactobacillus rhamnosus positively impacts GABA levels and lowers the stress-induced hormone corticosterone, which in turn reduced anxiety and depression-related behavior in test subjects. Some psychologists now treat anxiety and depression in part with probiotic therapy.

It's more widely known that psychologists have encouraged their clients to use meditation, journaling, and high intensity aerobic exercise. Perhaps part of the benefit these activities provide is that reducing stress helps the good gut bacteria to thrive again. According to Dr. Maggie Phillips, a psychologist who specializes in trauma recovery, psychologists have found that combining probiotic use and psychotherapy together has reduced symptoms of depression enough to require no traditional psychotherapeutic drugs within six months, with psychotherapy/probiotic treatment concluded after one year.

Histamine Intolerance

Histamine is a compound that our body makes. It acts as a neurotransmitter, regulates function in the gut, and plays a vital part of our local immune alert response. Histamine also occurs naturally in food, even very healthy foods. Our ability to handle histamines in our food is reduced when we are stressed.

Since histamine is a part of the trigger that activates our sympathetic nervous system, eating foods high in histamine can put us on the pathway toward inflammation, poor nutritional absorption, anemia, low iron, low calcium, low magnesium, low B-12, leaky gut and osteoporosis. This happens particularly when we are chronically stressed. Excess histamine in our diet beyond what we can process causes inflammation and damage in our intestinal tract. It plays a big part in reducing our body's ability to repair itself.

A damaged intestinal tract cannot digest food as well as a healthy, uninflamed one can. Our western diet is rich in histamines which occur naturally in aged foods like vinegar and cheese, smoked meats, cultured foods like yogurt, kefir and buttermilk, pickled foods and fermented foods like wine, beer, kombucha, and soy sauce. They are also found in citrus fruits as well as avocado, tomatoes, strawberries, raspberries, cherries, and apricots.

As foods age, they become higher in histamines, so it's important for people with histamine intolerance to buy fresh foods, cook what is needed, and try not to eat leftovers. We can freeze leftovers if necessary because freezing cooked foods halts histamine formation, but we need to eat these foods within a month. Lots of meats are aged to become more tender, so we need to use caution and ask questions of our butcher when buying meat. Buying fresh meat, or meat aged no more than 1-2 weeks after being butchered can make a difference, as can buying fish no more than 12 hours old.

The Importance of DAO and HNMT
Diamine oxidase (DAO) and histamine N-methyltransferase are enzymes that the body makes to break down histamine. It is common to take medications that block our ability to break down histamines, like NSAIDs (aspirin, ibuprofen/Advil, Aleve) and other medications like cimetidine, dihydralazine, NKC heparin and some chemotherapy drugs. It might be a good idea for cancer patients to ask their doctor and nutritionist if they should watch for excess dietary histamines and to build DAO as much as possible.

It is also important to make sure to get enough vitamin C, B-6, zinc, copper, and magnesium in our diets to support production of DAO. DAO is made in the small intestine by the body, but if the small intestine is damaged from chronic stress or mucus buildup because of bile not doing its job, then DAO production will not be optimized. DAO-supporting foods are olive oil and pea shoots grown without light.

It might be that one of the Mediterranean diet's biggest benefits comes from the protective quality of olive oil in maximizing DAO production and keeping the intestinal tract healthy.

HNMT is an enzyme concentrated in the liver and is responsible for breaking down histamine in the nervous system. It's possible to have too little of it too. Things like DAO deficiency, bacterial imbalances, HNMT genetic inheritance and HNMT inhibitors like the drugs diphenhydramine (found in Benadryl), amodiaquine (an antimalarial), and tacrine (an early Alzheimer's drug), can all reduce the amount of HNMT in the body.

Some people get obvious symptoms of histamine intolerance, like flushing after drinking some types of red wine that are high in sulfates, or they get hives when exposed to histamines, but many people don't have anything so obvious happen. If you suspect you might have a problem with histamine, you might be impacted the way I was. I didn't have flushing or hives, but I was frequently sick. I never connected that my coughing or having a slightly runny nose after eating had any meaning other than I was getting another cold. I had no idea why some foods made me produce phlegm. Since learning about the problem and making the connection, I can see that my histamine reaction was leading me to get sick. Many times, I've had a histamine intolerance reaction from the first bite of balsamic vinaigrette on a lettuce leaf. I start coughing uncontrollably and wheezing. Despite drinking water to try to flush away the irritating balsamic, it would directly lead to a week-long sore throat and sinus infection. For me, the balsamic vinegar hits the back of my throat, my body starts to attack it like it's an invader, my throat swells up with inflammation and the area becomes easy pickings for whatever bacteria is on site to penetrate the tissue. My immune system is already overwhelmed by constant invasion due to leaky gut, so in overreacting to the balsamic it misses the offending bacteria and voila, yet another cold.

Extra Virgin Olive Oil

I've added in two tablespoons a day of cold pressed extra virgin olive oil, usually to my salad, as a way of upping my DAO production. I find it helpful in reducing my symptoms both digestively and improving my quality of sleep (side effects of high histamine levels include anxiety and insomnia.) I'm adding organic pea sprouts, too, although it is incredibly inconvenient to grow them, so it's not as frequently as I'd like. Make sure to buy the kind of pea seeds meant for sprouting so they're not chemically treated. And if you find you have trouble with acid reflux, which can be connected to high histamine levels, ask your doctor if you should try melatonin. Studies show that taking melatonin is just as effective toward reducing acid reflux or heartburn as medication like Prevacid, and it might help your sleep. As always, discuss with your doctor first.

Hormesis

Hormesis is a term that I learned about from Dr. Douillard of Lifespa. It is very important to discuss this concept with your doctor or nutritionist before changing your diet. It turns out there are benefits to adding small amounts of hard-to-digest items like wheat, dairy, nuts, seeds, grains, legumes, or fruits to one's diet.

Some people should never eat wheat again or any food you have an allergic reaction to, so be very cautious here. For those whose doctors okay it, research has shown that small amounts of hard-to-digest items can help support a healthy microbiome, immunity, and more. For example, with wheat, research has shown that gluten decreases bad bacteria and supports beneficial bacteria, it boosts immune response, and lowers cholesterol. It's also been shown that gluten-free diets can raise mercury levels and can increase risk of heart disease. A big problem with wheat is that many of us eat it three or more times a day on most days: in cereal for breakfast, a sandwich for lunch, rolls with dinner, crackers for snacks, and in dessert, too.

Removing other foods that are harder to digest like nuts, seeds, nightshades, foods that are goitrogens (anti-thyroid), or oxalates can remove their important immune-boosting benefits. A weekly glass of wine has been shown to be helpful for health, while large amounts are known to be harmful to health. Another reason why balance and moderation are important.

Action Steps:
Easy:
If your doctor approves, add 1-2 tablespoons of olive oil and a probiotic to your daily diet. Chew your food well. Ask about melatonin for your heartburn.

Time your water intake to help rebuild your stomach acid and bile production.

Read *Spark* by John Ratey, MD. Dr. Ratey advocates high-intensity aerobic exercise for a number of conditions.

Read *The Self-Hacked Secrets*, by Joseph Cohen.

Read Mark Sissman's excellent blog at MarksDailyApple.com for more information about lectins and other nutritional advice with a paleo perspective.

Consider buying biodynamic and organic food at farmers markets whenever possible. My theory is that the true organic practices of enriching the soil aren't happening with the rise of corporate organics. Living soils allow fruits and vegetables to develop with the full complement of vitamins and minerals they're supposed to. Because of mineral depletion of the soils first noticed in the 1930s, fruits and vegetables may contain little very little nutrition. I want to support the biodynamic approach whenever possible and the surest way I can do that is to shop from my local biodynamic farmers at farmers' markets and from Community Supported Agriculture. (CSAs.)

Medium:
If you have insomnia or anxiety, consider timing when you eat higher histamine foods so that you're consuming them in the morning and at lunchtime rather than loading up on them at night. The caveat here is

that I believe the worst part of my leaky gut is in a particular section of my digestive tract. It takes about 6-7 hours of digestion time to reach it, just perfect for me to wake up at 3 a.m. to anxiety and insomnia.

If you have leaky gut and you've tried making other changes without success, try figuring out if you've got a similar situation with your doctor's help. This is part of the reason that eating dinner like a pauper as Dr. Douillard recommends (ideally for me a small, simple dinner low in histamines which includes pea sprouts and olive oil) helps me get a better night's sleep. Try an intestinal cleanse and gallbladder flush with an Ayurvedic practitioner. There are lots of Ayurvedic doctors in the US. You can look them up online by using the search terms "Ayurvedic doctors in the USA." Dr. Douillard's program is available through his website, www.lifespa.com.

More information about hormesis through Dr. Douillard's website at https://lifespa.com/hormesis-digestion-longevity, which has links to the research articles on the National Institutes of Health website.

Harder:
Stop eating leftovers if you have a problem with histamine.

We need the nutrition found in histamine-rich foods in order to heal, but it makes sense to reduce intake of high histamine foods which are not particularly nutritious, like beer and wine, until you heal.

Stop using aged foods like balsamic vinegar and switch to fresh cheese when possible, instead of aged cheese. You can get information on the latest research, great advice on how to heal, as well as nutritious recipes that appeal to both men and women at www.healinghistamine.com, run by Yasmina Ykelenstam, a former news journalist who became a health journalist after her own histamine issues forced her to research her way back to health. Yasmina passed away in 2018, but her family is continuing to run her website and programs.

Www.mindbodygreen.com also has some excellent resources

about histamine and DAO.

Dr. Maggie Phillips is at www.maggiephillipsphd.com.

Chapter 22
Nutrition You Can Live With

Nutrition Lite

When I was a kid my mother introduced me to butter and sugar sandwiches on white bread. Cap'n Crunch cereal was a daily feature. We regularly had ice cream and fudgesicles on hand for afternoon snacks. Ho-Hos and Twinkies made weekly appearances. Basically, it was a kid's dream, until it all came to a screeching halt when I was seven. What happened? My mother discovered nutrition. I never ate Wonderbread again. Instead, good ol' Mom became a nutritional drill sergeant. Store-bought whole wheat bread if we were lucky. Homemade whole wheat bread with soy flour added if we were not lucky. Wheat germ. Plain yogurt. Wheat germ *on* plain yogurt. And vegetables. Lots and lots of vegetables. One day, in my most scathing tone, I summed up my chief complaint about all the change, ''Mom, I can *taste* the vitamins!'' She struggled to keep a straight face.

While I didn't have a choice in the matter at the time, by the time I went off to college, I chose to keep eating healthy food. I know it's not easy to change. I feel for those of you who don't have a taste for healthier fare. I didn't either, but I'm also proof that it's possible to change, and to develop a taste for healthier food.

Our Unique Bodies

It's become clear to me that we are all so unique that there's no one diet right for everyone. The combination of genes and gut flora we inherited can make what heals one person hurt someone else. I've had

245

to learn how to listen to my body, and it's hard to do because I've found that often what we eat doesn't impact us for days, or weeks, or even months. What is true for everyone is that we can improve our body's ability to digest food and provide balanced blood sugar by getting out of constant sympathetic nervous system activation. No matter what type of diet we follow, it's clear that no one thrives on sugar and processed foods. I've cut back on these to a bare minimum. Instead, I look to eat plenty of nutrient-dense foods every day to provide my body the best chance it has at getting the building blocks it needs to maintain my health.

Look for the Aggregate Nutrient Density Index (ANDI) food score, which rates foods for nutritional density. It's available at www.drfuhrman.com. If you suspect you have leaky gut, you might need to be vigilant about what types of food you choose from the ANDI scale. For example, kale has the highest nutritional density, but if you choose curly kale, it is high in oxalates, which I am sensitive to. Lacinato/dinosaur kale is the type I use, though I don't use it much raw because it's not great for the thyroid. More explanation on oxalates is in the next chapter.

Stabilizing Blood Sugar

It is important to stabilize our blood sugar for the health of our body and brain. This means limiting our sugar and refined carbohydrate intake. High sugar intake has been linked to heart disease, though for years the blame was put on fat. Blood sugar swings from eating sugar and refined carbohydrates have also been shown to damage the brain.

For people who have blood sugar swings or who are light sleepers, the Ayurvedic suggestion to eat breakfast like a prince, lunch like a king, and dinner like a pauper might be of help. When I first tried this, it helped me sleep better because it helped stabilize my blood sugar levels as well as lessening the discomfort of digesting a large meal at night, which can disturb light sleepers. I believe that people with autoimmune diseases are most likely to be sympathetic nervous system dominant, which means they will have more of an issue with blood sugar stabilization. I've found that to be true for me, so I'm careful about avoiding most simple carbohydrates. I try to make sure the carbs I eat count, for example, by including resistant starch (a type of starch we can't digest which stays in our gut longer) in the mix to help feed good gut bacteria.

Getting Individualized Help on What to Eat

Over time, we might develop food hypersensitivities that keep our digestive tracts irritated and unable to repair themselves. These sensitivities are unique to each of us. If you are already sick, it could be of benefit to find out which foods are helpful and which foods are inflammatory for you. I got a lot of help from Dr. James Roach of Midway, Kentucky, better known as America's Doctor, on what not to eat so my body could heal. He gave me a blood test called the IgE to find out if I had hypersensitivities. When he discussed the results with me, it was clear that I did. It helped to know exactly what I could safely eat. The results were given as a list of common foods categorized into high, medium, and low inflammatory response. Some examples from my testing: no type of milk was okay. I'd thought goats' milk yogurt was fine, but the tests show that I had a high level of immune response to it. I had high reactivity to cherries, lots of types of beans as well as some herbs like rosemary that I was unaware of.

I've made some big changes because of these findings. It wasn't hard to give up things like beans and rosemary because I'm not overly fond of them. I needed good proof to give up yogurt because it was my go-to food. After I gave up eating those inflammatory foods, I felt noticeably better. I still have yogurt as a treat every few months, but it's less appealing to me because I've seen how much better I feel without it. I'd tried giving up yogurt before, but couldn't see a difference in how I felt, because I was still eating so many other things that irritated my body. The tests Dr. Roach ordered also showed what nutrients I was deficient in. Among other things, I was surprised to learn I had very low copper levels. Dr. Roach gave me directions on which supplements to take to help rebuild my health. More information about Dr. Roach is in action steps of this chapter.

Vegan Diets, Insoluble and Soluble Fiber

Some people are helped by vegan diets, but I had IBS attacks when I tried it because my body couldn't handle the insoluble fiber. I have a friend who's got a new lease on life thanks to his vegan diet, though. It's greatly improved his blood chemistry after discovering he had a clogged "widowmaker" left anterior descending artery.

When my life is in good balance, I can handle more raw vegetables in my diet. When I'm stressed, I can't. When I make a mistake in what I eat, I've been lucky to identify a soluble fiber (acacia fiber) that doesn't upset my stomach. Plenty of people can't use it, though, because they may have freeloading gut flora that like to eat acacia fiber. If you have trouble digesting foods with insoluble fiber, try hunting for a soluble fiber that helps you. Make sure to have some whenever you eat insoluble fiber. Some people swear by konjac flour, also called glucomannan. Whatever you buy, look for a reputable source.

A good intro book to explain insoluble fiber and soluble fiber is *Help for IBS*, by Heather Van Vorous. I take some of the book's information with a grain of salt, because she promotes wheat as being soothing during an IBS attack, while I know that wheat makes me feel worse during an attack and leads to sinus infections for me. She only suggests acacia fiber as a soluble fiber, but I know that some people can't use it, though for me it's been a godsend. Those issues aside, her book does a very good job of differentiating between foods with soluble and insoluble fiber, which foods are trigger foods, and how to calm the gut. As an example, her book helped me find my go-to foods when I was in the middle of an IBS attack: applesauce and instant oatmeal with no added sugar.

As suggested in *Help for IBS,* I've also found that small meals were essential when I had an ongoing attack, and I frequently sipped water with acacia fiber added, so that I rarely had a totally empty

248

digestive tract. If you suspect you might have IBS, Heather's book is a great place to start educating yourself. I also found her peppermint capsules (taken with food) and her fennel seed tea to be a big help during an IBS attack or to stave off an IBS attack.

Diets

I've been asked what my favorite diet is. I'd love to say the Mediterranean diet, but as much as I love its health benefits, I think that as traumatized people age, the Mediterranean diet is a prescription for weight gain. Many of us can no longer eat wheat, and gluten-free replacements, while much more palatable than they used to be, are often even more likely than wheat to cause weight gain. We also need to be careful with portion sizes on fruits, even low sugar ones like apples, berries, watermelon, and cantaloupe.

I believe there's hope--that it's not so much that people's metabolisms always get slow as they age, but instead, it's that we're seeing that accumulated traumas cause the nerve to be suppressed, which means blood sugar is no longer balanced. Trauma might also reduce the tendency to exercise, given that traumatized people are more likely to have chronic health issues that might discourage or prevent them from exercising. Research has shown that muscle mass doesn't have to take a downturn until about the age of seventy. That's a sign that we have more capacity than we think to keep our metabolism elevated. If we can put the long-term effort into healing, I believe we can reactivate our vagal tone, and along with a balanced exercise program and a healthy microbiome, reawaken our metabolic rate back to a normal level.

Pro-Veg, Pro-Organic

You could call what I eat a modified Mediterranean-Paleo diet. In general, I aim for a diet with lots of vegetables, some organic chicken, wild fish, and grass-fed meat. 100% grass fed beef is full of omega 3 fatty acids rather than the omega 6 fatty acids found in grain-fed beef. Our diets are too high in omega 6 fatty acids, so it's nice to have another source for omega 3s. I do not fear fat in a phobic way like a lot of people do these days, but neither am I eating lots of fat and meat at every meal. I'm careful of the fats I eat because I still don't make enough bile. I take milk thistle whole-herb capsules to try to improve my bile production. I've made sure to get olive oil in my daily diet, along with some coconut oil, which is full of medium chain fatty acids that are good for the brain. I add bioflavonoids as suggested by the research findings Yasmina Ykelenstam reports on her website Healing Histamine.

You could say I'm cautiously paleo, trying for 60% vegetables in my diet. I need to limit the carbs in my diet because of problems with hypoglycemia and a genetic tendency towards Type 2 diabetes. My hypoglycemia is much improved since I started intermittent fasting, eating only in an eight-hour window between noon and 8pm. Intermittent fasting has been shown to help people with diabetes, heart disease, epilepsy, fatty liver disease, and helps inhibit growth and spread of a type of childhood leukemia called acute lymphoblastic leukemia.

It is important to find balance however you eat. It seems that the biggest problem with red meat is that it encourages the growth of a type of digestive bacteria that raises our triglyceride levels; at least the grain-fed version does. The more red meat we eat, the higher those levels of bacteria and therefore the higher our triglyceride levels, which are inflammatory to our body.

Impact of Our Intestinal Biome on Our Mood and Cravings
It is important to realize the significance of bacteria in our bodies and how they interact with our DNA. Yeast overgrowth is more likely each time we use antibiotics if we do not continuously reseed with probiotics while we take the antibiotics. Yeast overgrowth is also more likely to occur because of high fructose corn syrup intake and high amounts of other sugars in our typical Western diet.

The bacteria and yeast in our bodies can affect the size of our appetite. Some bacteria and yeast are beneficial, but others are freeloaders and create poisonous toxins. One type of bacteria, C. difficile, is associated with a muscle stiffness found with autistic spectrum kids. The only way to have the good kind of bacteria is to feed it what it likes, (sadly, not sugar and processed foods) and the only way to get rid of the bad kind is to starve it by not eating what it likes (which means no or low sugar and processed foods.) Colonic irrigation and reseeding with probiotics can help that process along.

The good kind of gut bacteria is much more susceptible to dying off with stress than the bad kind--and that includes internal stress. This is another reason why it is critical to nurture our inner child and be careful about how we speak to ourselves. Reducing internal stress around eating can help improve the quality of our diet (for example, I respond better to self-encouragement to eat better next time when I make a poor food choice rather than shaming myself for having made a mistake.) Reducing internal stress helps me have a healthier microbiome. As everyone knows, it's best to stay away from the processed food aisles.

Rethink Dairy and Wheat

It's a good idea to rethink dairy and wheat at least until we regain our health, because both are inflammatory. Dairy can cause a cycle of constipation if our bile is poor quality or too thick. Without the right amount of good quality bile, fat will not be fully absorbed by the small intestine. This makes the body shut down peristalsis until all the fat is absorbed. Since fat is a liquid in the body, the body also absorbs additional water from our stool, leading to constipation.

Both wheat and dairy can cause immune issues if we have leaky gut syndrome. The particles can get into the body and cause a release of histamine, which creates mucus and congestion in our sinuses, leading to sinus infections. An example from my life: it took me three and a half months without wheat to notice a difference in my sinus health. But once I did, I have not had to take antibiotics for a sinus infection since, and that was seven years ago.

In my experience, as I've released more abdominal fascia, I've realized that fascial tension can keep us from proper peristalsis, which could contribute to problems with constipation or diarrhea. The more abdominal fascia I've released, particularly around the psoas muscles, the healthier my digestion has become.

The Benefits of Unrefined Salt and Iodine

In the book, *Salt Your Way to Health,* Dr. David Brownstein says, "Refined salt leads to nutritional deficiencies in trace minerals as well as sodium imbalance in your body."

Many commercial bread products are made using bromide which confuses the body. Our body needs iodine, but bromide and iodine are similar enough that the body will use bromide instead of iodine, especially if iodine is undersupplied, as it tends to be in the western world. The thyroid needs iodine. Bromide inhibits the thyroid; the thyroid is responsible for our metabolism, so if we eat commercial bread products, we may be reducing the activity of our thyroid.

This means we are lowering our metabolism, which could cause us to gain weight. Some states, like California, have banned the use of bromides or bromates in bread. In other states, buyer beware. It might be a good reason to bake your own bread using bromide-free flour. Ask your Ayurvedic doctor if he recommends supplementing with iodine—I've only found Ayurvedic doctors to be versed enough in its use to recommend it at high levels. Never take extra iodine beyond what's in table salt without talking to an Ayurvedic doctor first, because it's toxic if unneeded.

Dr. Brownstein recommends Celtic Sea Salt from Selina Naturally or Real Salt by Redmond Trading Company. Using regular iodized salt and adding in trace minerals like ancient sea minerals from your local health food store is a good compromise.

Iodine and Breast Cancer Rates

Japanese women have rates of breast cancer that are four to five times lower than women in the United States. They get a lot more iodine in their diet than U.S. women because of their seaweed consumption. Ayurvedic doctors think that feeding iodine to the thyroid reduces fibrocystic breast disease which reduces breast cancer risk. I had fibrocystic breast disease until I started taking iodine at Dr. Douillard's recommendation.

My gynecologist requested an ultrasound as well as a mammogram the first year that ultrasounds were offered because my breast tissue had always been dense and filled with cystic tissue. This was ten months after I had started taking iodine. When the ultrasound results came in, they told me my breast tissue was normal and that I did not need to have an ultrasound again. In the years since I have never been asked to have another ultrasound.

Medical Herbalists

We can be aided in our quest to heal by learning which medical herbs (no, I'm not referring to marijuana) can assist our conditions. It is said that herbs such as ginger can help with digestion, slippery elm bark and herbal licorice can soothe the tissue of our digestive tract, and that hawthorne is helpful for the heart. There are wonderful medical herbalists out there who are teaching people what they can do for themselves through identifying local plants and creating their own tinctures and salves. Medical herbalists can also advise which herbs are right for their clients and where they can find reputable sources to buy. I had the privilege of taking classes from Janice Ditchek when I lived in New York. She works with a local doctor too, to assist his patients. I really enjoyed her classes. Get your doctor's okay before proceeding with a medical herbalist.

Action Steps:
Easy:
Enjoy seaweed salads regularly and change to sea salt if your doctor approves, making sure to replace the iodine with seaweed or a supplement.

Be good about taking a daily probiotic. Add bioflavonoids to your diet. Ask your doctor if you should switch to bread made without bromide.

Moderate:

If you have blood sugar issues, try a consultation with an Ayurvedic doctor.

Try ART or MFR if you think you might have fascial restrictions in your abdomen. More at www.myofascialrelease.com.

Read the blog at marksdailyapple.com for sensible ways to reduce over-reliance on processed carbs—handy even if you're not paleo.

I've found Dr. Josh Axe's website to contain helpful nutritional information. You can find him at www.draxe.com.

See an integrative medicine specialist for potential IgG food hypersensitivities. Dr. Jim Roach can be contacted at www.themidwaycenter.com.

If you think you might have IBS, read *Help for IBS,* and talk to your doctor. It can take a long time to get diagnosed. Patient awareness can help point your doctor in the right direction and reduce the time it takes to get a diagnosis. Rheumatologists are the specialists who make this diagnosis.

Contact Janice Ditchek for a session or to sign up for a class at jditchek@gmail.com.

Harder:

Try rethinking your diet if you have signs of leaky gut syndrome. Ask your doctor if it's okay for you to add chlorophyll and/or chamomile tea to your diet. Both help the body repair the squamous epithelial cells that line our GI tract. I use the broken cell wall type of chlorophyll so it's easier for my body to get nutrition from it. A word of caution: I have to take soluble fiber with my chlorophyll. For me, chlorophyll powder mixed in water feels like each particle comes with its own tiny chainsaw. Most people have no problems with chamomile tea, but it started causing tachycardia for me, so I had to stop using it.

Add a good protein powder to your daily diet. Beware of the oxalate content in it and choose wisely.

Sign up to attend Dr. Roach's health seminar. The information is accessible to laypeople even though most of the attendees are doctors and naturopaths looking to gain the knowledge needed to prevent disease rather than trying to fix problems after the fact. More info at www.themidwaycenter.com.

Chapter 23
Internal Repair

Help for Irritable Bowel Syndrome (IBS) Woes

For those who have IBS, it's common at unexpected times to have large quantities of gas. Social situations can be a nightmare because sufferers never know when it is going to strike, or which foods are going to cause a problem. Odor could be a sign of inadequate stores of vitamins for the liver to produce albumen. (Albumen is needed to remove waste through urination.) It might be a sign that we aren't eating enough protein to allow for efficient peristalsis, (normal contraction of the digestive tract) to move food along. If that's the case, the food stays in the intestine long enough that some amount of decay sets in. It's also possible that past antibiotic use has allowed the digestive tract to be colonized by bad bacteria, or we're not drinking enough water, or we're chronically stressed, or some combination of all the above.

Seek the Help of Integrative Medicine Doctors, Ayurvedic Doctors and Naturopaths

Integrative medicine doctors, Ayurvedic doctors, and naturopaths can help us work on nutritional needs and rebuilding digestive capacity. Look for practitioners who have good word of mouth in the community—anyone can hang out a shingle, but a robust practice and happy patients are what I've found to be important to look for. Trying the BED (Body Ecology Diet) or GAPS (Gut and Psychology Syndrome) diet can help too. Elimination diets like the BED or GAPS diet are not easy, so it's important to be extra kind and patient with ourselves.

It's not uncommon to have a sense of fear or failure when trying something new like an elimination diet, even while under a doctor's guidance, so our inner critics may be very active. Heaping on self-praise and keeping a gratitude journal with at least three things you are grateful for every day can be a help in anything new you try. If you try an elimination diet, you might encourage yourself by telling yourself that each day you follow it is one step closer to figuring out your path to better health.

Why We Should Care about Glycoproteins

Glycoproteins are sugar molecules attached to protein molecules. They are essential for your body to properly function. Here are a few examples of what glycoproteins do: they're vital for white blood cell recognition, our antibodies are glycoproteins, they help bind fibers and cells of connective tissues and help calcium in connective tissue bind to bone. Many of our hormones are glycoproteins and they are an important component of mucus produced throughout the body.

From what I've read, it appears the body does best if it is stocked with the essential ingredients to make its own glycoproteins (which includes eight essential sugars, also called glycans, such as xylose, fucose, galactose, glucose, mannose, n-acetylglucosamine, n-acetylgalactosamine, and n-acetylneuraminic acid.) When I mention the foods that contain these eight essential sugars, if you are sensitive to oxalates, please be aware and limit or avoid high oxalate foods.

Xylose is found in guava, pears, blackberries, loganberries, raspberries, aloe vera, echinacea, boswellia, psyllium seeds, broccoli, spinach, eggplant, peas, green beans, okra, cabbage, and corn. It's said to prevent cancer of the digestive system.

Fucose is found in brown seaweed like kelp and wakame, some mushrooms and seeds. It helps support long-term memory and fights allergies.

Galactose is found in plums, mango, orange, prunes, peach,

rhubarb, cranberries, blackberries, raspberries, apples, currants, dates, pineapple, kiwi, apricot, pear, strawberries, passionfruit, Echinacea, chestnuts, leaks, onions, brussels sprouts, green beans, carrots, eggplant, cauliflower, asparagus, broccoli, avocado, celery, cucumber, potato, tomatoes, beets, mushrooms, parsnips, and green peas. It's said to improve the speed of healing from injuries as well as improve memory.

Mannose is found in blackcurrants, red currants, gooseberries and cranberries, aloe vera, green beans, cabbage, eggplant, tomatoes, and turnips. It helps reduce inflammation and reduces disease through its anti-bacterial, anti-fungal and anti-viral properties.

Glucose is found in honey, grapes, banana, mangoes, cherries, strawberries, cocoa, aloe vera, licorice, sarsaparilla, hawthorn, garlic, and Echinacea. Glucose is best eaten as part of a whole food rather than as table sugar stripped of fiber and nutrients.

N-acetylneuraminic acid is found in whey protein isolate and chicken eggs, as well as human breast milk. It's anti-bacterial and anti-viral and is said to be important in brain function, particularly brain development and learning.

N-acetyl-galactosamine is found in shark cartilage and bovine cartilage. Either one can be problematic to find a good, safe source, so be cautious if you're thinking of supplementing this. N-acetyl-galactosamine is reported to inhibit the spread of tumors, regulate inflammation, and help immune system functioning.

N-acetyl-glucosamine is found in shitake mushrooms and glucosamine sulfate. It's said to help the immune system, repair cartilage and the mucosal lining damaged by ulcerative colitis and Crohn's Disease.

Unfortunately, modern wheat contains inflammatory glycoproteins whether it is white or whole wheat according to Dr. Mark Hyman. Eating sugar and other high processed foods also increases the amount of inflammatory proteins that circulate in our bodies.

Just as we need a proper balance of omega-3, 6 and 9 fatty

acids in our diet, we need a proper balance of healthy glycoproteins and glycans (those essential sugars I mentioned earlier.) Unfortunately, in the same way our Western diets are weighted too heavily towards omega-6 fatty acids, which causes inflammation, our diets are weighted much too heavily towards only two types of sugars, glucose, and galactose. Too much of a good thing is not good for us.

Reduce the Amount of Circulating Inflammatory Glycoproteins
It is thought that having high levels of circulating inflammatory glycoproteins is what fuels the development of autoimmune disease, heart disease and type 2 diabetes. The C-Reactive Protein test measures this level. Inflammatory glycoproteins also play a role in cancer. If we are sick with a chronic illness or a life-threatening disease, we want to get the most healing properties possible from the food we eat. The last thing we want is to give the body fuel that leads to worsening health. Even if we are healthy, eating in an imbalanced way, without enough of some of the essential sugars and healthy glycoproteins, as well as excessive amounts of others, is asking for trouble down the road.

I know it's hard to make these changes. If it's hard for you to give up processed foods and sugar, I'd suggest adding in more of the missing six glyconutrients to your diet. Get your glucose with whole food sources. I'm adding in fresh aloe gel to lemonade that I make with stevia. Ask your naturopath or integrative medicine doctor if that would be good for you. Ask them for other suggestions on the remaining glyconutrients.

The Benefits of Cleansing
There are two important ways that we can improve our health quickly: by doing an intestinal cleanse and changing our diet at least while we are in a healing phase. A cleanse clears out mucus from our intestinal tract. As I mentioned before, mucus is produced to protect our digestive tract from stomach acid which has not been properly neutralized if our bile is of poor quality or is too thick to move from

bile duct to gallbladder to small intestine. Cleansing allows us to get the full nutritional benefit of the food we eat. It also sweeps away pockets of bad bacteria that are working against us and attacking the intestinal wall.

The Ayurvedic version allows intestinal repair by eating easy-to-digest food during the cleanse. It simplifies life for the digestive tract so that it can clear away unhealthy cilia and start growing new cilia where damage has occurred.

I'd suggest asking an Ayurvedic, integrative or naturopathic doctor, nutritionist (or oncologist during cancer treatment) if it would be healthy and safe to reduce mucus in the digestive tract as a support for the body. It makes sense also to selectively reduce foods with little nutritional value that are high in histamines. The Ayurvedic cleanses I've done can take as little as three days.

The Lowdown on Histamine

Let's talk about histamine in more depth. As I mentioned earlier, histamine is a neurotransmitter that communicates messages from the body to the brain. It causes an immediate inflammatory response. It's meant to be a red flag to the immune system, notifying the body of any attackers so it can find the location of the problem.

It is meant to send a quick signal and get broken down immediately by DAO (diamine oxidase) which is produced in the intestinal tract. Things can go wrong in the production of DAO if the intestinal tract is not in good health. The following can widen the cell spacing of the gut lining: gluten intolerance, leaky gut, SIBO (small intestinal bacteria overgrowth), intestinal inflammation and/or medication like aspirin, ibuprofen, and some anti-depressants like Cymbalta, Prozac, Zoloft, and Effexor. Widened cell spacing allows food particles to escape the digestive tract. Medicines such as some immune modulators, some antiarrhythmics, as well as some antihistamines and histamine blockers can all impair DAO production. As listed earlier, there are lots of foods that contain high levels of histamine. In addition to foods containing high histamine, some foods cause our bodies' mast cells to release histamine as if we were under immune attack. This list includes most citrus fruits, chocolate, cow's milk, papaya, shellfish, strawberries, tomatoes, nuts, and wheat germ, along with additives like sulphites, nitrites, glutamate, food dyes and benzoate.

DAO-blocking foods include alcohol, which makes beer and wine a double whammy, since they're high in histamines too. Other DAO blockers are energy drinks, black tea, green tea and matcha.

Stress and Histamine Intolerance
High stress levels could be causing histamine intolerance to dietary histamines. Additionally, our diet may be too high in DAO blockers. I have found that as I have reduced my stress levels and been consistent with yoga and meditation that I have more tolerance for dietary histamines.

Excess Dietary Histamines and the Pain/Poor Health/Insomnia Cycle
To give you an example about how strongly histamine can affect a person, my wakeup call came after following advice to make homemade yogurt cultured for 24 hours. I had been rebounding in health from all the changes I'd made in my life and by that point I could do hot yoga three times a week. Day One of eating that yogurt, I went into hot yoga and after 15 minutes I had to lie down on my back. I got up after 5 minutes and then had to lie down another 15 minutes. I spent the rest of the class like that. I felt like Superman encountering kryptonite for the first time—I couldn't figure out what had gone wrong! I hadn't learned about histamine at that point. It turns out that the longer we culture a food, the higher the histamine levels. I went back to hot yoga two more times and was weak as a kitten each time. After that last time, I stopped eating yogurt. I went to hot yoga the following day and was as strong as I'd been before eating yogurt; I powered right through the class. And that was the day I decided to boot yogurt from my life until I'm 100% better. If you

have leaky gut, it's possible you too might be impacted by histamines without realizing it.

Immune System Overreaction and Histamine Intolerance Response

As I mentioned before, sometimes when I ate salad with a strong vinegar dressing, I would start to cough and choke a bit. In the past, I just figured vinegar just hit my windpipe the wrong way, but then I realized it set off a huge immune response that caused so much inflammation that it allowed in the very bacteria or viruses it was trying to defend against. For me, even just one eighth of a teaspoon of vinegary dressing can lead to a sore throat that goes into the common cold and congested sinuses. I bet I am not the only one.

This explains how I could have gotten sick so frequently. We do not have the same reaction to each type of dietary histamine; for me vinegar is the worst offender. If you think histamine could be impacting you, try to figure out which type is the worst for you. That way you can customize your diet to eat as many of the foods you love as you can while minimizing any hardship.

Leaky gut leads to molecules being released into the bloodstream that are intended to stay within the gut. The body makes histamine when this happens. I have a problem with wheat from leaky gut, so when wheat gets into my bloodstream, I start to have sinus congestion (histamine leads to mucus being formed in the sinuses). This led me to get chronic sinus infections.

Most people with chronic fatigue syndrome (now called either SEID or M.E./CFS) and fibromyalgia have the genetic problem of not being able to use some B vitamins unless they are already in a converted, ready-to-use state. The body has to do up to four steps before some B vitamins are ready for use. Fortunately, there are methylated forms of B vitamins available for those who, like me, have an issue.

Unfortunately, rebuilding wellness is complicated, and the process can lead to feeling worse initially instead of feeling better right away. It is important to find the right doctor to help. In my experience, I have found that integrative medicine doctors, Ayurvedic doctors, and naturopathic doctors understand this best. Some people swear by functional medicine doctors, though I have never been to one.

In trying to heal the body once chronic conditions have set in, it is important to repair the gut by following one of the diets such as GAPS or BED or a diet that tries to limit high histamine foods that don't build health. The best way to rebuild our health is through adding bioflavonoids (in other words, not fearing healthy high histamine foods), as the website HealingHistamine.com suggests. Unfortunately, these diets don't have much overlap. I suggest that you evaluate your biggest problem; is it intestinal distress or is it pain, fatigue, or insomnia? Treat the worst condition first if your doctor okays it. I'll discuss GAPS and BED later in this chapter.

Oxalates in Food

Oxalate and oxalic acid are organic acids that come from some plants, fungus such as aspergillus and candida, as well as metabolic processes in the body. Oxalates are powerful oxidants that can cause tissue damage, pain, and inflammation. Most of us don't have to think twice about oxalates because the flora of the gut will metabolize them, or the oxalates will be taken out of the digestive process by the lymph as it removes toxins and instead sent to the stool for elimination.

Unfortunately, those of us with inflammation in the gut, low storehouse levels of magnesium or calcium, or leaky gut can absorb damaging levels of oxalates. A healthy person might absorb 1-2% of dietary oxalates and an unhealthy one might absorb 50% of dietary oxalates. *Never cut oxalates out of your diet all at once because it can cause a potentially fatal reaction as the body tries to remove them from where they've been stored.* We need to slowly dial down how much oxalate we eat. Here is a list of health conditions with good reason to avoid oxalates: if you are on the autistic spectrum, if you have digestive issues like leaky gut, if you have any autoimmune illness, cystic fibrosis, COPD/Asthma, kidney stones, thyroid issues, breast cancer or a family history of breast cancer, fibromyalgia, chronic fatigue syndrome (also known as ME/CFS,) anxiety, depression, arthritis, infertility, interstitial cystitis (chronic bladder pressure and pain) or vulvodynia (chronic pain in the vulvar region which includes burning or irritation.) Remember this book is meant for informational purposes only and you need to talk to your doctor before making any dietary changes.

Proper levels of nutrients like calcium and magnesium are important to help eliminate oxalates safely. This is an area where not a lot of medical research has been done and where there isn't a standard best practices pathway. It's best to get help from a knowledgeable integrative medicine doctor and a nutritionist to reduce oxalates. *Proceed with extreme caution!*

Susan Owen is an oxalate researcher who was recommended by Yasmina Yekelenstam of Healing Histamine. Ms. Owen has created a Facebook support group called Trying Low Oxalates; again, I can't stress enough to please work through something like this with your doctor on board too. As an oxalate researcher, she is most likely more aware of the latest information than your doctor is, but your doctor has knowledge she doesn't have, so use both. The highest levels of oxalates in any food by far are found in spinach, which I first cut back on and then cut out of my diet. I've also cut out other foods that are considered high in oxalates. I have such a restricted diet that I would rather not cut out medium level oxalate foods, but I may try it in the future. I have noticed a significant difference in pain levels with just cutting out high oxalate foods. I highly recommend Susan's Trying Low Oxalates Facebook group. Susan is constantly striving to advance oxalate research into how it impacts multiple illnesses that seem unrelated, and I've made the final strides towards optimal health from what I've learned in the group. Susan has a related group which offers spreadsheets on which foods are high, medium, and low oxalate, as well as a third group with recipes to help eat a low oxalate diet without having to give up good-tasting food along with information on food preparation to reduce oxalate load. Dealing with oxalates is particularly important for people who have a problem with uptake of vitamin B1. People with this issue can have an increased risk of developing Alzheimer's. Oxalates have also been shown to be linked to an increased risk of developing breast cancer.

Lectins

As I mentioned in Chapter 21, lectins are found in all forms of life. When trying to rebuild our health, it's important to look to avoiding nuts, beans and grains that are not soaked or fermented, or cooked at a specific temperature for a certain length of time. Sally Fallon has a cookbook called *Nourishing Traditions* that is a resource. So is Sandor Katz's book *Wild Fermentation.*

There are dozens of cookbooks and blogs out there to help you, but a word of caution: go slowly. If you have a leaky gut, these fermented bacteria are getting into your bloodstream and taxing your immune system. Soaking seems like a safer way to go, at least until you've overcome your leaky gut. Research how to prepare foods that are high in lectins—for example, as few as four or five raw kidney beans can trigger lectin poisoning. Red kidney beans can only be safely eaten after having been boiled for 30 minutes and should never be prepared in a slow cooker for that reason, as the temperature never gets high enough. Have a tablespoon of a fermented bean dish, not half a plate. Evaluate how you feel after that tablespoon. If you're experiencing any symptoms of histamine intolerance like headaches, migraines, anxiety, arrhythmia or accelerated heart rate, difficulty falling asleep, dizziness, nausea, vomiting, or hypertension, back off the soaked and fermented food and have a talk with your integrative, naturopathic, or Ayurvedic doctor. Report how you're feeling and ask further advice about how to rebuild gut health.

Glutamic Acid

Glutamic acid is an amino acid found in plant and animal protein. Glutamate is the most common form of glutamic acid in our bodies.

Glutamate is a neurotransmitter that is vital to help our brain learn, grow, develop, and recall. The issue with glutamate is when it is free —no longer bound in a whole food source—and therefore able to be absorbed rapidly. Free glutamate is found in high concentrations in some natural foods, and it is also found in a lot of processed foods. Certain people are more susceptible; namely if you have problems with leaky gut, there is a possibility that low level chronic inflammation could have led to problems with a leaky blood-brain barrier. Additionally, there's a suggestion of genetic susceptibility for children with autistic spectrum or ADHD, Huntington's Disease and people who suffer from migraines.

Natural sources for free glutamate are matured, cured, or preserved foods, such as cheeses like Parmesan and blue cheese and cured meats like salami. Other sources include mushrooms, tomatoes, broccoli, peas, walnuts, grape juice, bone broth as well as long-braised meats, wheat gluten, dairy casein, malted barley, and aged sauces like fish sauce and soy sauce.

Free glutamate in processed foods can be listed in many ways: monosodium or monopotassium glutamate, yeast extract, anything hydrolyzed, autolyzed yeast, textured protein, gelatin, soy protein (both isolate and concentrate), whey protein (both isolate and concentrate), milk powder, carrageenan, kombu and other seaweeds, bouillon, broth, stock, maltodextrin, pectin, citric acid, corn starch, corn syrup, modified food starch, and often flavors, such as "natural vanilla flavor".

Free glutamate is overstimulating to the brain. Some areas of the brain, like the hypothalamus, do not have an impermeable blood brain barrier, according to the American Nutrition Association. Excess free glutamate can injure and even kill neurons. The ANA says that at least 25% of the US population react to free glutamate from food sources, and these reactions range between mild and transitory to debilitating and life-threatening. A disparate number of disease conditions such as ALS (Lou Gehrig's Disease), Alzheimer's disease, seizures, and stroke are associated with glutamate cascade.

So are symptoms like tachycardia, hives, diarrhea, chest pain, dizziness, weakness, chills, unusual perspiration, a flushing sensation in the face or chest, tinging, skin rash, stiffness, joint pain, flu-like achiness, extreme rise or drop in blood pressure, sciatica, slurred speech, lethargy, sleepiness, insomnia, runny nose, asthma, shortness of breath, nocturia, (excessive urination at night), mouth lesions, panic attacks, and depression. Babies and small children are the most vulnerable. While many manufacturers removed monosodium glutamate from their food, they often left free glutamic acid such as "autolyzed yeast" and "hydrolyzed vegetable protein" in their products. Symptoms may be immediate or take up to 48 hours to appear.

I must admit I love some processed foods, both for convenience and even taste. In today's busy world, it's hard to be a purist and I don't aim to be. I'm just more careful because of leaky gut issues as I rebuild my health. I also limit them because of my genetic predisposition towards Type 2 diabetes. I'm mindful to enjoy the heck out of them whenever I do indulge.

Candida

I think it's possible that people who are in sympathetic nervous system dominance are more susceptible to candida. Taking a cell wall suppressor (something which prevents candida from forming a cell wall, which makes it more vulnerable to our immune system) is one way to reduce yeast overload. At the same time, it is important to reduce emotional holding patterns and stress levels, as well as to reset the amygdala.

Women going through perimenopause and menopause are often under high levels of stress which can cause histamine intolerance. That can sometimes be relieved by reducing our intake of dietary histamines and including more self-care and holistic therapies in our lives. Making sure to take a probiotic while on antibiotics is important to help keep candida in balance, as can keeping sugar intake low and removing other candida-supporting foods from the diet.

BED or GAPS Diet to Starve the Bad Bacteria and Reseed with Good

BED stands for the Body Ecology Diet by Donna Gates. The GAPS Diet is described by Dr. Natasha Campbell-McBride in her book *Gut and Psychology Syndrome.* These diets look to reduce the intake of short chain carbohydrates found in foods which are poorly absorbed in the small intestine. Omnash University in Melbourne, Australia created the term FODMAP to describe these short chain carbohydrates: fermentable oligo-, di-, monosaccharides and polyols.

FODMAPs are short-chain polymers of fructose called fructans, galactose (galactans), disaccharides (lactose), monosaccharides (fructose) and polyols which are sugar alcohols like sorbitol, mannitol, xylitol and maltitol. FODMAPs can feed any bad bacteria you have in your digestive tract, so it is worth figuring out what kind of FODMAP your bad bacteria like.

It is rare that we have the same reaction to each type of FODMAP because we tend to predominate in a few types of bad bacteria. Each type of short chain carbohydrate is tested in an elimination diet, so we can see which bacteria are causing us digestive distress.

Once we figure it out, we can help reduce the worst offenders by avoiding that type of FODMAP for a certain amount of time. Taking probiotics will help reseed the space left in the digestive tract that the offender occupied. It doesn't have to be perfect; being in better balance will help our bodies heal.

Ultimately, adding nutritionally dense, healthy foods high in bioflavonoids is the way to go daily.

Action steps:

Easy: If you have leaky gut, avoiding multiple high histamine foods at once could reduce how hard your immune system has to work. For example, make it a treat rather than the norm to eat a salad with avocado, aged cheese and balsamic dressing while having a beer. Reduce how often you pair drinking wine while eating a corned beef sandwich, melted cheese and a pickle.

Consider your reaction to high free glutamate foods and take steps to cut back if needed. Read more about the issue at americannutritionassociation.org.

Ask your doctor if it's okay to take a daily probiotic.

Be careful if you have leaky gut, because probiotics are particularly alarming to the body when they circulate in your blood stream. Certain types are better than others, but ultimately let your body be your guide.

Www.healinghistamine.com has e-cookbooks to give people with histamine issues an idea about how to cook to heal.

Mark Sissman is also concerned with rebuilding gut health and his blog has archives on how to navigate histamine issues. Whether you're on a paleo diet or not, it's a good educational tool. It's at marksdailyapple.com.

Dr. Josh Axe has a good website with lots of educational material focused on using food as medicine. It's full of recipes for rebuilding health. His website is at www.draxe.com.

The most important information on diet includes awareness of oxalate levels in food. More information is available at Susan Owen's Facebook group Trying Low Oxalates, and at her website www.lowoxalate.info.

Moderate: Try making dietary changes. Buy a cookbook on the subject and see if you can add in some healthy, nutrient-dense foods.

I've been helped by colonic irrigation with a licensed practitioner, at times using hydrogen peroxide, other times chlorophyll, to assist the intestinal tract in healing. The hydrogen peroxide helped reduce bacterial attack and speed up repair. The chlorophyll gave me energy. Ask your doctor if colonic irrigation is safe for you to try.

Harder: Work with an integrative medicine doctor or naturopath. You can find an integrative medicine doctor through Andrew Weil's Center for Integrative Medicine's website at https://integrativemedicine.arizona.edu/alumni.html. You can find a naturopath through the American Association of Naturopathic Physicians at naturopathic.org. Dr. Roach is at themidwaycenter.com. Dr. James Pilc's fusion and meditation practice is at www.completewellnesswny.com. (By the way, he's got a great voice and I enjoy his meditation CD's.) My local doctor, Dr. Lizzie Clapham, is a naturopath and I've gotten a lot of great help from her. She is at www.pathways2nh.com.

Dr. Sara Whitney has been a huge help for me with cutting edge Lyme treatment. She consults with doctors at the top of their field in Lyme disease and brings both their expertise and hers to Los Angeles. She is at www.theroxburyinstitute.com.

Find an Ayurvedic doctor and try a cleanse if recommended for you. You can find one through the National Ayurvedic Medical Association at ayurvedanama.org. You can reach Dr. Douillard at www.lifespa.com.

Chapter 24
Cognitive Hypnotherapy

Improve Digestion, Nutritional Absorption, and Internal Repair with Hypnotherapy

I'm writing about cognitive hypnotherapy in this section rather than in the psychology section because of its importance in improving our digestive health. Reworking how we live in the world and our unconscious beliefs is something that a good cognitive hypnotherapist can help us with. While we do so, we are also healing our immune reactions to foods we ate during times of emotional upsets in our lives.

We each come into the world with our unique traits and pairing a sensitive child with a harsh environment (or even a not particularly sensitive child with a harsh environment) can mean that our fight-or-flight alarms are triggered for the rest of our lives. Even for adults, life events like breaking a bone, the death of a loved one, divorce or job loss can trigger PTSD. We can become sensitized to foods that we eat because our immune system associates the trauma of an event with food that was eaten around the same time. The good news is that it doesn't have to stay this way. Examining our unconscious beliefs, how we interact with our emotions, our self-talk—all of these can be worked with. It's never too late to redo the way we interact with the world. Additionally, despite all the other work I've done, cognitive hypnotherapy helped me quickly release additional deeply held beliefs that were keeping me from moving forward.

There are a variety of cognitive hypnotherapy programs available online. The one I took was offered by Yasmina Yekelenstam of Healing Histamine, who partnered with a cognitive hypnotherapist, Hazel Gale, to develop a program which decouples those lifelong connections. It's not a cure, but it can help reduce symptoms.

Choose What's Right for Your Budget and Ability
The Healing Histamine hypnotherapy program was a four-week program with a daily calming meditation to put us in a parasympathetic state. It also had us journaling daily. We were led through the process of examining the first time we felt a particular emotion and what beliefs we'd accepted about ourselves and the world, so that we could change the programming and enlist our internal abilities to heal.

The downside of online group cognitive hypnotherapy programs is that they are not tailored to individual needs. For example, looking at the user posts on the program's Facebook group, I could see that some people were unable to start working on the program because their unconscious fears were so triggered. Hazel and Yasmina did a great job of helping people through the process. I confess I was somewhere in the middle on this one—I got several weeks into it and life "suddenly got too busy" to proceed with it. I'm always suspicious that my unconscious fears are stalling my progress when life events step in like that. If you try a group hypnotherapy program and get stalled, you might want to try individual therapy. That said, I was enormously helped by those first two weeks. One of the first things we did was create an "anchor", which is a word or phrase to calm the nervous system down. I still use that anchor when I'm stressed. I did need to get one-on-one help to finish the program.

Another Way to Understand Allergies and Asthma Triggers
It's not widely known that our bodies can make connections between food and trauma. The body can develop an autoimmune response to the food we ate at the time when we were traumatized. A lot of people

don't realize that this is what allergy partly is—that there is connection between our emotions and our immune system. The same process causes triggers for asthma too, according to Dr. Buteyko, whom I mentioned in Chapter 15. So, one reason a person might have an inflammatory response to a food could be because when they first ate it, a parent yelled at them harshly, or right after they ate it, they got word that someone in the family had died, or they ate that food and then got bullied in school. It's all completely unconscious.

Going through hypnotherapy can help reset the mind and body to improve our relationship with food, our ability to digest and absorb the nutrients in our food, and our ability to be in a parasympathetic state so we can repair our bodies. Perhaps the result of this might eventually be a reduction in medication, too, but this needs to be worked through with your doctor. Please don't stop taking medications without getting a doctor's approval. Allergies and asthma are life-threatening conditions.

Action Steps:
Easy: try Les Fehmi's Open Focus meditation if you have anxiety, PTSD, or histamine issues.

Moderate: get one-on-one help from a cognitive hypnotherapist about whatever issues you are facing. You can find therapists through psychologytoday.com, the Association for Behavioral and Cognitive Therapies at abct.org, and the National Association of Cognitive-Behavioral Therapists at nacbt.org. Hazel Gale can be reached at www.hazelgale.com.

Harder: combine cognitive therapy and meditation with dietary changes that your doctor or nutritionist okays.

Chapter 25
The Power of Intention

What Intention Can do For You

When I was a little girl living in Taiwan, my father belonged to the Rod and Gun Club formed by American military personnel stationed in Taipei. A few times every summer, they would charter a Chinese junk to take them and their children out fishing in the South China Sea. It was warm and muggy there, with jade green water. The waves were generally gentle, which was good because old-style fishing junks don't have railings. There was a foot-tall edge around the boat and that was it between you and the ocean. We had so much fun out there catching things like eels, parrot fish–which are bright green with yellow fins and orange and blue markings–and other similarly exotic-looking fish. One time, one of my fellow anglers had a good-size fish on the line, about two feet long. Try as he might, he couldn't land it. It kept getting away from him, line hissing back out as soon as it caught sight of the surface. In all my times fishing, I was shocked by what happened next: one of the deckhands grabbed a flat rattan basket and dove into the ocean. The next time the fish got close, he swam down to it with the basket in front of him, bringing it up underneath the fish, and bringing the fish to the surface completely without a struggle. And that, my friend, is a metaphor of what Intention can do for you.

What is Intention?

It is what you want to have happen in your life but haven't achieved yet. It's a positive, active, present time goal you're working on.

Examples:

- *I am healthy and love eating nutritious food*
- *I excel at test-taking and stay positive and calm during tests*
- *I enjoy being fit and love exercising*
- *I am seen for the incredible work I do at my job*
- *I make excellent strategic decisions for my company*

Intention is one way to signal to the unconscious that there is education coming in. There will be inner children who resist the message, so it is not enough. Repetition of intention helps, but again, that is not enough, either. What I have found works is to think of myself (my conscious self) as a partner to the higher level of the unconscious. I set an intention and then ask for its input via a session on myself on what emotions need to be processed and released in the session. This involves the specialized kinesiology you've read about in Chapter 15. I ask if anything needs integration, then work on fixing other energy that the body is connected to. And once all of that is complete, I always notice that walking, bending, and turning is easier and less painful, my muscles are looser, my mood is upbeat, and my sense of possibility for that intention coming true is strong. I've also decided that this tandem cooperation is more important than what my ego alone wants for me.

I've learned the hard way that ego will get me into trouble if it is all I listen to and I'm tired of that. I want connection and instruction on what my soul wants from this life, and a partnership between ego and soul in order for me to consciously be able to assist it, so that both ego and soul are aligned. This way, everything I think I want, I'm double checking to see if it is for my highest and best good before proceeding. This is also a process that I guide clients through, as well as teach. I believe that this is the way we climb out of the brain stem and emotional brain's reach and ascend into the higher capacities of the cortex. As a wise friend once told me, power lies on the other side of our emotions. I have lived life both ways and find it to be true.

A Word About Empaths

People who are traumatized as children have learned to tune in and listen to other people's emotional states before their own, as a way to stay safe. This is called being empathic. The problem is that empaths do not learn to listen to their own internal states, so they are often not sure what they think or believe or feel.

They often find their feelings inconvenient or downright dangerous at times—feelings did not help their survival as children, so they stuffed them. Most likely they don't seem helpful in adulthood either. Anger over their treatment in childhood or as an adult may have endangered them or their relationships and required them to suppress it. Empaths think they can push their feelings aside or bury them because that is what they've always done, and it has always worked.

They tend to repeat the patterns of their childhood and find relationships that echo the problems they encountered as children. Those problems are familiar--and familiar feels safe to the unconscious, even when it isn't safe to the rational mind. Being empathic can be a perfect breeding ground to become codependent.

Empaths can be extroverts or introverts. Introverted empaths can lose their way and remain frozen or trapped by others' needs or fears. The juggling act involved in trying to read mirror neurons in a room full of people is exhausting for them.

On the path back to health, introverted empaths must be aware of their internal state, figure out what emotion they are feeling, and assign that feeling as much value as another person's feelings. In this way, they can break free of co-dependency.

The Aladdin Factor

As Jack Canfield and Mark Victor Hansen say in *The Aladdin Factor*, "The truth is all facts are facts and all events are meaningless. You are the one who makes up the meaning and once you make the event mean something, that meaning becomes an unexamined box that can limit or disempower you." Introverts have a mountain of unexamined boxes which limit and disempower us. It all starts with a willingness to examine a box. You can choose to welcome the opportunity to start examining those boxes. If you do, you'll live life like Bill Murray in the movie *Groundhog Day* after he finally starts giving his life a positive meaning. Everything that has happened to us this far is what was necessary to have us wake up and start taking positive steps. No more beating ourselves up for the-might-have-beens.

Happily Self-Parenting for Life

Start parenting your inner self in a kind way. What we've said to ourselves over the course of a lifetime has likely been far harsher than optimal. As Jack Canfield mentions in *The Success Principles*, according to researchers, we think an average of 50,000 thoughts a day, 80% of which are negative and most of those are about ourselves.

There surely is someone out there whose parents didn't love them, whose friends have never been there for them and have only used them. But telling yourself these types of things is only going to shut you down and paralyze you more because it scares the unconscious. If you have tried the logical and rational left-brained way, telling yourself such dire things, and have gotten sick, it makes sense to try a different way. If you live in fear, paralysis, avoidance, or anger, try being kind to yourself. You need to positively parent your inner child. Would anyone say tens of thousands of negative things to a three-year-old child every day? If they did, that child would be a wreck.

You are Loved

Try telling yourself for a week that everyone loved you and wanted the best for you to the best of their abilities. Repeat this sentence multiple times a day. If you notice you feel better at the end of the week, continue it. It is ultimately a gift to yourself. You deserve to have it be true. You are worthy. Telling yourself that it is true will free you up to enjoy your life in ways you didn't think possible. Don't you deserve to enjoy your life to the fullest?

Telling yourself what you logically perceive as true is keeping you a victim of your actual parenting. Begin the re-parenting process if you feel in need. If this rings a bell for you, you will need to promise that inner three-year-old that you will take care of him or her, now that you have learned how. Apologize for letting that three-year-old down and tell him or her that you will listen.

Imagine hugging your three-year-old self. Remember how adorable and loving you were. See how worthy you were of love and kindness. You may not have gotten it then but from here on out you can provide it. You can happily and successfully learn to be a better self-parent.

Weekly Self Care

What do you do to help encourage yourself every week? Try taking a bath with Epsom salts (or if pressed for time, a shower with a sugar scrub). Think about all the parts of your body which have helped you, and thank them one by one: from organs to glands, from skin to muscle, from fascia to bones, etc.

Judgments Poison

Become aware of the times that you judge. As Jesus said, "Judge not lest you be judged." While we are wired to be human judgment machines, we don't have to be that way. When we judge others, we wind up being a harsher judge of ourselves than if we try to let go of our judgment of others.

We often internalize the most judgmental adults in our lives as our inner critic when we were young. They live on in how we put ourselves down, and in turn how we focus on others' faults, so that we have relief from judging ourselves. Far better to ease up on the inner critic's hold on you. When that self-judgment shows up, thank it for helping and tell it that you're running the show now.

Experiment with this for yourself and see if it holds true for you. You deserve to be happier. If you believe in God or a universal energy, be sure to add that element to your self-talk, reminding yourself that God or The Universe loves you. Even if you do not believe in God or a universal energy, even if your prayer consists of, "Hey _____, I don't believe in you but here's what's going on," (fill in the blank and add a sentence on to it that you are loved by this thing), it can help reduce your stress. If it sounds interesting, you can choose to try it for a week and see if you are happier or calmer. Above all, you still get to be you during this process.

Final Thoughts
As this book winds down, I want to make sure it leaves you with a path out of whatever health issues and/or pain you currently have. You always have the choice to not take any suggestions from this book. It's your decision to make. If you think you'd like to start taking a step, maybe pick an easy one. One easy start down the path back to health is to begin taking a supplement of trace minerals if your doctor okays it. Another choice might be to start timing when you drink water before meals to aid your stomach acid production.

The important thing is to not load up on too many steps at once. Why not treat yourself kindly? Whether you add the second step in after a week or two, or after a month or two, or six or eight, it is forward momentum, and you'll get there.

Give yourself a pat on the back; you have earned it. If you're shy, go on, find somewhere private and give yourself a real pat on the back. Get used to doing silly things like that. You would be amazed at how much it means to your inner child, and really, no one else needs to know. Learn how to muscle test so you can ask your inner child what it wants for breakfast, or to wear for the day, or what way to get exercise.

When somebody first learns how to juggle, they are not using multiple balls at once and expecting to be successful right away. They start simply and get the feel for the first step; then once that is mastered, they add another ball. The ones who succeed at juggling are the ones who make the learning process enjoyable by being kind to themselves. Wherever we've succeeded in our lives, it's because either we or someone else in our lives provided a safe space for us to practice mastery until we acquired it. Now that you consciously know that, you can master anything if you are willing to take the time to learn how to provide a safe space for yourself as you practice.

Those who truly succeed in life are the ones who make the learning and living process enjoyable by being kind to themselves. We all need to show ourselves the same courtesy. Once we have set our intention, we should realize its power to carry us through the change. Visualize it often in detail. Reaffirm it regularly and enjoy your best health ever.

Action Steps:

Easy: Read *The Aladdin Factor*, by Jack Canfield and Mark Victor Hansen.

Ask your doctor if it's okay to take trace minerals like what you'd find in health food stores, or Ancient Earth Minerals from www.bodyecology.com.

If your doctor has advised you to do so, be sure to drink eight glasses of water every day, timing it so that you're drinking a glass 15-30 minutes before eating.

Look back through the other chapters at the easy steps and see which appear truly easy to you. Make a list of easy steps for you to take and put them in order of priority so you can add them in whenever it feels right.

Moderate: Make a commitment to stop judging others so harshly. If you are Christian, realize that 'thou shall love thy neighbor as thyself' doesn't mean love the easy people. It means all of the people. Every single human being. It's really a way of loving *ourselves* because the parts of ourselves which we find unlovable are hidden away in our unconscious mind until other people who are like those 'unlovable' parts trigger us. Often our unconscious reasoning is why should other people get to be like those parts of ourselves that our parents or others shamed us about or punished us for, and so we lash out against other people rather than ourselves or our parents. Instead, by treating others with kindness, we begin to heal our inner child ren and start rebuilding our health.

Harder: Keep a journal about the emotions you experience. Notice the conclusions you make and how often you are right in predicting how something is going to turn out when you're in the middle of strong emotion. If you're like most people, you're rarely right. Notice if that makes it any easier to let go of your emotions. Remind yourself that research shows mentally bracing for disaster is not effective in actual emergencies. Instead visualize positive outcomes. Allow yourself to be hopeful as you wait for life to play out.

Try getting support for your growth from psychologists and specialized kinesiologists near you.

Learn how to Focus. More info at www.focusing.org.

Once you've integrated all the lessons you've chosen from this book, I suggest you take stock of your life three or four times a year by looking at the Monday through Friday lessons. On Monday, make sure you've still got flow in your life and that you've taken steps to reduce stress. On Tuesday, ask yourself about your pain levels, etc. Remember that if you've fallen short, that's a judgment, so be sure to give yourself a positive word of encouragement for your intention.

Here is to the miracle you already are; may you come to fully see it for yourself.

Love,
Elizabeth

P.S. A reminder that the ACE test as well as all updated links in this book are available by signing up at www.rightbrainuniversity.com/guide.

Bibliography / Recommended Reading

Adams, Case PhD   *Natural Solutions for Food Allergies and Intolerance*

Agus, David MD *The End of Illness*

Amand, R. Paul MD   *What Your Doctor May Not Tell You About Fibromyalgia*

Amen, Daniel MD   *Healing ADD*

Amen, Daniel MD   *Change Your Brain, Change Your Body*

Amen, Daniel MD   *Use Your Brain to Change Your Life*

Arrowsmith Young, Barbara   *The Woman Who Changed Her Brain*

Ball, Ron   *Freedom at Your Fingertips*

Barnes, John   *Healing Ancient Wounds*

Bennett-Goleman, Tara   *Mind Whispering*

Berceli, David Phd   *The Revolutionary Trauma Release Process*

Blaich, Dr. Robert   *Your Inner Pharmacy*

Bolte Taylor, Dr. Jill   *My Stroke of Insight*

Boyle, Dr. Neil   *Why Be In Pain?*

Brostoff, Jonathan MD   *Food Allergies and Food Intolerance*

Brown, Brene   *Daring Greatly*

Brown, Brene   *The Gifts of Imperfection*

Brown, Brene   *Rising Strong*

Browning, Tovi   *Gentle Miracles: Holistic Pulsing*

Brownstein, David MD   *Salt Your Way to Health*

Cain, Susan   *Quiet*

Cameron, Julia   *The Artist's Way*

Campbell, Phil *Ready, Set, Go! Synergy Fitness*

Campbell-McBride, Dr. Natasha   *Gut and Psychology Syndrome*

Canfield, Jack   *The Aladdin Factor*

Canfield, Jack   *Chicken Soup for the Soul Series*

Canfield, Jack   *Tapping into Ultimate Success*

Capacchione, Lucia PhD   *Recovery of Your Inner Child*

Carlin, Dr. Debra   *Build the Strength Within*

Carlson, Neil   *Foundations of Physiological Psychology*

Carrigan, Catherine   *Unlimited Energy Now*

Chaitow, Leon *Fibromyalgia Syndrome*
Challem, Jack *The Inflammation Syndrome*
Chilton, Floyd PhD *Inflammation Nation*
Chilton, Floyd PhD *Win the War Within*
Cohen, Dr. Michael *Feel it? Heal it*
Cole, Jonathan *Pride and a Daily Marathon*
Cooley, Bob *Resistance Flexibility 1.0*
Covell, Cathy *Feeling Your Way Through*
Cryder, Chad *Men are DAWGS and Women are CATS: A Field Guide for Human Relationships*
Csikzentmihalyi, Mihaly PhD *Finding Flow*
D'Adamo, Dr. Peter *Eat Right 4 Your Type*
Dahlin, Dondi *The Five Elements: Understand Yourself and Enhance Your Relationships with the Wisdom of the World's Oldest Personality Type System*
Davis, Adelle *Let's Get Well*
Davis, Adelle *Let's Eat Right to Keep Fit*
Dennison, Paul & Gail *Brain Gym® Teachers Edition*
DeSalvo, Louise *Writing as a Way of Healing*
Doidge, Norman MD *The Brain That Changes Itself*
Douillard, Dr. John *Body, Mind, Sport*
Douillard, Dr. John *Eat Wheat*
Douillard, Dr. John *The 3 Season Diet*
Douillard, Dr. John *Colorado Cleanse*
Eden, Donna *The Little Book of Energy Medicine: The Essential Guide to Balancing Your Body's Energies*
Eden, Donna *Energy Medicine: Balancing Your Body's Energies for Optimal Health, Joy and Vitality*
Fehmi, Les PhD *Dissolving Pain*
Feldenkrais, Moshe *Awareness Through Movement*
Feldenkrais, Moshe *Master Moves*
Fields, Jonathan *Uncertainty*
Forbes, Bo *Yoga for Emotional Balance*
Ford, Debbie *The Dark Side of the Light Chasers*

Fredrickson, Barbara PhD *Positivity*
Gendlin, Eugene *Focusing*
Gilbert, Daniel *Stumbling on Happiness*
Gilbert, Elizabeth *Big Magic*
Gilbert, Elizabeth *Eat Pray Love*
Goleman, Daniel *Social Intelligence*
Gottchall, Elaine *Breaking the Vicious Cycle*
Hannaford, Carla *Smart Moves: Why Learning Isn't All in Your
    Head*
Hartwig, Dallas & Melissa *It Starts with Food*
Haynes, Anthony *Food Intolerance Bible*
Heath, Chip & Dan *Switch*
Heller, Laurence PhD *Healing Developmental Trauma*
Hitzmann, Sue *The MELT Method*
Hubert, Bill *Bal-A-Vis-X*
Hyman, Mark MD *The Ultramind Solution*
Ingebretson, Susan *Fibrowhyalgia*
Ingram, Dr. Cass *The Respiratory Solution*
Ivker, Robert *Sinus Survival*
Jackson Nakazawa, Donna *Childhood Interrupted*
Jackson Nakazawa, Donna *The Last Best Cure*
Kalsched, Donald PhD *The Inner World of Trauma*
Kaplan, Melvin *Seeing Through New Eyes*
Kaplan, Melvin *The Secrets in Their Eyes*
Karnis, Joyce *Comprehensive Myofascial Self Treatment*
Kerson, Dr. Don *Getting Unstuck: Unraveling the Knot of
    Depression, Attention and Trauma*
Keyes, Ken *The Power of Unconditional Love*
Kraftsow, Gary *Yoga for Transformation*
Levine, Peter PhD *Waking the Tiger*
Lipski, Elizabeth PhD *Digestive Wellness*
Lozoff, Bo *We're All Doing Time*
Masgutova, Svetlana *Masgutova Method*
Meyer, Joyce *Living Beyond Your Feelings*

Mullin, Gerard MD *The Inside Tract*

Mullin, Gerard MD *Integrative Gastroenterology*

Musil, Donna *Brats: Our Journey Home (DVD Documentary)*

Neff, Kristen PhD *Self-Compassion*

Nelson, Dr. Bradley *The Emotion Code*

Northrup, Christianne MD *Goddesses Never Age*

Oleska, Paula *Your Secret Brain (DVD)*

Ornstein, Robert *The Right Mind: Making Sense of the Hemispheres*

Pagano, John *One Cause Many Ailments: Leaky Gut Syndrome*

Pennebaker, James PhD *Opening Up: The Healing Power of Confiding in Others*

Perl, Sondra *Felt Sense: Writing with the Body*

Perlmutter, David *Brain Maker*

Pert, Candace PhD *Molecules of Emotion*

Ratey, John MD *Spark*

Rimland, Bernard *Dislogic Syndrome*

Roach, Dr. Jim *God's House Calls: Finding God Through my Patients*

Roach, Dr. Jim *Vital Strategies in Cancer*

Robbins, John *Reclaiming Our Health*

Rock, David *Your Brain at Work*

Rome, David *Your Body Knows the Answer*

Sarnow, Dr John *The Divided Mind*

Seligman, Martin PhD *Authentic Happiness*

Seligman, Martin PhD *Flourish*

Seligman, Martin PhD *Positive Psychology*

Shimoff, Marci *Happy for No Reason*

Shimoff, Marci *Love for No Reason*

Shumway-Cook, Anne *Motor Control Theory and Practical Applications*

Simon, Bebe *How I Teach Focusing: Discovering the Gift of Your Inner Wisdom*

Singer, Michael *The Untethered Soul: The Journey Beyond*

Yourself

Solden, Sari   *Women with Attention Deficit Disorder*

Stone, Hal & Sidra   *Embracing Ourselves*

Stutz, Phil   *The Tools*

Tanner Boll, Pamela   *Who Does She Think She Is? (DVD Documentary)*

Thie, Dr. John and Matthew   *Touch for Health: The Complete Edition*

Truman, Karol   *Feelings Buried Alive Never Die*

Truman, Karol   *Healing Feelings from Your Heart*

Van Vorous, Heather   *Help for IBS*

Wangyal, Tenzin (Rinpoche)   *Healing With Form, Energy and Light*

Wangyal, Tenzin (Rinpoche)   *Sound Healing (Book and DVD)*

Warner, Priscilla   *Learning to Breathe: My Yearlong Quest to Bring Calm to my Life*

Weill, Andrew MD   *Spontaneous Healing*

Wells, Steve   *Enjoy Emotional Freedom*

Zukav, Gary   *The Seat of the Soul*

Zukav, Gary   *Soul to Soul*

Acknowledgements

To Dr. Jill Bolte Taylor, whose TED talk and book *My Stroke of Insight* helped provide support for this book.

To my friends for putting up with my one track mind over the years:-)

In appreciation to my family: Michael, Alex and Dylan, Pop, Kate, Ian, Adam, Simon, and Nic.

To my mom, Jan Wharton, for starting me on the path, and to Oprah Winfrey for being a guiding light with *What I Know For Sure*.

With thanks to Dr. James Roach, Dr. John Douillard, Dr. Valerie Girard, Dr. Sara Whitney, Dr. Lizzie Clapham, Matthew Thie, M.Ed., Hazel Gale, Dr. Anne Jensen, and Paula Oleska.

Deep thanks to another dear friend and fellow author, Chad Cryder, for your wit, wisdom, and encouragement.

My mentors Julie Newendorp and Annegret Wolf Rice, who helped me build a life worth living.

To two standout therapists who've helped me integrate mind and body, Alan Levin and Cheryle Van Scoy.

Index

ACE test: p. 21, 50, 284
Action steps: p. 27, 36, 44, 52, 59, 67, 72, 82, 91, 99, 108, 119, 125, 129, 185, 194, 201, 211, 219, 228, 242, 253, 269, 275, 283
Acupuncture: p. 127, 128, 129
ADHD/ADD: p. 48, 56, 64, 141, 206, 214, 202, 267
Adrenal/Adrenaline: p. 13, 27, 31, 41, 111, 112, 116, 233, 235
Alcohol/Alcohol Use Disorders: see Drug and Alcohol Use
    Disorder
Anxiety: p. 9-12, 16, 27, 29, 33-38, 44, 48, 49, 56, 58, 64, 66, 104, 122, 127, 150, 176, 184, 186, 192, 204, 207, 211, 214, 215, 222, 225, 238, 241-243, 265, 266, 275
Arrhythmia: p. 266
Asthma: p. 191, 192, 194, 198, 265, 268, 274, 275
Avoiding Emotion: p. 112, 115, 147
Biodynamic organic farming: p. 242
Bön: p. 55, 56, 59, 214, 217
Bones: p. 70, 75, 85-89, 97, 104, 105, 140, 151, 159, 160, 166, 224, 237, 258, 267, 273, 281
Bowen Technique: p. 97, 99
Brain Gym®: p. 45, 120, 125, 143, 146, 179, 183, 185-187, 211, 286
Brain stem: p. 24-28, 31, 55, 58, 62, 81, 87, 88, 104, 111, 112, 119, 147, 183, 216, 234, 278
Breath/Breathing: p. 24, 42, 44, 55-57, 59, 88, 91, 93, 119, 135, 139, 140, 189-195, 197, 198, 201, 205, 217, 227, 268, 289
Cancer: p. 21, 23, 106, 239, 252, 253, 258, 260, 261, 265, 266, 288
Cognitive Hypnotherapy: p. 83, 273, 274
COPD: p. 21, 265
Cortex/prefrontal cortex: p. 24-26, 40, 42, 56, 114, 133, 177, 178, 183, 205, 208, 216, 278
Conscious/ unconscious: p. 10, 12-16, 19, 20, 22, 23-26, 33, 34, 36, 37, 41, 49, 50, 77, 78, 80-83, 88-90, 112, 121-123, 141-143, 176-178,

181, 183, 184, 189, 190, 192, 223, 224, 226, 227, 273-275, 278-280, 283

Dance: p. 30, 48, 64-67, 115, 120

Depression: p. 10, 11, 16, 21, 27, 33-37, 64, 66, 77, 104, 113, 122, 127, 141, 155, 211, 214, 215, 222, 223, 238, 265, 268

Digestion p. 24, 27, 28, 41, 42, 90, 127, 128, 213, 231, 232, 234, 235, 237, 238

Dizziness: p. 105, 266, 268

Drug/ Alcohol, Drug and Alcohol Use Disorder: p. 21, 112, 141, 238-240, 262

Drum circle: p. 61, 66, 67, 218, 219

Dura/Dural: p. 104, 105, 198,

Educational Kinesiology: p. 143, 148

Ego: p. 33, 36, 51, 61, 82, 176, 182-184, 278

Emotion/al: p. 20, 21, 24-26, 33-35, 41-43, 47, 49, 50, 55-59, 61-63, 65, 70, 72, 76-78, 81-83, 86-90, 92, 97, 98, 100, 104, 111-124, 127, 132, 133, 139-183, 185, 187, 191, 192, 194, 207, 209, 210, 216, 217, 222-228, 231, 234, 268, 273-275, 278, 279, 284

Executive function: p. 116, 180, 210, 216, 217, 220

Exercise: p. 28, 36, 37, 64, 66, 69, 80, 86, 94, 99, 105, 111, 119, 132, 133, 139, 140, 189, 193, 197-201, 204, 210, 214, 218, 219, 223, 238, 242, 249, 282

Fascia/Myofascial: p. 68, 70-72, 83, 86, 88-91, 94-97, 99, 101-104, 106-108, 120, 128, 193-195, 201, 235, 237, 251, 252, 254, 281, 287

Fatigue/chronic: p. 64, 73, 94, 97, 143, 181, 198, 264, 265

Fibromyalgia: p. 4, 11, 22, 64, 73, 76, 90, 91, 95, 97, 102, 104, 105, 107, 143, 211, 217, 263, 265

Flow: p. 15, 32, 43, 47-49, 51, 52, 86, 87, 89, 95-97, 102, 113, 116, 125, 144, 226, 284

Gratitude practice: p. 37, 48-50, 52, 123, 258

Headaches: p. 28, 104, 105, 207, 266,

Heart Disease: p. 17, 21, 241, 246, 250, 260

HeartSpeak: p. 227, 229

Histamine: p. 44, 66, 238, 239-244

Hormesis: p. 243
Hypertension: p. 266
Illness (chronic): p. 16, 26, 27, 33, 37, 65, 76, 143, 184, 185, 193, 215, 217, 221, 222, 233, 236, 260, 265
Infertility: p. 35, 127, 128, 265
Inner Chronic Stress: p. 19
Insomnia: p. 105, 127, 241-243, 262, 268
Intention: p. 56, 79, 123, 277, 278, 283, 284
Interactive Metronome: p. 37, 45, 48, 214-216
Internal repair: p. 43, 257, 273
IQ: p. 30
Journaling: p. 49, 50, 52, 111, 178, 238, 274
Left Brain: p. 24, 25, 31, 32, 33, 50, 56
Left/right handshake: p. 24
Limbic (emotional) brain: p. 24, 26, 33, 55, 58, 81, 111, 112, 114, 115, 117, 147, 183, 278
Meditation: p. 37, 38, 41, 43, 44, 52, 55-59, 83, 96, 108, 111, 113, 114, 118, 119, 121, 122, 124, 125, 190, 200, 214, 217, 223, 237, 238, 262, 271, 274, 275
Migraines: p. 96, 105, 190, 204, 266, 267
Mirror neurons: p. 20, 41, 77, 142, 279
Multiple sclerosis: p. 30, 37, 76
Musculo-skeletal: p 85
Myelin: p. 29-31, 37, 41, 42, 199, 213, 214, 216-218
Myofascial: see Fascia
Nausea/ted: p. 95, 127, 266
Numbness: p. 75, 104, 115, 180
Nutrition(al)(ist): p. 37, 40, 43, 77, 86, 231, 238, 239-243, 245, 246, 252, 254, 257, 261, 265, 267, 269, 273, 275
Obesity/overweight/weight loss/weight gain: p. 17, 21, 187, 223, 249
Outer Chronic Stress: p. 19
Oxalates: p. 128, 242, 246, 258, 264-266, 270
Pain/ful: p. 3, 4, 15, 16, 20, 22, 23, 34, 57, 61, 64, 70, 71, 75-78, 81-83, 85, 86, 89-91, 94, 96, 98, 103, 104, 106, 115, 116, 118, 121, 122,

127, 128, 132, 133, 139-141, 143-145, 181, 182, 208, 211, 217, 262, 264, 265, 268, 278, 282, 284

PanHarmonic Healing: p. 96, 120, 125, 141, 143, 147, 148, 155, 178, 179, 182-187, 194

Parasympathetic nervous system: p. 15, 41, 42, 114, 189, 190, 192, 197, 208, 235, 274, 275

Parkinson's: p. 30, 37

P-DTR: p. 98, 99

Positive psychology: p. 37, 47, 48

Prefrontal cortex: see cortex

Primary/primitive reflexes: p. 29, 40, 42, 187, 204-206, 208, 209, 211, 216

PTSD: p. 10, 16, 22, 28, 141, 147, 224, 225, 273, 275

Repetitive movement: p. 29, 30, 199, 217-219

Rhythm and Reflex: p. 37, 45, 216, 220

Rhythm and timing: p. 42, 43, 213, 214, 216, 218, 219

Right brain/hemisphere: p. 24, 25, 28, 29, 31-33, 37, 41, 45, 50, 56, 87, 90, 113, 121, 146, 189, 215,

Right Brain University: p. 146, 216

Russa yoga: p. 63, 64, 66, 67

Specialized kinesiology: p. 115, 118, 120-122, 128, 131, 132, 141, 143-145, 147, 179-182, 184, 185, 200, 206, 208, 214, 216, 217, 227, 278

Spine: p. 24, 64, 86-89, 91, 107

Stress: p. 9-12, 15, 16, 19-23, 27-29, 32-34, 37, 40, 41, 44, 49, 56, 57, 70, 77, 78, 80, 83, 86-89, 91, 94, 99, 101, 104, 106-108, 113-115, 119, 123, 124, 132, 140, 144, 146, 184, 187, 191, 204, 206, 208, 209, 211, 216, 217, 227, 231, 234, 236, 237-239, 248, 251, 257, 262, 264, 265, 268, 274, 282, 284

Stroke: p. 26, 28, 128, 267

Suicide: p. 9, 10, 17, 21, 32, 34-36

Surrendering ego: p. 33, 185

Sympathetic nervous system: p. 40, 41, 56, 83, 105, 189, 208, 235, 237, 238, 246, 268

Synaptic connections: p. 40, 56, 83, 105, 189, 208, 235, 237, 238, 246, 268

Toastmasters: p. 228, 229

Touch for Health: p. 96, 118, 120, 125, 131, 139, 143-146, 179, 183, 185-187, 211

Trauma/tic: p. 12, 13, 16, 21, 27, 34, 40, 50, 51, 76, 78, 86, 89-91, 93-95, 97, 99, 107, 108, 112, 113, 117, 141-143, 147, 180, 183, 185, 204, 206, 221, 223-225, 228, 238, 249, 273, 274, 279

Unconscious: see conscious

Vagus nerve: p. 41-45, 249

Vision Therapy: p. 43, 48, 65, 96, 203-211, 214, 215, 220

Yoga: p. 11, 23, 30, 31, 37, 43, 55, 61-65, 67-69, 83, 86, 87, 95, 97, 98, 101, 104, 108, 115, 120, 189, 190, 200, 217-219, 237, 262

Made in the USA
Columbia, SC
22 November 2021

49499474R00163